PICKLES, PIGS
~ & ~
Whiskey

· RECIPES FROM ·
MY THREE FAVORITE
· FOOD GROUPS ·
(and then some)

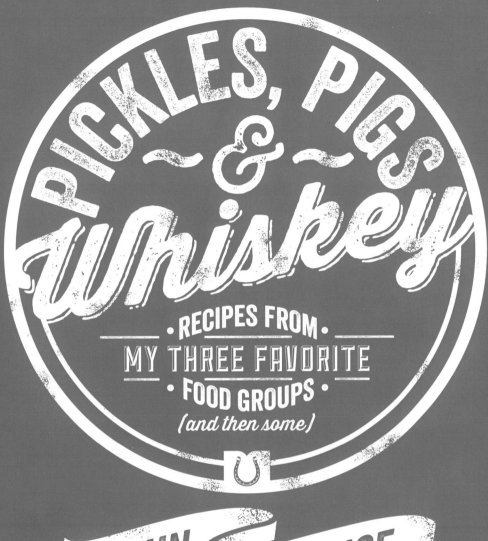

PICKLES, PIGS & WHISKEY

RECIPES FROM MY THREE FAVORITE FOOD GROUPS

(and then some)

JOHN CURRENCE

FOREPLAY *by* JOHN T. EDGE

PHOTOGRAPHY *by* ANGIE MOSIER

Andrews McMeel
Publishing, LLC

Kansas City • Sydney • London

Andrews McMeel Publishing, LLC
an Andrews McMeel Universal company
1130 Walnut Street, Kansas City, Missouri 64106
www.andrewsmcmeel.com

13 14 15 16 17 TEN 10 9 8 7 6 5 4 3 2 1

ISBN: 978-1-4494-2880-8

Library of Congress Control Number: 2013940033

Design: The Splinter Group
Photography: Angie Mosier
Digital/Photo Assistant: Lizzy Johnston
Prop Stylist: Angie Mosier

Photo Credits:
Page v: Bruce Newman
Page viii: Besh and Currence, Alon Shaya; Joe York and Pig, Pableaux Johnson; JTE, JC, AC at Poole's, Matt Fern
Page xi: Ann-Marie Wyatt
Page xiv: Brandall Atkinson
Page xv: Turnip, Chris Grainger
Page xvi: JC and pig, Justin Fox Burks
Page xvii: Staff, used with permission of Jody Eddie, pic by Chris Granger

www.citygroceryonline.com

ATTENTION: SCHOOLS AND BUSINESSES
Andrews McMeel books are available at quantity discounts with bulk purchase for educational, business, or sales promotional use. For information, please e-mail the Andrews McMeel Special Sales Department: specialsales@amuniversal.com

DEDICATION

For the town and people of Oxford, Mississippi.

I am incapable of expressing this dedication in the typical one- or two-line format these things are normally relegated to, as I owe a debt of gratitude that limited space will not fully satisfy. This book is dedicated to the town and people of Oxford, Mississippi, who have taken me in as a son of their own. You have made me family. You have made me friend. You have supported and encouraged me without coddling and have never pulled punches. You have kept me honest. You have taught me about honor, loyalty, and integrity at every turn. We have grown up together in the last twenty-one years, from fledgling aspiration to lauded achievement. I could not have accomplished what we have in the last couple of decades anywhere else in the world.

Thank you, Oxford. You trusted me. You tested me. You pushed me. You helped me understand my place in the South. You have made me a better man. You have helped me become a chef. You have helped launch the careers of untold numbers of people who made their start with us. You have given me a place to call my own and you have welcomed me into your community. Oxford, you are my home and my heart.

I thank you with all of my heart.

Hotty Toddy!

John

Contents

ACKNOWLEDGMENTS — IX

FOREPLAY BY JOHN T. EDGE — XI

INTRODUCTION: THE WORD, ACCORDING TO JOHNNY SNACK — XII

MY MANIFESTO: HOW I COOK — XIX

Chapter 1   STIRRING, SHAKING & MUDDLING — 1

Chapter 2   BOILING & SIMMERING — 26

Chapter 3   PICKLING & CANNING — 56

Chapter 4   SLATHERING, SQUIRTING & SMEARING — 88

Chapter 5   CURING, PRESERVING & STUFFING — 108

Chapter 6   FRYING (PAN & DEEP) — 130

Chapter 7   SAUTÉING & SEARING — 152

Chapter 8   ROASTING & BRAISING — 176

Chapter 9   BRINING & SMOKING — 196

Chapter 10   BAKING & SPINNING — 218

METRIC CONVERSIONS & EQUIVALENTS — 250

INDEX — 252

ACKNOWLEDGMENTS

It took a village—a very large village—to raise this idiot. Simply put, this book would never have happened without the help of a tremendous number of people. My college roommates can attest to the fact that I rarely, if ever, turned in anything on time. (For the record, neither of them did either. We were constantly fighting over access to the Flintstones'-era printer in our house at 4 A.M.) This manuscript was no different. Here's to the inhabitants of Idiot Village who helped make this little dream a reality:

Thankfully my editor, Jean Lucas, and the head of the cookbook division at Andrews McMeel, Kirsty Melville, saw enough promise in this project that they tugged me through to the finish line. Their patience and encouragement is the stuff of legend. It has been a joy working with and getting to know you both. I am deeply grateful to everyone at Andrews McMeel who helped us along. You guys are truly a DREAM publishing house.

David Black, the best Jewish bulldog a man could have on his side. I love you immensely, especially because you are the only person I know capable of using "fuck" more frequently in a sentence than I can, while having it seem entirely natural and almost inoffensive. I think I speak for us all when I say we are proud to have you as an honorary fucking Southerner.

A coconspirator in a project like this is a must. Angie Mosier, brilliant photographer and stylist, does a surgical strike like Seal Team Six. I love every minute we spend together. Thank you for making this so beautiful and making me laugh when I was in the depths of self-loathing. You are amazing. By the way, all that shit you stole while you were drunk and harassing Ole Miss frat boys, well . . . it's still on my porch.

My dear friend Lane Wurster and the entire team at the Splinter Group in Chapel Hill, who designed this book for us; what you have lent us in the way of credibility with what you have done with our whole graphic design program is just remarkable. The fact that we got to work with you guys on this made the project. You were the linchpin. For all of you who are unaware, Lane was the general manager at Crook's when I started there as a busboy and was the man who fired me for insulting the dickwad frat boy who was picking on his girlfriend. Lane, you are at once the man who fired me from my first restaurant job, but rehired me into the kitchen and started me along this path. Have I told you that your father sculpts the nicest figurines from soap?

John T. Edge, Wright Thompson, and Joe York, each as diplomatic as the August day is hot, managed to find dozens of ways around telling me that this or that sucked about different pieces of this book, while always encouraging me to forge ahead. You are all wonderful friends and your guidance, criticism, and time have been invaluable. Please make me a drink and make it a double . . .

To the staffs at all of the restaurants and in particular to the guys who got behind helping me get this finished, whether it was affording me the time to write or helping put together the food for the photo shoots. I could not have done this without you. Jim Weems, my brother, vanilla bean–scraper, minister of culture, raconteur, sky rooster, and sole quality control director of our company's Heineken inventory: I'll never be able to thank you enough for everything you have given. Vishwesh Bhatt, I am equally grateful to you for what you have helped us build. You are as amazing and gifted a chef as I have ever had the pleasure of working with. Thanks for helping cover my tracks.

For my business partner Stefano, our publicist Sarah Abell, and our team at Baltz and Co. and my insanely organized assistant Angie who have all wondered for the last year why the fuck I am not doing whatever the fuck it is I am supposed to be doing. It has taken precisely that long to write this sentence. You rock like the Stones . . . circa *Some Girls* . . . not this geriatric bullshit they are pulling these days.

For an army of chef, artisan, farmer, and writer friends who all inspire me to be better at whatever I do every day, I thank God for all of you. Jessica Harris, John Edgerton, Leah Chase, Sean Brock, Ashley Christensen, Frank Stitt, Ben and Karen Barker, Mike Lata, Hugh Acheson, Linton Hopkins, Steven Satterfield, John Fleer, Edward Lee, Tandy Wilson, Tyler Brown, Kelly English, Andrew Ticer, Michael Hudman, Bryan Caswell, Bill Smith, Michelle Bernstein, Donald Link, Steven Stryjewski, Drew Robinson, Eli Kirshtein, David Crews, Floyd Cardoz, Allan Benton, Billy Reid, Nick Pihakis, Tim Hontzas, Richard and Lisa Howorth, Brett Anderson, Sandy Whann . . . I'd go into battle for any of you fuckers, any day of the week. And, Besh . . . well, Johnny Boy, you're like the much older, uglier brother I never had. I love all of you guys.

Mom, Dad, Richard, Mathilde, a man could ask for no better support, encouragement, love, or source of humorous material than you guys. Thank you for believing in me even when the ideas seemed a little suspect. The fact that you tended toward trusting me and my ability rather than waxing cynical means more than I will ever be able to say. Thank you.

My dear, sweet, beautiful, and amazingly smart wife, Bess, has read every word of this book dozens of times as well as five or six years' worth of throwaway crap material prior to getting the manuscript rolling in earnest. You are amazingly patient and massively adept at taking my C+ effort and turning it into A+ material. You are an inspiration, my dear. I love you very much.

See? Huge village to raise this idiot . . .

John Currence
OXMS
April 13, 2013, after just changing the first diaper of the day (not mine, my daughter, Mamie's . . .)

FOREPLAY BY JOHN T. EDGE

I'm godfather to his firstborn. He's my frequent drinking companion. And I'm his sometime critic. He cooked the rehearsal dinner for my wedding. My son and I eat breakfast twice each week at one of his restaurants. My wife and I eat dinner once each week at another.

That is all to say, I'm biased. And I'm not alone. John Currence has legions of friends and admirers. He's the kind of guy who can quote William Faulkner's *Light in August* from memory. He's the kind of chef who can keep his head down, man the line, and hold his whiskey at the after-party.

Currence was born and raised in New Orleans. He owes a debt to that place, one he began to pay down after the Hurricane Katrina levee failures, when he worked as a volunteer crowbar jockey and general contractor, tearing apart and then putting back together Willie Mae's Scotch House, a Treme fried chicken joint.

New Orleans still matters to him. But Currence, who has called Oxford, Mississippi, home since 1992, is now a full citizen of our little courthouse square–centered town. By way of City Grocery, his plank-floored flagship, and three other local restaurants, he has fostered a culinary scene that cities twenty times our size envy.

As a chef, Currence pulls no punches. From sweet potatoes pickled in star anise–infused champagne vinegar, to confited chicken gizzards, inspired by local gas station cafés, the dishes he documents in *Pickles, Pigs & Whiskey* are muscular and playful.

The language Currence employs here is playful, too. He compares the names of various salts to the names of marijuana strains. He draws analogies between hothouse tomatoes and strippers. He compares pork rillettes to potted meat. And he thinks Barry White and braising have something in common.

At a time when many thinking eaters are looking south for inspiration, Currence serves as the curator-in-chief of modern Mississippi foodways. Take his Szechuan catfish, developed after visits to a Chinese-owned grocery hereabouts. Or his pecan-smoked duck, lacquered with molasses, born of Delta rice field hunts. Both showcase a Mississippi rarely glimpsed by outlanders. Both tell resonant stories about the state.

Lots of chefs who write books declare that their cuisine is very personal. Half the time, I don't buy the rhetoric. This time I do. John Currence has written a book that sounds like him, a book that smells like him, with recipes that conjure his past and his present and pay homage to the place he calls home.

INTRODUCTION:
THE WORD, ACCORDING TO JOHNNY SNACK

I grew up in New Orleans, in a house where cooking was an immense part of the daily landscape. My mother, who was a full-time history teacher, made hot breakfasts, packed us lunches, and cooked supper every day. She was a fucking maniac . . . it's the only way I can describe it. I have no idea how she did it, and my respect for her is boundless for that alone. Watching her in the kitchen, I learned a strong work ethic. I came to appreciate foods I would not likely have had the chance to taste otherwise, I observed selflessness, and I came to understand the importance food and eating together play in the role of a healthy family life. I was not musing this shit over my bowl of SpaghettiOs. It has come to me as an adult.

Mom at a frommagerie *in Cannes.*

Our kitchen was the heart of our home. My brother and I sat at the counter doing our homework every night while Mom cooked dinner and watched the evening news. She effortlessly threw together pots of chili, pasta Bolognese, and beef stew. My dad cooked beans, duck gumbo, or court bouillon on the weekends to the soundtrack of college and professional football. It was the birthplace of countless dinner parties, Tulane tailgate gatherings, pre–Mardi Gras parade rendezvouses, and birthday celebrations. And over the course of my childhood, my mom transformed from a young housewife providing meals for a husband and two sons into an accomplished cook and crackerjack entertainer.

My brother, Richard, and I spent summers between our grandparents' homes in North Carolina and Georgia. My mom's people operated a general store on the outskirts of Lenoir, North Carolina, and raised a couple acres of vegetables every summer. I passed my time with them, almost

exclusively, harvesting, processing, cooking, and canning or freezing all that came out of that garden. Years later, these experiences provided me with an understanding of and appreciation for those individual vegetables and fundamental building blocks for a variety of preservation techniques. At City Grocery and Snackbar, we now put up hundreds of quarts of canned vegetables and pickles each summer and make thousands of pounds of different sausages and hams each year, such as our Pickled Peaches (page 76) and Tasso Ham (page 119).

When I was 10, Dad, an "oil and gas man," was transferred to Edinburgh, Scotland, where we lived for several years. In their infinite wisdom, Mom and Dad seized the opportunity to pull us out of school regularly for long weekend trips around western Europe, knowing the exposure to those places and living that history was as valuable as anything we would absorb in a classroom at that age. Eating was as important on those trips as visiting museums or cathedrals, so I had the opportunity to see and taste classic dishes in the places they originated. Later, as a young chef, those experiences gave me a true understanding of the classic dishes I would be preparing stateside and an appreciation for how those dishes were co-opted by settlers in America and made part of the canon of foods of the New World. My Hill Country Cioppino (page 167) and the Duck Confit (page 118) are versions of dishes I first had at those European restaurant tables.

With Dad dove hunting in Mexico.

With my brother Richard at the Superdome.

In my very early twenties, as I began working in restaurants, I fell into the lap of Bill Neal at Crook's Corner in Chapel Hill, North Carolina. Unbeknownst to me, I was working side by side with the man who was fast becoming a giant in Southern cooking and is credited with legitimizing the food of the Southern family table. (As a side note, Frank Stitt was doing exactly the same thing on the western frontier, in Birmingham, Alabama, significantly more refined, but much less spoken of. He is as responsible for leading us out of culinary obscurity as anyone else and continues the "good work" every waking moment.) It was in those years that I received my first glimpse of the actual beauty of the food of my grandparents' table and the dishes from my mom's kitchen. Stewed Okra and Tomatoes (page 55) and Chicken Skin Cornbread (page 225) were foods we could be proud of, foods that told a story about our lives, our history, and our families. It was not food that needed to be relegated to those home tables, it was food to be explored, examined, and celebrated.

All of my experiences would eventually make for a great "destined-to-be-a-chef" story, but at that point it never really occurred to me that becoming a chef was a viable or acceptable career option. The mid-1980s was not the era of celebrity for restaurant employees. Service work was still looked down upon as patently plebeian, and in few places more so than Uptown, old-money New Orleans. Kitchens at that time were, for the most part, pirate ships full of derelicts, washouts, and fuckups. The job suited the lifestyle of the nocturnal ne'er-do-wells and was something that required little in the way of qualification. If you could get along with the other reprobates, hold your liquor, show up ready to fight the battle every day, and follow orders, more often than not, you were in. For all of these reasons, it suited me perfectly.

I was lured home to New Orleans in the late 1980s to help a high-school friend get his first restaurant off the ground. The kitchen at Gautreau's became ground zero for my passion. Our chef, Larkin Selman, was maniacally plowing new ground. The food in New Orleans at that time was languishing in staid mediocrity. The giant Creole French institutions had stopped cooking for their clientele and were using poor technique and poorer quality ingredients. Larkin saw the opening and dove in. His food, in those early days, was smudged with the thumbprints of his mentors, Jonathan Waxman and Alfred Portale. He was taking dishes from his experiences with those chefs and making them his own. He paired classic duck confit with marinated red beans instead of the traditional stewed lentils. Northeastern crab cakes took a turn into a Creole-spiced neighborhood, and über-traditional seafood bisques were spiked with Louisiana shellfish. It was his passion for food and drive for excellence that inspired me to forge head-on down this path.

At the same time, Emeril Lagasse was first going out on his own after Commander's Palace. After leaving Paul Prudhomme, Frank Brightsen had planted his flag, opening the eponymous Brightsen's, and Susan Spicer had graduated from the Bistro at the Maison de Ville and opened the venerable Bayona. It was an amazing time to be part of that scene. Observing each of these chefs early in their careers, it was easy to see how their individual food was influenced by experience but at the same time was taking its own shape. They were each telling a personal story, informed by a desire to illustrate their own interpretations of New Orleans and what they loved about it, through food. It was exciting at the time but like what I took from my time with Bill Neal, it would take maturation and experience to truly understand.

Cooking at Daniel Boulud's Palm Court in Palm Beach, Florida.

In the dining room at City Grocery.

The dining room and kitchen at Gautreau's were tiny and could not have been any more intense. It was a monument to insanity, replete with drugs, groupies, sociopaths, hustlers, booze, gambling, sex, and most any other vice you might imagine. How I survived to tell the tale of my two years in that kitchen is something I can't explain. It was comparable to the fire-breathing psychopathy captured in *Kitchen Confidential*, but I'd square Gautreau's kitchen off with that of Les Halles any day for comparison of psychoses, substance abuse, and general slap-dickery. We played ridiculously hard while putting out, arguably, the best food in the city at that time. We lightened traditionally heavy fried soft-shell crabs with a quick sauté or smoke, tinkered with local soybeans (an otherwise ignored ingredient at the time) and we were sourcing locally grown vegetables and locally raised proteins. It's food that I still hang my hat on today and that led the way in the reinvention and reinvigoration of the New Orleans food scene. For the most ridiculous of reasons, this all struck the perfect chord in me. Though I had fallen in love with restaurant work under Bill Neal's tutelage, it wasn't until I returned to New Orleans and that insane kitchen that I realized that this was my future, in spite of its implications, what it may have signaled to my peers, and the consternation it stirred in my parents.

In the spring of 1992, I made an unexpected trip to Oxford, Mississippi, to visit my best childhood friend. The net result of that visit was that my best friend became my business partner and we opened my first restaurant, City Grocery, early that summer in that beautiful little burg. We were successful, in spite of ourselves, from the minute we opened, which makes it extremely easy to admit that I had no idea what I was doing and sure as shit had no business opening a restaurant. Work ethic and passion are almost entirely responsible for our survival . . . well, that and understanding that whatever I did, if I tried to reach beyond my abilities, I would surely tumble off the edge of the cliff.

With the first Grocery team at the Beard House, 1994.

Orleanians do not consider themselves "Southern." I had no conception of what my food was in those early days, what it was "supposed" to say, or how it fit into the larger Southern traditions. I simply went in at the crack of dawn, cooked desserts, made stocks, finished sauces, butchered, prepped mise en place, washed dishes, and tried to simply craft dishes I knew our guests could connect with. I wanted to give them comfort and offer unyieldingly high quality. I didn't have a firm hold of my place in the South because New Orleanians do not consider themselves "Southern." This is not out of arrogance; it is simply due to the fact that it is a unique place, both physically and psychologically, that it just "is." Southernness is just not something that New Orleans folks spend a lot of time discussing, cultivating, or considering. Turns out a move north from NOLA to Oxford is what it would take to come to that understanding of my place in the South.

Although I didn't truly realize it, my formative experiences in those years were building a foundation for what my food would ultimately become. The lightning bolt of understanding struck in the summer of 1998 on an extended work-play trip to the south of France. At the end of my second week there, I began craving everything I knew was exploding out of the ground in our garden back home. I wanted lemon-sautéed squash, sliced heirloom tomatoes, skillet-fried corn, and fresh green beans more than I had ever craved anything in my life. I wanted those Sunday suppers from my grandmother's garden and table.

Beard House kitchen, 2000.

On my last day there, we made our daily trip to the outdoor market in Cannes, and the chef I was working with approached me with a pod of okra and accosted me with questions about this curiosity he had never experienced. We returned to the house with exactly all of the okra from the market, and I launched into an afternoon tutorial. We prepared boiled okra with black pepper, pickled okra (page 61), stewed okra with fresh tomatoes (page 55), fried okra, and simmered seafood gumbo chock-full of okra. We were both blown away—him with the possibilities for this ingredient and me with the immediate understanding that his response to this food that I would never have considered bringing to the table at City Grocery had just become the centerpiece of my food philosophy and what would propel City Grocery into the brewing conversation about Southern food.

In that moment, cooking became a greater joy than I had ever known. I was telling a story through the food we created. It was personal, it was impassioned, it had meaning. Fifteen years later, that food reflects exactly who I am and speaks to my entire life's experience. Like Southern food as a whole, it continues to evolve slowly and is influenced by every brush with another cuisine that comes to inhabit our corner of the country.

With giant local turnips.

At le Cep in Beaune, France.

Above: Front door at BBB. Top right: Picking up a hog at Stan's Meat Market. Center right: After an event for the First Lady at the Casa Blanca. Bottom right: With my mom, dad, and godmother at the Beard House, 1994.

My approach to cooking, like my career journey, is untraditional. I wanted the structure of this book to reflect my greater interest in how things work. When I was a child, the running joke around our house was about how long I would play with Christmas toys before I started dismantling them to see what made them tick. The chapters herein reflect that interest. I am fascinated by technique. I love the fact that taking a sausage blend and beating it in a mixer at a certain temperature will produce a completely different result than simply casing and cooking that same sausage blend unemulsified. I am amazed that whisking egg yolks vigorously and thus relaxing their proteins gives you the ability to drop in molecules of fat and create things like mayonnaise and hollandaise. Creativity defines lots of chefs, but understanding and mastering technique is what sets them apart. Technique is forgotten when it comes to traditional chapter structure in cookbooks, as we tend to think about food in courses. *Pickles, Pigs & Whiskey* reflects my desire to continue taking apart my favorite toys and showing you exactly how they work.

Good luck, good timing, and a tiny little bit of common sense led me to my home here in Oxford, Mississippi. Hard work, dedication to quality, and respect for tradition and history have carried me forward; the recipes in *Pickles, Pigs & Whiskey* paint that picture. They reference points all over the globe, but they all reflect influences that have formed the food of the South. Complex, intelligent, and at times altogether healthy, that food is far from what some people would have you believe. This is my interpretation of it. This is my story in about 130 recipes. . . .

Top: The City Grocery Staff c. 2010. Above: Smoked Carrots (page 212).
Right: Pan-Roasted Duck Breast and Lardons (page 185).

MY MANIFESTO: HOW I COOK

The exercise of cooking is, at its very core, a joy, or it should be. We cook out of necessity, but sharing that food is an intensely personal experience. When cooking for others, you are delivering something that is elemental and personal because you have prepared it for them and frequently have prepared that dish for a reason. Even delivering something as simple as pasta with red sauce conveys something about the person cooking it.

I have a very old copy of the *Joy of Cooking*. As I understand, it belonged to my great-grandmother, was given to my grandmother, and then to my mom, who in turn gave it to me as I got into cooking. It is a beautiful edition from 1942 that wears a magnificent kitchen patina and threatens to come apart if not handled with due respect and care.

I love this book dearly. At home I reach for it to pick out certain ratios that escape me these days. It was with this book that I learned to cook, and it's because of what's inside of it that I came to understand cooking. It isn't just the recipes contained in the yellowing pages of this tome that have helped me understand the basic tenets of cooking. It's the three generations of handwriting on the pages, noting slight adjustments to the recipes here and there, that ultimately helped me understand that recipes, no matter how simple, are just a guideline for the cook.

I can open my copy of *Joy of Cooking* and quickly thumb to a recipe that has been adjusted by one of three generations before me. My great-grandmother made the best chocolate chip cookies I have ever tasted, and I know the difference is that she used half lard and half butter instead of the all butter that was called for in the *Joy* recipe. Her notes are written neatly in faded pencil on page 595. There are notes written on yellowed, lined index cards and pieces cut from faded newspaper stuck among the pages. It's a great little piece of personal history.

I hope this book is the same for you. I want you to cook from it. I want you to find the joy in preparing these things for people. Take these recipes and make them your own. Each one will make an excellent dish as is, but experiment with them. Play with your food. Use this book. Abuse this book. Go buy three more copies and use and abuse them all, too.

Here are a few of my basics, which just might make things cook a little easier and taste a little better.

MOOD

Enjoy yourself. Remember that, more than anything else, these recipes are guidelines. The end results of each of these will get you to a place you can enjoy, but don't be shy about trying to improve them. The Veal Country Captain (page 157) may have more curry powder than you like, so make yours with less and increase the fresh thyme. Stuff like that. This book is made with paper that can take ink, graphite, blood, wine, or coffee. Use any of these to make notes on how each of these can be better. (Secret: They can all be done better.)

Make a drink or pour a glass of wine before you start cooking. Create a joyful working environment. Cooking is work, no question about it, but it doesn't have to be drudgery. Make it fun. Find recipes that strike you, put on some music, relax, and surrender yourself to the process.

Listen to music. It has played a big role in my life. I started listening to the Carpenters and the Beatles on reel-to-reel with my great-uncle when I was so young that all I can remember is the machine itself and what songs we listened to. As soon as I was able to start destroying my mother's record collection, I listened to the Moody Blues, Cat Stevens, and Simon & Garfunkel until I was dragged away from the record player. I listened to my grandparents' copy of *Live from San Quentin* so many times that it eventually mysteriously "disappeared." I played in the marching band in junior high and a frat-house pop band in college and the ensuing years.

Music is intertwined with every moment of my life. I remember "Beat on The Brat" playing on my Walkman when the space shuttle exploded; "Freaky Tales" by Too $hort on the stereo the first day I walked into the kitchen at Gautreau's; "Dancing Queen" the first time I held hands with a girl I liked, skating at the Roller-rama at my best friend's birthday party; "Bennie and the Jets" in the car with my parents on the way to the beach as a little boy; "Purple Haze" on the same trip with friends as a teenager, and on and on. The kitchens of our restaurants are rarely without music, just like our kitchen at home. It creates a soothing environment, and songs themselves can become a motivator when things get sluggish.

Each of the recipes contained in this book has a song paired with it. So you don't have to purchase all of them individually, I have created a playlist at spotify.com. All you have to do is to tune in and you can listen to these selections as you work through that recipe. I will warn you now that you will not like every song on the list. They span the spectrum from Mozart to Beefheart, from Meat Loaf to the Meat Puppets. You'll get a little Bee Gees and Elton John while touching on Ministry and Minor Threat. Each means something to me, and I have selected them to suit the mood of each of these dishes.

Read the recipe all the way through before you start cooking. I tell my cooks this almost every day. When you do it, you familiarize yourself with ingredients, technique, and equipment you might not be familiar with otherwise. You won't end up being surprised that you need an ice bath set up in the middle of your process, and end up overblanching something as a result. Reading gets you comfortable with the process and builds confidence as you launch in for the first time.

INGREDIENTS

Buy good ingredients. Our crap food is killing us and, more important, laying the groundwork for obesity and diabetes in our children. So much of the garbage food is loaded with the highly processed, genetically engineered corn that converts to fat more easily than any of the simple starches out there. Buy natural, and buy local when you can. Search out hormone-free proteins and indulge in raw fruits and vegetables. I don't want to sound like one of these whiny, didactic shitheads trying to run your life or

guilt you into doing the right thing, but for God's sake, we have got to begin to change what we consider acceptable to put in our bodies. Please go get a Michael Pollan book, watch *Food, Inc.*, or simply consider what you are throwing into your cart the next time you are in the snack aisle.

Proteins are arguably the most important part of this conversation. The growth hormones and antibiotics given to factory-raised animals are contributing to our daughters and sons developing at earlier ages, to the resistance we are building to disease-fighting antibiotics, and to the proliferation of food allergies. This is important stuff, and only we can make a difference by demanding change through consumer habit.

When I call for **salt**, it is always kosher salt. Buy a box, and pour it into a small cup. Grab it and feel it in your fingers. You can actually pick it up, as opposed to table salt, which just slips through your fingertips. You can actually sprinkle it. Taste it next to your regular iodized salt, which will comparably seem chemical and almost artificial.

Occasionally, I call for a **finishing salt**. These are larger-flake, natural salts that don't dissolve as quickly. Maldon is the most readily available brand, but there are hundreds available (and they sound like names of weed): Hawaiian Big Flake, Mayan Sun, Himalayan Pink, Cyprus Black Lava, and so on. They are excellent for sprinkling over sliced meat just off the grill, lightly sautéed fish, or roasted bird. I do not recommend trying to roll and smoke any of them, no matter how enticing they sound.

Immediately throw away any pre-ground **black pepper** you have. It is disgusting and in almost no way representative of the flavor of freshly ground. Black pepper is always freshly cracked and preferably should be lightly toasted before it's ground. My advice is to purchase a spice grinder just for pepper, because once you have ground some pepper in it, it will be little good for anything else. They are inexpensive, so a small splurge will free up the time you would otherwise

spend grinding by hand with a pepper grinder. If you are a purist and must hand-grind (more power to you), consider the Vic Firth or Peugeot brands. They are pricey but produce exceptional results. The little orange Vic Firth given to me by Mary Sue Milliken is the best I have ever owned.

I make no excuses for the occasional use of **standard grocery store products** such as French's yellow mustard, Duke's or Kewpie mayonnaise, Vlasic sweet pickle relish, or quick-release pan spray. Sometimes there just isn't anything that quite substitutes for these items. They exist for a reason. If you eat anything other than yellow mustard on a fried bologna sandwich, well, you're just a chump.

"Light" or "low-fat" *anything* means you are sacrificing flavor. That's all there is to it. Rather than skimp on flavor, moderate your portion size. Substituting light mayonnaise or sour cream, low-fat buttermilk, or whatever ingredient will inevitably affect the outcome of the recipe. And for God's sake, low-fat cheese doesn't even remotely taste like cheese; it's more like rubberized cardboard. This is where my sweet wife, Bess, and I cross swords, and though she is improving in the kitchen, my food tastes better than hers for this reason alone.

Make your own bread, even if it means buying a countertop bread maker to do it. Homemade is not only usually superior to store-bought bread, but it also fills your home with a smell that stops fighting, makes the crossest folks content, and convinces everyone who comes over that you are the next coming of James Beard himself.

Eat tomatoes when they are in season . . . only when in season. Be the first to bore your friends to tears with a stimulating lecture on "eating in season." Referring to winter tomatoes as "hothouse tomatoes" is the equivalent of calling a stripper a "dancer." They certainly resemble one another, but have little else in common. And while I think a cast of strippers doing *The Nutcracker* would be hilarious, the joke gets short in a hurry.

Tomatoes only taste like they are supposed to during the season when the good Lord intended for them to grow. The hours in the days are long and hot. Only then can their sugars develop the complexity and depth they are capable of producing. Everything else is simply second-rate at very best.

I know this is opening a can of worms, but here it is. The peekytoe, stone, king, or whatever other crappy **crab** you eat because you can't get delicious, fresh Gulf blue crabs are but a pale comparison to the finest crabmeat in the world. Blue crab is sublimely rich, velvety, and worth trading your beloved mother into white slavery for. Wait until you can get it to cook recipes herein containing said gift of God, or understand that no matter your conviction, your final product will suffer. Unless your tastes run toward things like kerosene, tire fires, or dirty diapers, whatever you do, *avoid at all costs* any variety of crabmeat that has been pasteurized, is "Crab" spelled with a "K," or shows any hint of unnatural orange or red markings. Just trust me on this.

Stop wasting time sifting flour. I've never had any discernibly different results in a final product because of sifted versus unsifted flour. Self-rising flour is perfect for biscuits and pancakes. It's simply all-purpose flour with just the right ratio of baking soda for a typical rise and a touch of salt. It's okay for saving a step, but I would not use it for cakes or cookies where you want to control the rise and final texture. (Thank you, Louis Osteen.)

Step away from the white chocolate . . . *it isn't really chocolate* . . . and it's a pain in the ass. Seriously, even the very best white chocolate is chocolate that has had all of the cocoa solid removed, so it's nothing but cocoa butter and sugar. It is the "dry hump" of the pastry world.

Stop making such a big deal about lard. It is no less healthy than other fats, and it is more delicious. Nothing makes as flaky or as delicious biscuits or piecrust as ones made with part lard. And there is simply nothing better for frying. You eat the rest of the animal (including parts that are likely much more offensive), so buy a tub of fresh lard to keep in your refrigerator. Use it and be proud that you are working to bust a stupid stigma about a completely natural ingredient. Don't engage the lard enemies, as more often than not, they have no fucking idea what they are talking about. Go beat your head against a wall instead. You'll end up happier.

Save your bacon fat and *use it.* You can add it to olive oil or butter when cooking almost any meat. It will add layers of flavor to crappy factory-farmed chicken that you would never have dreamed possible. It is great for spur-of-the-moment gravy and makes an excellent addition to homemade mayonnaise and hollandaise.

While we are on the subject of fat, for the most part, store-bought **olive oil** sucks monkey ass. If it's all you have available, at least infuse it with fresh garlic to give it a lift. Really good olive oils take a little digging and tasting to identify. They are most frequently found in specialty stores, but higher-end grocery stores will stock them from time to time. After you have made your flavored oil, you can take the garlic, mash it up with a little sea salt, and spread it on some crusty bread . . . impress your friends with your "garlic confit bruschetta." You are on your way to becoming a true bullshit chef. Congratulations!

Take a little time and **clarify some butter** to cook with. It doesn't take very long and, once made, it will keep in the refrigerator for a long time. Butter is basically made up of three things: 1) fat, 2) milk solids, and 3) water. When you clarify butter, you are basically separating those three things by slowly warming them and then very slowly simmering. The result is pure butterfat, which has a much higher smoking point. Butter blackens quickly because when used whole, the milk solids drop to the bottom and literally burn.

To Make Clarified Butter

Place 4 sticks (1 pound) of butter in a medium saucepan. Place the pan on the stove over low heat. Melt the butter and let simmer very slowly until you see the milky solids separate and drop to the bottom of the pan. This will take 20 to 30 minutes, if done properly. Ladle the butterfat off the top and store chilled until needed. Discard the solids.

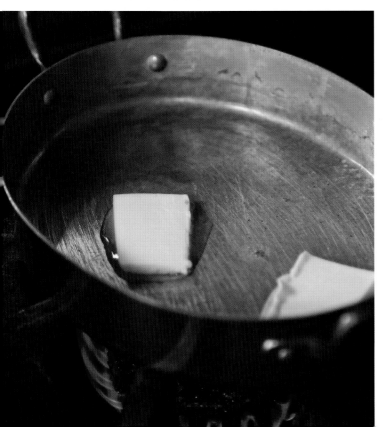

EQUIPMENT

Get some **good tools**. Without the right tools, you'll just hurt yourself and/or your final product. You'll be happier using good-quality equipment.

Knives: I like Shun knives. They are excellent-quality steel, and the lack of a bolster on the handle end of the blade makes then a cinch to sharpen. Wüstof and Henckels make outstanding knives, but whatever you do, buy the professional grade of, at least, a chef's knife. An 8-inch length is ideal. A good utility knife or paring knife is also handy. And make sure to get yourself a good diamond steel for sharpening them.

Cookware: Get yourself a couple of heavy stainless-steel pieces.
10-inch sauté pan
2-quart saucepan
1½-gallon soup pot
A larger braising/roasting pan with a handle (such as Calphalon)
10-inch Lodge cast-iron skillet
6-quart Dutch oven

Lodge makes the best cast-iron cookware in the world. The pieces have hundreds of uses and are very easy to clean. They come pre-seasoned now, so they look used. As a result, you can begin making up the bullshit story about your grandmother's cornbread skillet even as you are signing the receipt at the store.

Countertop: These two items are essentials in my kitchen. Vitamix blender: I don't know how I did anything before this gal came into my life. Nothing ever before has ever approached the Vitamix. It purees soups and sauces to a smoother consistency than I can describe.

KitchenAid 4½-quart stand mixer: Tried and true, these guys have stood the test of time. The larger sizes seem to fail increasingly as the size increases, so we stick to the standard size. Don't be fooled by the "professional" 6 quart. The main gears are plastic, and they can't begin to handle the larger batches of doughs without crumbling.

Miscellaneous: Here are a few really helpful items to round out your equipment.

An inexpensive Japanese mandoline for prepping vegetables is an outstanding tool to have. They cost about $25 and will pay off in spades when you see how much work they can save you. Benriner makes an excellent model, and they are available everywhere online.

John Boos's maple cutting boards—Boos Blocks—are the best out there. Buy one and you'll pass it on to your kids, and they will pass it on to theirs. Maple is an excellent surface to work on with a good knife, because it provides a solid resistance with a surface that doesn't wreak havoc on your knife blade. From a sanitation standpoint, they are the safest surface to maintain, with the possible exception of glass.

Get a FoodSaver or some other brand of vacuum sealer. These are absolutely invaluable in professional kitchens for a number of reasons, but when it comes to freezing product, this little bugger will free up tons of space in your freezer because everything can be bagged and laid flat to freeze, eliminating bulky packaging. They also completely eliminate freezer burn.

The pressure cooker is a tool that languishes on the outskirts of serious consideration and is rarely part of the conversation when it comes to professional cooking. This could not be any more unfortunate. Pressure cookers, though annoying, deliver flavors and texture almost unattainable with traditional cooking methods and in a fraction of the time. Get one, cook some dried beans in it, and see if that doesn't change your opinion in a heartbeat.

Get a Microplane. This instrument, which had its beginnings as a woodworking tool, is absolutely indispensable.

It is the tool that finally allows anyone to harvest zest and the resulting citrus oils from lemon, lime, orange, and grapefruit without getting any of the bitter white pith. They are also excellent for shredding Parmesan cheese, nutmeg, tonka beans, and truffles.

TECHNIQUES

Cook over open fire whenever you have the chance. *It just tastes better*. It takes practice, and you will overcook or undercook things here and there, but we all do sometimes. It's a joyful learning process. Nothing, though, re-creates the flavor, even remotely, of open-flame cooking. When wood or charcoal flame kisses protein and fat, magic happens that will never occur in a pan, on the stove, or in the oven. If you use charcoal, source real charcoal and not briquettes. Briquettes are compressed, charred wood chips and sawdust that are treated with a pile of petrochemicals and will leave your food with a bitter aftertaste if they are not treated properly. The best thing you can do is burn actual hardwood down to coals and cook over that. Granted, that isn't something everyone can accomplish, so bagged charcoal is the next best thing. It burns hot and very quickly, so be prepared to stoke your fire regularly if you are cooking anything that takes very long to cook.

When baking, always whisk wet mixtures into dry ingredients to avoid clumping. Mix a little slowly.

The final product you cook is only as good as the sum of its parts. **Season everything**. If you are frying chicken, don't skip seasoning the flour because you think there is enough salt on the chicken itself, because then you end up with a flavorless crust. Season your cooking oil with garlic for meat, lemon zest for fish, red pepper flakes for whatever. You are simply taking the extra step to making your final dish that much better. Remember that this isn't work—you're having fun.

BASIC RECIPES

Here are a few recipes for things you should keep handy or that you can whip up in a second.

GARLIC OLIVE OIL

4 cups pure olive oil
¾ cup garlic cloves, peeled

MAKES 4 CUPS

Pour the oil into a medium saucepan and add the garlic cloves. Place on the stove over medium heat. Bring up to 325°F on a candy or frying thermometer and then decrease the heat to low. Let simmer for 30 to 45 minutes. Remove from the heat, cool, strain through a fine-mesh sieve, and then put the oil into bottles for use. Reserve the cloves for use in bruschetta, mashed potatoes, for salad garnish, and so on.

SEASONED FLOUR

3 cups all-purpose flour
2 teaspoons salt
2 teaspoons freshly ground black pepper
2 teaspoons smoked paprika
1½ teaspoons garlic powder
1½ teaspoons onion powder
1 teaspoon cayenne

MAKES 3 CUPS

Toss the flour, salt, black pepper, paprika, garlic and onion powders, and cayenne in a stainless-steel bowl and combine well. Store in an airtight container until needed.

CREOLE SEASONING

¼ cup smoked paprika
3 tablespoons salt
3 tablespoons garlic powder
5 teaspoons onion powder
4 teaspoons freshly ground black pepper
4 teaspoons dried oregano
1 tablespoon red pepper flakes
1 tablespoon dried thyme
1 tablespoon fennel seeds, roughly crushed
2 teaspoons cayenne

MAKES 3 CUPS

Combine the paprika, salt, garlic and onion powders, black pepper, oregano, red pepper flakes, thyme, fennel seeds, and cayenne in a small bowl. Store in an airtight container in a cool, dry place for 4 months.

EGG WASH

3 large eggs
1 cup whole milk
¼ cup heavy cream
1 teaspoon salt
1 teaspoon freshly ground black pepper
3 dashes of Tabasco hot sauce

MAKES 3 CUPS

Whisk the eggs, milk, cream, salt, pepper, and Tabasco together well. Store in a sealed container in the refrigerator for 3 days.

FRESH HERB VINAIGRETTE

¾ cup chopped fresh herbs (*see Note*)
3 tablespoons Dijon mustard
1 large egg
2½ cups pure olive oil
¾ cup extra-virgin olive oil
2 medium shallots, finely diced
½ tablespoon finely minced garlic
¾ cup apple cider vinegar
Finely grated zest and juice of 2 lemons
2 tablespoons sugar
Salt and freshly ground black pepper

MAKES 4½ CUPS

Place the herbs, mustard, and egg in a blender and puree until smooth. With the blender running, drizzle in the oils until fully combined. Add the shallots and garlic and mix until smooth. Blend in the vinegar, lemon zest and juice, and sugar. Season to taste with salt and black pepper. Store in a sealed container in the refrigerator for 2 weeks.

Note:
Okay, here's your first chance to get all "cheffy" with the herbs. The ratio of ingredients here is not really important. That being said, I would not recommend making this entirely with lavender. Mix a variety of rosemary, basil, thyme, tarragon, oregano, sage, cilantro, flat-leaf parsley, and so on. Use what you like best.

LEMON-SHERRY VINAIGRETTE

2 cups pure olive oil
¼ cup extra-virgin olive oil
½ cup sherry vinegar
¼ cup Dijon mustard
1 medium shallot, finely minced
Finely grated zest and juice from 2 lemons
2 teaspoons fresh thyme leaves
Salt and freshly ground white pepper

MAKES 3 CUPS

Whisk together the oils, vinegar, mustard, shallot, lemon zest and juice, and thyme in a stainless-steel bowl and let stand at room temperature for 30 minutes. Season to taste with salt and white pepper. Store in a sealed container in the refrigerator for 2 weeks.

chapter 1
STIRRING, SHAKING & MUDDLING

CITY GROCERY BLOODY MARY — 4
ROSEMARY-CHERRY LEMONADE — 7
EUGENE WALTER'S ICED TEA — 8
LAST-WORD FIZZ — 11
"SMOKED" SAZERAC — 12
ABSINTHE FRAPPÉ — 14
BOURBON MILK PUNCH — 15
NEW OLD-FASHIONED — 17
SPICED CIDER — 18
UNIVERSITY GRAYS PUNCH — 21
DEADLIEST SIN CHAMPAGNE PUNCH — 22
MINT JULEP REDUX — 24
THE VOLUNTEER — 25

Chapter 1

STIRRING, SHAKING & MUDDLING

STIRRING, SHAKING & MUDDLING

Beverages come first here, for a number of reasons. First, when cooking at home, little sets the tone for an evening in the kitchen like a cocktail. My delightful wife, Bess, never lets me get started without offering to make me a drink. This tradition is nothing we ever discussed or considered. She's not a doting wife in that sort of way at all. This ceremony just began naturally the moment we started spending time in the kitchen together. It's simply the civilized way to initiate the process and it came to us organically. As a result it only makes sense that we tackle this subject straight out of the gate, so we can all get to work.

Second, other than wine and, to a lesser extent, beer, little academic consideration is given to the beverage world. Granted, the current interest in craft cocktails might suggest otherwise, but except to a precious few folks, cocktails are still whimsical and more "kicked back" than they are "considered." Oddly, though, every meal is rounded out by an accompanying beverage—whether it is coffee or apple juice with breakfast, iced tea with a barbecue sandwich at lunch, or the cocktail we choose before supper, they are an integral part of the experience of each of these meals and are almost always tasted before the first bite of food crosses our lips. These pages contain some of my favorites, alcoholic mostly, but a few for the family. All are for enjoyment.

BUFFALO TRACE DISTILLERY, INC.
FRANKFORT, KENTUCKY 20w
DSP #113 KY.
90.4 proof. Van Winkle
PURPOSE: TESTING O.E.P.:
PROOF: _____ LINE: _____
BATCH #: _____
TANK LOCATION: _____
BARREL S/N: Personalized Barrel
BARREL LOCATION: _____ DIST. DATE: _____
DIST. CO: _____
SCHEDULE #: _____ REF. #: _____
R.D. NO: _____
Cits Grocery
CONSIGNEE: For J. Van Winkle

CITY GROCERY BLOODY MARY

I have spent a significant portion of my life working on different Bloody Mary recipes because I love this basic flavor combination and, let's be honest, sometimes it's the only thing that will bring you back from the brink. Each is distinctly different, but like gumbo, each has its place, time, and raison d'être. When we opened the Grocery, though, I met my match with regard to how seriously I took this drink. Randy Yates, our bar manager (and ultimately business partner), insisted we craft a special recipe and make us *the* destination in town for this libation. The result is spicy, fun, effervescent, and bright.

"Welcome to the Jungle" —Guns N' Roses

ingredients

4 cups V8 juice

1¾ cups vodka of your choice
(good quality, but not "top shelf")

3 tablespoons Worcestershire Sauce *(page 97)*
or store bought

5 teaspoons prepared horseradish

2½ teaspoons finely grated shallots

1½ teaspoons minced garlic

2 tablespoons dill pickle juice

2 teaspoons Tabasco hot sauce

¾ teaspoon celery seeds

2½ teaspoons freshly ground black pepper

1½ teaspoons kosher salt

Finely grated zest and juice of 1 lemon

Finely grated zest and juice of 1 lime

Ice cubes

6 pickled okra pods

12 cocktail onions

6 good-quality pitted olives

6 lime wedges

SERVES 6

Combine the V8, vodka, Worcestershire, horseradish, shallots, garlic, pickle juice, Tabasco, celery seeds, pepper, salt, and lemon and lime zest and juice in a large pitcher and stir well to combine. Place the pitcher in the fridge and let chill (this will keep the drink from diluting as much when you pour it over ice).

Fill 6 short glasses with ice. Skewer 1 okra pod, 2 onions, and 1 olive on 6 skewers and place one in each glass.

Pour the chilled mixture over the ice. Sprinkle the top of each drink with a little more pepper and top with a wedge of lime.

Variation

Turn this into a Bloody Pig by adding 2 teaspoons Goya brand ham concentrate. It's my favorite and is available at Latin specialty markets. It also makes an excellent "rimming" ingredient (like salt on a margarita glass). Add crumbled bacon to the cocktail and garnish with a trimmed romaine lettuce leaf, a pepperoncini pepper, and/or a pickled jalapeño.

ROSEMARY-CHERRY LEMONADE

I worked with a young Italian chef early in my career who lived by very set rules in his cooking. One he never stated but that was extremely clear was: Where there is rosemary, let there be lemon . . . and vice versa. We did lots that involved this combination, so when our first big street festival event came around in Oxford, I rolled out this old girl for a refreshing new twist on an old favorite. People went nuts for it. Only use fresh rosemary because the oils in the rosemary leaves are what give this its punch.

"Cherry Bomb" —Joan Jett and the Blackhearts

In a nonreactive pan, combine the sugar with 2 cups of the water and warm over medium heat until the sugar dissolves. Remove from the heat and set aside to cool slightly. Stir in the rosemary and let cool further to room temperature. Remove the rosemary sprig and discard.

Combine the cherries with 1 cup of the water in a nonreactive saucepan and bring to a simmer over medium heat. Remove from the heat immediately and set aside to cool to room temperature.

In a pitcher, combine the cooled rosemary syrup, the cherries and their liquid, the lemon juice, and the remaining 5 cups water. Stir to combine. Serve over crushed ice with a lemon wheel on each glass.

ingredients

1 cup sugar
8 cups water
2 sprigs fresh rosemary
½ cup chopped dried cherries
1 cup freshly squeezed lemon juice
Crushed ice
Lemon wheels, for serving

MAKES 1 MEDIUM-SIZE PITCHER

EUGENE WALTER'S ICED TEA

Little has bothered me (from a beverage standpoint) throughout my life more than cloudy and/or stale iced tea. There isn't much in the world more off-putting to me than ordering a barbecue sandwich somewhere you know is going to be excellent and then drawing a glass of tea that is flaccid and stale. Iced tea should be bright and crisp.

I drink lots of tea when it is warm, and it is warm most of the time in Mississippi. I developed an unapologetic love for tea made very sweet when I was young, and in spite of my mildly diabetic condition, this is still something I indulge in. If sweet tea kills me, well, so be it.

Years ago I read an account of how Eugene Walter made iced tea—or I have completely imagined it and now attribute this perfect recipe to his memory. He was a man (writer, actor, puppeteer, poet, extraordinary cook, and bon vivant) nearly impossible to sum up in words, but one who had definite opinions on everything he addressed, including iced tea. It is the addition of ice cubes to the hot concentrate that cements the brightness of tea made from this recipe. It has an almost infinite life in the refrigerator. I have literally left the country with some in the fridge and returned two weeks later, and it looks and tastes just-made.

My dear friend John Egerton suggested the addition of baking soda, which takes a touch of bitterness off the tea. I don't notice bitterness very much when using Luzianne tea bags, but tasted side by side, there is definitely a touch of difference when baking soda is included.

ingredients

6 family-size tea bags
8 cups boiling water
¼ teaspoon baking powder
1½ cups sugar *(optional)*
8 cups ice cubes
½ cup chopped fresh mint *(optional)*

SERVES 12

"Adam Raised a Cain" —Bruce Springsteen

Place the tea bags in a large glass or plastic pitcher, pour the boiling water over, and steep for 15 minutes. Stir in the baking soda and sugar, if using.

Add the ice and stir briefly to begin to melt. Remove the tea bags and discard. Place the pitcher in the refrigerator; the tea will keep for up to 2 weeks.

For Mint Iced Tea: Once the tea has begun to cool, wrap the mint in cheesecloth and add to the tea. It will give it a nice flavor after steeping overnight.

Variations
If half iced tea and half lemonade gives you an Arnold Palmer, then half iced tea and half rosemary lemonade gives you a Rosie Arnold!

For a John Daily, combine 1 part iced tea, 1 part lemonade, and one half part bourbon.

A NOTE ON "GROWN-UP" DRINKS

I enjoy a reputation as a man who likes his whiskey. As much as some may think that has unsavory potential, I am *actually* a man who truly enjoys it. I love everything from the way a bottle feels in my hand to the beautiful and varying hues of caramel that the family of brown liquor spans to the *fffpooop* sound the cork makes coming out of the top of the bottle for the first time to the feeling that very first sip has as it slides slowly down your esophagus to your stomach and bounces so quickly back to the pleasure center in the brain. I alternately blame and credit my dad for this, depending on whether it's a painful morning or a joyous evening. Few people have truly appreciated a glass of whiskey like my dad.

I enjoy good wine, but I drink it only with food. I'll have the occasional beer when I am fishing or playing golf, but for most of my life, a glass of whiskey on the rocks has been my simple recipe for contentment. This started for me at a debutante party in New Orleans when I was about 19. My mom was out of town, so Dad and I hit the party together. In an attempt to illustrate that I was becoming a man of the world, I ordered a Scotch with him. He didn't notice . . . I sipped. I liked. I sipped more. I really liked.

It was in this moment that I understood why Dad enjoyed his first glass of Scotch after work so much. I was washed over with a warmth that was as seductive as anything I remembered. It was good.

When we got ready to open City Grocery and I was putting thought into the beverage program, I remembered, throughout my life, Dad talking about particular restaurants that he liked because he didn't feel like he was getting squeezed when he ordered a drink. I remember him, when I was a youngster, marveling over a tumbler at Antoine's and espousing the virtues of a place that served "grown-up" drinks. A "grown-up" drink was one made for a man who knew exactly what he wanted, was serious about what that was, and didn't want to waste time ordering multiple times. So one drink was usually as big as two or three "regular" drinks. A restaurant that served such was reason enough to patronize that particular place. We returned for these "grown-up" drinks in spite of what the food may have been like at several places that dot the landscape of my lifetime.

"Grown-up" drinks became the order of the day at City Grocery, and that he *did* notice. We pour a man's drink at the Grocery and always have. There's no telling how much frigging booze I've given away just to be able to say that I serve big-boy drinks for big boys and big girls, but what I do know is that it keeps my dad coming back.

LAST-WORD FIZZ

My friend and super-stud mixologist at French 75 in New Orleans Chris Hannah turned me on to the Last Word. I don't much go in for overwrought, *froufrou* cocktails, but this one changed my opinion on the craft cocktail with my very first sip. It is a masterful blend of citrus, floral, sweet, and herbal, with a gin base. We make it and finish it with an egg white to spin it up into a fizz. It's lovely, though deadly in the right quantity.

"Kiss the Sky" —Sean Lee's Ping Pong Orchestra

In a cocktail shaker, combine the gin, Chartreuse, Luxardo, lime juice, sugar, and egg white. Shake vigorously for 20 seconds. This is called a "dry shake." Add a few crushed ice cubes, and shake again for another 15 seconds.

Strain into two cocktail glasses. Top with a small splash of soda water. Rub each rim with and garnish with a lime twist. Drizzle with cherry juice and serve.

ingredients

¾ ounce gin
¾ ounce green Chartreuse
½ ounce Luxardo maraschino liquor
¾ ounce freshly squeezed lime juice
1 tablespoon confectioners' sugar
1 egg white
Splash of soda water
2 lime twists, for garnish
1 teaspoon cherry juice

SERVES 2

"SMOKED" SAZERAC

There are so many things wrong with this drink that I can't even begin to say. I have never been one for smoke in my cocktails, but my friend Greg Seider (the brains behind the Summit in New York City) changed my mind with a smoky version of the Mint Julep in the summer of 2011 at the Big Apple BBQ Block Party. With a deft hand, a little smoke brings an interesting depth of flavor. I serve this one over cubed ice . . . apologies to my hometown. Little could offend some people more than a Sazerac not served straight up but then again we drink Martinis on the rocks in New Orleans, so I take my liberties.

"Hang On St. Christopher" —Tom Waits

ingredients

1½ teaspoons absinthe

1 drop of liquid smoke

Ice cubes

4 dashes of Peychaud's bitters

3 ounces rye whiskey

1½ teaspoons sugar

4 smoked ice cubes *(see Note)*

Lemon peel, for serving

SERVES 1

Pour the absinthe and a drop of liquid smoke into a large old-fashioned glass and swirl.

In a cocktail shaker half-filled with ice cubes, combine the bitters, rye, and sugar. Using a long bar spoon, stir quickly for 15 seconds. Wrap the smoked ice cubes in a bar towel and crack with a muddler. Swirl the absinthe in the glass again and discard. Place the cracked smoked ice into the glass and strain the rye over the top. Rub the rim with the lemon peel and drop into the drink.

Note:

To make smoked ice, place water in a heatproof dish inside a smoker for 45 minutes. Remove the water from the smoker, pour it into ice-cube trays, and freeze.

ABSINTHE FRAPPÉ

There is a reason for the legends around absinthe. That reason is that, if consumed in some quantity, it will mess you up nine ways from Sunday. I know; trust me, it leaves a mark. That being said, I've never seen a green fairy. I did see a couple of rats fall through a ceiling tile in the filthiest diner on the planet and fight to the death while screwy on some very nice Swiss blue absinthe, but I digress. In moderation, good absinthe is a really nice way to end a meal. This cocktail gives you the option of something other than sipping the straight watered devil. It's basically a mint julep with absinthe instead of bourbon. As odd as the combination of anise and mint may seem, it's astonishingly bright and refreshing.

ingredients

"Fuckin' with My Head" —Beck

8 fresh mint leaves

1 teaspoon sugar

1½ ounces absinthe

¾ ounce simple syrup
(dissolve 1 tablespoon + 1 teaspoon sugar in 1 tablespoon warm water)

2 ounces sparkling or soda water

½ teaspoon freshly squeezed lemon juice

Crushed ice

SERVES 1

Muddle the mint leaves with sugar in an old-fashioned glass.

In a cocktail shaker, combine ½ cup crushed ice, the absinthe, and simple syrup. Shake vigorously for 10 seconds. Pour into the glass with the muddled mint. Stir in the sparkling water and lemon juice, and top with more crushed ice.

BOURBON MILK PUNCH

Unbeknownst to most folks, Bourbon Milk Punch (or Brandy Milk Punch, depending on who's making it) is the choice beverage of the gentlemen who work the floats on Mardi Gras day on St. Charles Avenue and ply the masses with plastic beads and aluminum doubloons. Fat Tuesday can be very long for the guys who ride in the parade early in the morning, have been up (more than likely) late the night before, and will attend one of the Mardi Gras balls that night. Milk Punch is both a good entry point on those mornings and easy on what can be a sensitive Mardi Gras belly.

"Pancho and Lefty" —Emmylou Harris

ingredients

Pour the milk, half-and-half, vanilla, and bourbon over cracked ice in a cocktail shaker. Spoon in the sugar, and shake vigorously. Pour into a large old-fashioned glass, sprinkle nutmeg over the top, and serve.

4 ounces whole milk
2 tablespoons half-and-half
1 teaspoon vanilla extract
2½ ounces Buffalo Trace bourbon
4 teaspoons confectioners' sugar
Freshly grated nutmeg, for garnish

SERVES 1

NEW OLD-FASHIONED

One of my favorite memories as a child was heading west out of New Orleans into Cajun country with my mom and dad. Whenever we did, they always stopped at the last outpost west of the city in LaPlace, called Airline Motors. It was this giant mom-and-pop-owned truck stop that had a great diner that also mixed great drinks. Mom and Dad would always pick up giant Styrofoam cups of their signature Old-Fashioned for the 3-hour straight shot across the south Louisiana swamp to Lafayette, and I was always allowed one little taste. It was here I fell in love with the bourbony, sweet, orangy, cherry combination that is the brilliance at the center of an otherwise sophisticated cocktail. Here's our twenty-first-century version. God bless you, Airline Motors.

"Mondo Bongo" —Joe Strummer and the Mescaleros

ingredients

In a large old-fashioned glass, muddle the sugar, cherries, lemon peel, bitters, and half of the blood orange slice with the soda water. Fill the glass with cracked or crushed ice. Add the bourbon and stir briefly. Wipe the glass rim with the other half of the blood orange slice and use to garnish the rim.

Note:

Fernet-Branca is a bitter, Italian, herb-flavored digestif. It is from the family of spirits known as *amari* and is arguably the sophisticated distant cousin of Jägermeister. If it is not available, you can just as successfully plump the cherries in bourbon.

2 teaspoons sugar

3 dried cherries, soaked in Fernet-Branca to plump *(see Note)*

1 medium piece lemon peel

3 to 4 dashes of Orange Bitters *(recipe follows)*

1 slice blood orange, cut in half

1 very small splash of soda water

Cracked or crushed ice

2½ ounces Old Fitzgerald bourbon *(or whichever you choose)*

SERVES 1

ORANGE BITTERS

Making bitters is a very easy process. Other than waiting for a couple of weeks for your flavors to develop, there isn't much to simple bitters-making.

4 blood oranges *(or your favorite variety)*
3 whole cloves
2 whole cardamom pods
2 whole star anise
10 black peppercorns
3 allspice berries
½ teaspoon ground gentian root *(see Note)*
½ teaspoon cinchona bark *(see Note)*
2 cups inexpensive vodka *(over 90 proof)*

MAKES JUST OVER 2 CUPS

Wash and peel the oranges. Chop the peel into ⅛- to ¼-inch pieces and place in a dehydrator overnight (or in a 150°F oven), or until completely dried.

Place the dried peel with the cloves, cardamom, star anise, peppercorns, allspice berries, gentian root, and cinchona bark in a quart-size jar and cover with the vodka. Let stand for 2 weeks, giving the jar a shake every day.

After 2 weeks, strain the liquid and reserve. Crush the ingredients remaining in the strainer with a mortar and pestle and place the solids into a saucepan along with 1 cup water. Bring to a boil, then decrease the heat to low and simmer for 10 minutes, or until reduced by about half. Strain the liquid and discard the solids. Add the liquid to the vodka mixture. The bitters are ready to use and will keep for up to 6 months at room temperature in glass bottles.

Note:

Gentian root and cinchona bark are bittering agents used to give these bitters their unique characteristic. They are available widely from botanical supply companies on the Internet. We use dandelionbotanical.com.

SPICED CIDER

I am not sure who the bartender was at City Grocery about 15 years ago who commandeered a Farmer Brothers' glass coffeepot and started making the City Grocery Spiced Cider, but I do know I want to kiss him. There is very little on this earth better on a cold night than combining warm apple cider and bourbon with a blend of exotic spices. The smell fills the room, and more than a couple of these will put you on your ass. Believe . . .

ingredients

"Kentucky Rain" —Elvis Presley

4 cups apple cider

Peel of ½ medium orange

Peel of 1 lemon

1 stick cinnamon

4 whole cloves

3 allspice berries

2 cups W. G. Weller bourbon

Lemon twists, for garnish

Freshly grated nutmeg, for garnish

SERVES 8 TO 10

Combine the cider, orange and lemon peels, cinnamon, cloves, and allspice berries in a large saucepan and bring to a boil. Decrease the heat to low and simmer for 3 minutes. Remove from the heat and let steep for 7 to 10 minutes. Strain the liquid into a coffeepot, discard the solids, and add the bourbon. Serve warm in coffee mugs with a twist of lemon and grated nutmeg.

UNIVERSITY GRAYS PUNCH

There are scores of punch recipes attributed to different artillery, cavalry, and infantry divisions from the Revolutionary and Civil wars. Most are similar in that they are combinations of multiple liquors, sugar, and fruit. They are really just quasi-sophisticated versions of the "jungle juice" punches we used to make for high-school keg parties. The intention was exactly the same . . . only we hadn't been fighting hand-to-hand combat.

This recipe is one that Jayce McConnell (director of our cocktail program at Snackbar) made in honor of the twentieth anniversary of City Grocery. The University Grays, the Confederate infantry division from Oxford, was made up of almost all Ole Miss students. They suffered an almost 100 percent mortality or injury rate during Pickett's Charge at Gettysburg. This stuff is about as lethal as the foe they faced.

"Oh! You Pretty Things" —David Bowie

ingredients

2 cups **Old Grand-Dad bourbon**
2 cups **Appleton Estate V/X rum**
2 cups **Hennessy VSOP Cognac**
6 cups **Champagne**
½ cup **freshly squeezed lemon juice**
2 cups **Lemon-Thyme Shrub** *(recipe follows)*
3 **lemons, sliced ⅛ inch thick**
12 **sprigs fresh thyme**
Ice ring *(see Note)*

SERVES 20

Stir together the bourbon, rum, Cognac, Champagne, lemon juice, shrub, lemon slices, and thyme in a large punch bowl. Float one large ice ring in the center and ladle the punch into punch cups or cocktail glasses.

Note:

To make an ice ring, fill a Bundt pan halfway full with water, dot with herbs and flowers, if you like, and freeze. Unmold and place in the punch when ready to serve.

LEMON-THYME SHRUB

12 lemons
¾ cup freshly squeezed lemon juice
¼ cup fresh thyme leaves
5 cups sugar

MAKES ABOUT 2 CUPS

Shrubs come in a couple of varieties; some are acidic (vinegar-based), and others are more syrupy (just sugar and fruit). Both are vehicles for preserving (at least in the short term) summer fruits. Traditionally both varieties are cooked, strained, and then used to mix both alcoholic and nonalcoholic beverages. The nonalcoholic varieties are likely what preceded modern-day "sodas." This recipe is actually uncooked so that every bit of the brightness in the lemon and the oil in the thyme leaves are uncompromised. These oils lose their potency when subjected to heat.

Wash and peel the lemons, being very careful to get as little as possible of the white part (pith) of the lemon with the peel. Place the peels in a 1-quart glass jar. Carefully remove any extra white pith from the fruit and discard. Slice the flesh of the lemon and add to the jar. Add the juice, thyme, and sugar. Cover and let stand at room temperature for 3 days, shaking a couple of times a day.

Strain the liquid through a fine-mesh sieve and pour into a glass jar. Discard the solids. This will keep for 3 months at room temperature.

DEADLIEST SIN CHAMPAGNE PUNCH

A good punch is an outstanding way to get a party rolling. They are typically loaded with both booze and sugar, so they go down easy and sneak up on you quickly. There are few better legal ways to get folks to loosen up at an event. Like so many other things, when used in moderation punch will take you exactly where you want to go; used irresponsibly, you'll likely wake up in a ditch somewhere. This is a great summer variety. It's light, bright, and fun.

"Sin City" —Emmylou Harris and Beck

ingredients

1 (750-ml) bottle brut Champagne

2½ cups Cognac

3 tablespoons molasses

2 cups **Citrus-Strawberry Shrub** *(recipe follows)*

1 lemon, sliced, including rind

1 orange, sliced, including rind

1 lime, sliced, including rind

5 sprigs fresh rosemary

Ice ring *(see Note, page 21)*

SERVES 10

Stir together the Champagne, Cognac, molasses, shrub, the lemon, orange, and lime slices, and the rosemary in a punch bowl. Float one large ice ring in the center and let chill for 10 to 15 minutes. Remove the rosemary sprigs and ladle the punch into punch cups or cocktail glasses.

CITRUS-STRAWBERRY SHRUB

1 lemon

1 lime

1 orange

3 tablespoons freshly squeezed lemon juice

3 tablespoons freshly squeezed lime juice

3 tablespoons freshly squeezed orange juice

2¼ cups sugar

1 cup sliced strawberries

5 teaspoons chopped fresh rosemary

MAKES ABOUT 1 QUART

Wash and peel the lemon, lime, and orange, being very careful to get as little as possible of the white part (pith) of each fruit with the peel. Place the peels in a 1-quart glass jar. Carefully remove the white pith from all three citrus fruits and discard. Slice the flesh of the lemon, lime, and orange and add to the jar. Add the lemon, lime, and orange juices, sugar, strawberries, and rosemary to the jar. Cover and let stand at room temperature for 3 days, shaking a couple times each day.

Strain the liquid through a fine-mesh strainer, and pour into a glass jar. Discard the solids. This will keep for 2 months at room temperature.

MINT JULEP REDUX

The Mint Julep only saw the introduction of bourbon as its anchor spirit after being adopted as the companion beverage to the Kentucky Derby. The original versions of the Julep were made with brandy, and some called for the addition of berries and orange for garnish. Other recipes call for gin, Madeira, rye, claret, and so on, but the original was crafted with brandy. I was skeptical at first, but the drink itself is remarkably tasty and refreshing. We add a little orange to brighten it. Damn, people used to like to drink! And they did it *way* better than we do.

ingredients

"Rip Her to Shreds" —Elvis Presley

2½ teaspoons sugar

6 fresh mint leaves

1 piece orange peel, plus extra for rimming the glass

1 teaspoon orange flower water *(optional)*

Splash of soda water

Crushed ice

3 ounces brandy

Fresh sprig mint, for garnish

Fresh blueberries, for garnish

SERVES 1

In a large old-fashioned glass, combine the sugar, mint, orange peel, orange flower water (if using), and soda water and muddle until the mint is pulverized. Fill the glass with crushed ice and pour the brandy over. Stir well, and garnish with the mint sprig and fresh blueberries. Rim the glass with a fresh orange peel.

THE VOLUNTEER

On behalf of the city of New Orleans, I want to thank each and every good soul who swept in, in the months following Hurricane Katrina, and helped clean up the shit mess that the Corps of Engineers' levee failure delivered to the city. Had it not been for you, we would likely still be cleaning up the wreck our fair city was. Fortunately, you came in church groups, you came as families, you came as individuals, you came out of the goodness of your hearts to help. Some of you relocated to the city, others found a new love in it, some gained a greater appreciation, but *all of you* earned our eternal gratitude. I know this because I was there for the better part of two years working on rebuilding Willie Mae's Scotch House in the Treme neighborhood, and I hosted and hugged many of you. New Orleans is now a greater city than it was before August 29, 2005, in part thanks to what you gave of yourselves. Landmarks were saved, lives were rebuilt, spirits were bolstered because you came. A large number of you were Latins, so this one has a decidedly south-of-the-border twist. To all of you, we raise a glass and say thank you. Whip up a batch of these, kick back on the porch, and survey the good you have done. Or stop by City Grocery any time, let me buy you a drink, and tell me your story.

"Louisiana 1927" —Randy Newman

ingredients

In a small glass or stainless-steel bowl, combine the cucumber, 1 tablespoon of the lime juice, the cumin, and 1 pinch of salt. Cover with plastic wrap and place in the refrigerator for 1 hour to "pickle."

Place the melon, jalapeño, the remaining pinch of salt, and cilantro in a blender and puree. Cover and let stand in the refrigerator for 30 minutes. Strain the contents through a fine-mesh strainer, pressing the solids with a ladle or back of a large spoon to get all of the juice out. Discard the solids.

In a cocktail shaker half filled with ice, add ¾ cup melon juice, the remaining 2 tablespoons lime juice, agave, tequila, and Grand Marnier. Shake vigorously for 20 seconds. Strain over cracked ice into an old-fashioned glass. Garnish with several pieces of the "pickled" cucumber. (Place the rest in a shallow bowl to snack on.)

Note:

Charentais is, for lack of a better description, a miniature, intensified, French cantaloupe. At the peak of the season, they are about as sweet as anything natural you will put into your mouth. They pop up stateside in specialty markets in the summer. In a pinch, use a good ripe cantaloupe or substitute a really sweet watermelon.

½ cup peeled, deseeded, very small-dice cucumber

3 tablespoons freshly squeezed lime juice

¼ teaspoon ground cumin

2 pinches of salt

4 cups deseeded, small-dice Charentais melon *(see Note)*

1 tablespoon deseeded and minced jalapeño pepper

1 tablespoon chopped fresh cilantro

2 tablespoons agave nectar

4 ounces Patrón Silver tequila

¾ ounce Grand Marnier

Cracked ice

SERVES 2

01/15/2006

chapter 2

BOILING & SIMMERING

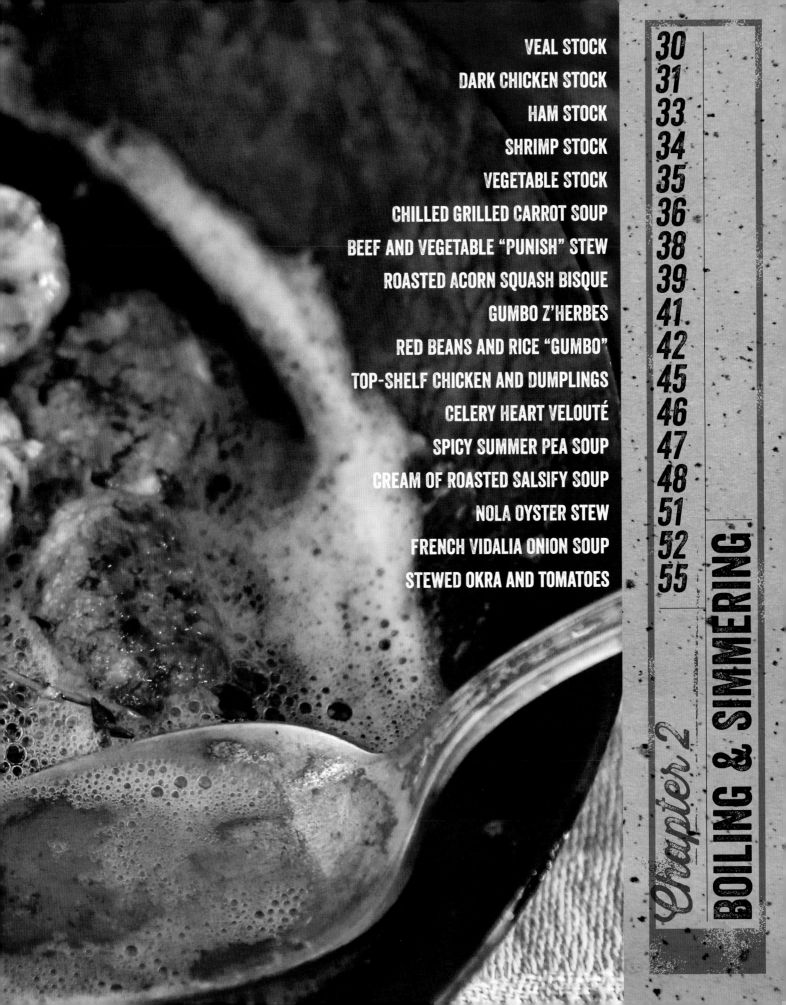

VEAL STOCK — 30
DARK CHICKEN STOCK — 31
HAM STOCK — 33
SHRIMP STOCK — 34
VEGETABLE STOCK — 35
CHILLED GRILLED CARROT SOUP — 36
BEEF AND VEGETABLE "PUNISH" STEW — 38
ROASTED ACORN SQUASH BISQUE — 39
GUMBO Z'HERBES — 41
RED BEANS AND RICE "GUMBO" — 42
TOP-SHELF CHICKEN AND DUMPLINGS — 45
CELERY HEART VELOUTÉ — 46
SPICY SUMMER PEA SOUP — 47
CREAM OF ROASTED SALSIFY SOUP — 48
NOLA OYSTER STEW — 51
FRENCH VIDALIA ONION SOUP — 52
STEWED OKRA AND TOMATOES — 55

Chapter 2
BOILING & SIMMERING

BOILING & SIMMERING

My mother traumatized me with soup as a kid. I hated it, and it was her fault that I hated it. That's right—I am coming out of the gate calling Becky Currence to the mat. I hated soup not for what it was, but for what it wasn't. What it wasn't was a meal, and I had very definite feelings on the matter. A "meal" consisted of protein, starch, and vegetable (and preferably sauce, if we must be really picky) in *individual, discernable piles*. Are you getting this, Mom? My dad and brother, the consummate ass-kissing mollycoddlers, fawned all over Mom's creations in the gumbo pot. They were particularly fond of her beef and vegetable stew. My blood boiled, as a wise young tot, every time I approached the dinner table and saw it set with soup bowls. Soup, to my Jungian mind, meant I was being cheated out of calories, sustenance, and experience.

On a particularly chilly February night in the very early 1970s, Mom and I collided over her tragically omnipresent beef stew. It was Mardi Gras season, and on this particular night, all the neighborhood kids and parents were rendezvousing at our house to go to the night's parade. Strategically, I decided that this was my opportunity to plant my flag of protest. I pushed my bowl away and roundly refused to eat. Mom insisted that if I didn't eat my stew, I would not go to the parade with all my friends. Young MacArthur decided he had an upper hand with friends and parents converging on the house and that there was no way she would fail to buckle. It was, it turns out, total miscalculation on my part. Everyone came and went, and Mom and I remained at the table with the aforementioned bowl of awfulness. We sat there until everyone returned and my brother trundled off to bed under the weight of his evening's Mardi Gras bounty.

Ultimately it was me and Joan Crawford locked in the battle of wills as the house and neighborhood fell completely silent. I was eventually excused and sent to bed, but that f-ing soup was waiting for me at the breakfast table. I ate . . . she won. I learned a valuable lesson: Her will outweighed mine.

I respected Cruella, but I hated her soup and what it represented. In the years that followed, I would continue to be traumatized by the "non-meal." For example, my first ever assignment to make a special for service was in the kitchen at Crook's Corner. A load of acorn squash was dumped on my butcher block one Friday afternoon, and I was instructed to make soup from it. Not only did I hate soup, but I also had never laid eyes on an acorn squash. Before it was over, Bill Neal and I would have a famous clash over that pot of soup. It was the last time I ever spoke with him. I hate that that is my last memory of the man. I blame soup.

When we first opened the Grocery, we didn't even have a soup on the menu. Though my opinions on the subject had mellowed, it just wasn't anything I gave much thought to, and, strangely, nobody said a word about its absence. I knew instinctively, however, that I would have to face the demon soup if I were ever going to be worth half my weight in salt, and so I set about crafting recipes that met my sensibilities. As soon as I set my mind to it, my opinions began to change, and I now love a good bowl of soup more than most people on the planet. I finally arrived.

If all that weren't quite enough, the first time I went to my mother-in-law's house, she was making my bride's favorite meal. Bess could not have been any more excited to be home from New York City and share her greatest culinary treasure with me. We sat down at the table, set with soup bowls, a loaf of crusty country bread, and a steaming tureen of stew. I was oddly ill at ease and couldn't quite put my finger on why. The top came off the pot and the smell filled the room and it hit me all at once. It turns out it was the exact same stew I had missed my parade over on that cool February night of my childhood. On this occasion, I sopped up the last of my soup with some sourdough bread and asked for more. It turns out that some things are just more important than others.

My sweet little bride, Bess, thinks this is hysterical. She calls it "Punish" Stew. Go ahead, Bess, pick on the fat kid. You'll get yours soon enough.

Now I like soup so much that the recipes included in this chapter make slightly larger batches, because they all rewarm and freeze so nicely for an easy second (or third meal).

VEAL STOCK

Stocks are the principle building block of so much of what we do in the kitchen that it is staggering. We go through thousands of gallons of veal, chicken, shrimp, ham, pork, and fish stocks a year. It's so serious that we have one guy who does individual stocks for each of the restaurants, all day, every day. If the stock is not dead-on, the final product will never be better than the quality of that stock. While it may seem tedious, making a stock rather than using a store-bought one will completely change whatever you are making with it. Plus it makes your house smell wonderful and you'll feel like a total badass telling people what you did.

"Monkey Man" —The Rolling Stones

5 pounds veal leg bones, knuckles, and/or neck, cut into 2- to 3-inch pieces

¾ cup tomato paste

2 cups peeled and roughly chopped carrots

2 cups roughly chopped celery
(leaving the leaves on is fine)

2 cups roughly chopped yellow onions

⅓ cup crushed garlic

5 fresh bay leaves *(or 3 dried)*

10 sprigs fresh thyme

4 sprigs fresh rosemary

15 sprigs fresh flat-leaf parsley

1 tablespoon black peppercorns

2 cups dry red wine

MAKES ABOUT 6 QUARTS

Preheat the oven to 450°F. Arrange the bones in a single layer in a couple of baking dishes or roasting pans and place in the oven. Check the bones every 7 minutes or so and, as they begin to brown, turn them until they are nicely lightly browned on all sides. Remove the bones from the oven and evenly brush the tops with the tomato paste. Return the bones to the oven and roast until the tomato paste browns, but be careful it doesn't burn. Remove the pan from the oven, and then transfer the roasted bones to a large stockpot. Reserve the fat in the roasting pans.

Add the carrots, celery, onions, and garlic to the roasting pan and stir to coat with the fat. Place the pan back in the oven and brown the vegetables lightly for an additional 10 to 15 minutes, stirring once or twice.

In the meantime, wrap the bay leaves, thyme, rosemary, parsley, and black peppercorns together in cheesecloth (or a coffee filter) and tie with a length of butcher's string.

Remove the browned vegetables from the pan and place in the stockpot with the bones. Place the roasting pan on the stovetop and turn on low heat underneath. Pour the red wine into the pan and stir with a wooden spoon, scraping the caramelized bits from the bottom of the pan. Pour this all off into the stockpot. Add enough cold water to the pot to cover the bones and vegetables and add the herb sachet. Bring the pot to a boil over medium heat and immediately decrease to a very low simmer. Cook for about 12 hours (the pot should just barely bubble). Turn the heat off, cover the pot, and let it cool to room temperature. Refrigerate to chill.

The next day, return the pot to the stove and bring back to a boil over high heat. As soon as it reaches a boil, decrease the heat to low, and simmer for an additional 4 hours.

Remove the bones, and strain the stock into a smaller pot. Discard the bones and vegetable solids. Return the stock to the stove and bring to a simmer over medium heat. Lower the heat, and slide the pot just off center of the heat source; the simmer will push the fat floating on the top more to one side of the pot. Using a ladle or large spoon, skim off as much of the fat and scum as you can and discard. Cool to room temperature, and then refrigerate until any residual fat congeals on top of the stock. Remove this hardened fat with a spoon and discard. (You can also reserve the fat, refrigerated, to use for cooking. For example, carrots are excellent cooked in beef fat.)

The stock can be used immediately, or refrigerated for up to 5 days. Frozen, it will keep almost indefinitely.

Note:
It is best to start this recipe early in the morning because in order to execute it properly, it needs a full 24 hours of attention.

DARK CHICKEN STOCK

For your sake, find a good ethnic or local grocery store. They will carry things you don't usually consider, like chicken backs and necks. Ours has jars of catfish "stink bait" arranged on top of the chicken cooler. (That is fermented chicken innards. Apparently catfish find that sort of thing appealing . . . but I digress.) Wherever you can find some chicken parts that are mostly bone and cartilage, they are exactly what you want, ideally. You can also buy whole chickens, debone them, and freeze the meat and the carcasses to use when you need them.

Stock is an essential element to a high-quality finished soup or sauce. Skip making stock and you immediately compromise your final product. Making stocks is good cooking practice, and they will keep almost forever when frozen.

"Love for Sale" —Talking Heads

Preheat the oven to 450°F. Arrange the bones, onions, carrots, celery, fennel, and garlic in a single layer in a large roasting pan. Roast for 10 to 15 minutes, until the tops begin to brown. Stir well to expose the unbrowned parts. Continue to roast and stir until the bones and vegetables have lightly browned all over.

Remove the pan from the oven and place the contents in a stockpot. Place the roasting pan over low heat and add the white wine. Stir with a wooden spoon, scraping and loosening all of the caramelized bits from the bottom of the pan. Pour this liquid into the stockpot and place the pot on the stovetop over high heat. Add cold water to cover the bones and bring to a boil.

In the meantime, wrap the bay leaves, thyme, parsley, and peppercorns in cheese-cloth (or a coffee filter), tie with a length of butcher's string, and add the sachet to the stockpot.

As soon as the liquid comes to a boil, lower the heat so the liquid just barely simmers. Cook for about 3 hours. Remove the pot from the heat and strain the liquid into a smaller pot. Discard the solids. Return the stock to the stove and bring to a simmer over medium heat. Lower the heat, and slide the pot just off center of the heat source; the simmer will push the fat floating on the top more to one side of the pot. Using a ladle or large spoon, skim off as much of the fat and scum as you can and discard. Cool to room temperature, and then refrigerate until any residual fat congeals on top of the stock. Remove this hardened fat with a spoon and discard. Use the stock within 4 days, or freeze for up to 6 months.

ingredients

4 pounds chicken bones

2½ cups roughly chopped yellow onions

2 cups peeled and roughly chopped carrots

2 cups roughly chopped celery

1½ cups roughly chopped fennel stalks *(optional)*

8 cloves garlic, crushed

2 cups dry white wine

5 fresh bay leaves *(or 3 dried)*

10 sprigs fresh thyme

12 to 15 sprigs fresh flat-leaf parsley

1 tablespoon black peppercorns

MAKES ABOUT 6 QUARTS

MAKING GOOD STOCK

Making a good veal stock is an art. *Sauciers* in traditional French kitchens are some of the most revered among the ranks. A well-made stock, whether veal, chicken, shrimp, or pork, can make or break a dish. Almost all are slow and deliberate to achieve the desired outcome: a clear, flavorful stock. With the fattier stocks, like veal, pork, and chicken, the real challenge is to make a flavorful broth without the final product becoming too cloudy. Cooking over low heat and slightly off center from your heat source will cause the fat to float and to pool on one side of the pot, making it easy to skim off. A cloudy stock comes from cooking it at too high a temperature and boiling too hard. When a stock rolls at a boil, it causes the fat molecules, which naturally want to float at the top of the stock, to be drawn to the bottom of the pot. At 212°F they explode and cause the stock to cloud. This can be rectified by making a "raft" of ground chicken and egg whites and slowly clarifying the stock, but that is a tedious and, arguably, expensive process. So, if you take on stock, be patient and accept that it is a time-consuming process. Taste the crappy, store-bought broth next to your incredible homemade version, and I guarantee you'll throw the factory stock in the garbage forever.

HAM STOCK

Ham stock is a great substitute for chicken stock, especially when preparing dried beans. It has a little more of a robust flavor. We make ours with smoked ham hocks, which add a touch of smokiness to the final product.

"Cock the Hammer" —Cypress Hill

ingredients

Combine the ham hocks, onions, celery, carrots, garlic, bay leaves, rosemary, parsley, and peppercorns in a stockpot. Add enough cold water to cover. Bring to a boil over high heat. Immediately decrease the heat to maintain a low simmer. Cover the pot and cook for 5 hours. Remove from the heat and cool briefly.

Strain the liquid into another soup pot and discard the solids. Return the stock to the stove and bring to a simmer over medium heat. Lower the heat, and slide the pot just off center of the heat source; the simmer will push the fat floating on the top more to one side of the pot. Using a ladle or large spoon, skim off as much of the fat and scum as you can and discard. Cool to room temperature, and then refrigerate until any residual fat congeals on top of the stock. Remove this hardened fat with a spoon and discard. The stock will keep for up to 5 days in the refrigerator or frozen for up to 8 months.

3 pounds smoked ham hocks

1½ cups roughly chopped yellow onions

1 cup roughly chopped celery

1 cup peeled and roughly chopped carrots

2 tablespoons roughly chopped garlic

5 fresh bay leaves *(or 3 dried)*

3 large sprigs fresh rosemary

10 sprigs fresh flat-leaf parsley

1 tablespoon black peppercorns

MAKES ABOUT 6 QUARTS

SHRIMP STOCK

This is a good stock to have around for seafood gumbo, cioppino, court bouillon, or a simple root vegetable soup. The flavor is a little strong, so I recommend that you cut it with a little bit of chicken stock (about 25 percent) for anything that you don't want to be too "shrimp forward" in its flavor profile.

Shrimp stock is a very quick stock to make, typically about 45 minutes from start to finish. It takes only a little bit of chopping, and the most difficult part is assembling the shrimp shells to make it. The best thing to do is when you get fresh shrimp, peel them and place the shells in a ziplock freezer bag, press out all the air (or vacuum-seal with a FoodSaver-type machine), and freeze until you need them. Shells can be frozen for up to 5 months.

ingredients

"Home in Your Heart" —Solomon Burke

8 cups shrimp shells

½ cup brandy

2 cups roughly chopped celery

1½ cups roughly chopped yellow onions

8 cloves garlic, thickly sliced

3 dried bay leaves

1 tablespoon black peppercorns

6 sprigs fresh thyme

6 sprigs fresh flat-leaf parsley

1 cup white wine

MAKES ABOUT 6 QUARTS

Heat a medium stockpot over high heat for about 2 minutes. Add the shrimp shells and stir constantly for 3 to 4 minutes, until the shells have all turned pink. Pour in the brandy and stir. If you tilt the lip of the pot toward the heat, the brandy may ignite. If it does, do not panic. Agitate the pan and the flame will burn down quickly. Immediately add the celery, onions, garlic, bay leaves, black peppercorns, thyme, parsley, and white wine and combine well. Add 4½ quarts water and bring the stock to a boil over high heat. Decrease the heat to medium-low and simmer for 30 minutes. Remove from the heat and cool for 10 minutes. Strain through a fine-mesh sieve and discard the shells and vegetable solids. The stock will keep refrigerated for about 5 days or frozen for up to 5 months.

VEGETABLE STOCK

If you had asked me 20 years ago whether I would ever write a recipe for vegetable stock, much less employ one professionally . . . well, there is a nation of ex-cooks from our kitchen who are having a huge laugh on me right now. Ours was a kitchen of vegetarian hate; we were intolerant and insufferable. We cursed vegetarians and made fun of their lame ways. We forced ourselves to honor their demeaning requests. We were tragically immature in our disdain. Age frequently softens these sharp edges and, perhaps, we mature. This stock is perfect for summer vegetable treatments, when you need a flavor vehicle but don't want to compromise the flavors of whatever you are cooking. Okay, laugh it up, assholes . . . I'm making vegetable stock.

"I Need Some Sleep" —EELS

ingredients

Preheat the oven to 400°F. Toss the onions, carrots, celery, tomatoes, fennel, turnips, green peppers, and garlic in a large stainless-steel bowl with the olive oil, salt, and pepper. Spread the vegetables in a single layer in a large roasting pan and roast for about 15 minutes, or until the vegetables begin to brown. Stir the vegetables with a large spoon and return to the oven. Continue roasting and stirring until the vegetables are tender and browned all over, about 25 minutes total.

Dump the roasted vegetables into a stockpot and place the roasting pan on the stovetop over a low heat. Add the white wine and scrape the bottom of the pan with a wooden spoon to loosen all of the caramelized bits. Pour this off into the stockpot with the roasted vegetables. Place the pot on the stovetop. Add the parsley, thyme, tarragon, rosemary, bay leaves, and peppercorns and cover them with about 4 quarts water. Bring to a boil, and then lower the heat to maintain a low simmer for 1½ hours.

Strain the stock into a bowl and discard the solids. The stock keeps in the refrigerator for up to 1 week or frozen for up to 3 months.

3 cups roughly chopped yellow onions
2 cups peeled, roughly chopped carrots
2 cups roughly chopped celery
2 cups roughly chopped tomatoes
¾ cup roughly chopped fennel bulbs
2 cups peeled, roughly chopped turnips
1 cup deseeded and roughly chopped green bell peppers
10 cloves garlic, crushed
5 tablespoons pure olive oil
2 teaspoons salt
1 tablespoon freshly ground black pepper
2 cups dry white wine
12 sprigs fresh flat-leaf parsley
10 sprigs fresh thyme
4 sprigs fresh tarragon
2 sprigs fresh rosemary
5 bay leaves *(or 3 dried)*
2 tablespoons black peppercorns

MAKES ABOUT 3 QUARTS

CHILLED GRILLED CARROT SOUP

Carrots are all too frequently glossed over. You dump them into stocks, they play a role in soups and sauces, and they are an easy go-to for color in a salad. However, they rarely hit center stage. I love the damn things and they are usually dirt cheap, so they make a great menu item, especially because no one ever sees them coming. This recipe really nails everything that is beautiful and surprising about the lowly carrot. The grill brings out something wonderful in their sweetness, and a touch of garam masala elevates their flavor to something truly special. This is a great spring soup. By the way, it is just as good served hot.

"10:15 Saturday Night" —The Cure

ingredients

1½ pounds carrots, peeled and halved lengthwise

2 tablespoons pure olive oil

1 teaspoon ground cumin

2½ teaspoons salt

1½ teaspoons freshly ground black pepper

2 tablespoons unsalted butter

¾ cup finely chopped shallots

1 tablespoon finely minced garlic

2 tablespoons fresh marjoram

3 tablespoons fresh cilantro

4 teaspoons Garam Masala *(page 157)*

¼ teaspoon cayenne

6 tablespoons dry vermouth

6 cups Vegetable Stock *(page 35)*

1 cup sour cream

3 tablespoons heavy cream

2 teaspoons freshly squeezed lemon juice

¼ cup fresh whole cilantro leaves

SERVES 8 TO 10

Build a hot fire in your outdoor grill. Allow the coals to burn down until there is no fire, but the coals are white-hot.

Toss the carrots together with the olive oil, cumin, 2 teaspoons of the salt, and the pepper in a stainless-steel bowl. Grill the carrot halves until they are marked well on both sides. Remove, cool, and chop roughly.

In a soup pot over medium heat, melt the butter and sauté the shallots and garlic until transparent. Add the chopped carrots, marjoram, and cilantro and sauté until warmed through. Sprinkle in 3 teaspoons of the garam masala and cayenne and stir until the carrots are coated. Stir in the vermouth and reduce it briefly. Add the stock and bring to a boil. Lower the heat to maintain a low simmer for 25 minutes.

Blend with an immersion blender (or let cool and puree in batches in a counter-top blender) until smooth. Season to taste with salt and pepper. Adjust the garam masala and cayenne as needed to suit your taste.

Whisk together the sour cream, heavy cream, lemon juice, the remaining ½ teaspoon salt, and the remaining 1 teaspoon garam masala.

Served the soup chilled with a drizzle of seasoned sour cream and fresh cilantro leaves.

BEEF AND VEGETABLE "PUNISH" STEW

Here it is, folks . . . the stuff stories are made of. I really do love this stew, but it does invariably take me back to the dining room table on "that" night (see page 28). This is perfect with some torn crusty bread and a drizzle of a good-quality extra-virgin olive oil. And it freezes beautifully for up to 3 months.

ingredients

"I Saw the Light" —Hank Williams

1½ pounds beef stew meat,
cut into ¾-inch cubes

2 teaspoons salt

1 tablespoon freshly ground black pepper

3 tablespoons pure olive oil

1¾ cups small-dice yellow onions

2½ cups peeled, medium-sliced carrots

2 cups medium-sliced celery

2 cups peeled, small-dice potatoes

1½ cups peeled, small-dice turnips

2 tablespoons minced garlic

4 cups chopped fresh tomatoes

2 tablespoons fresh thyme leaves

2 tablespoons chopped fresh rosemary

1½ cups dry red wine

1 tablespoon Worcestershire Sauce *(page 97)*
or store bought

8 cups Veal Stock *(page 30)*

3 cups elbow macaroni or other small pasta

3 tablespoons chopped fresh flat-leaf parsley

3 tablespoons chopped celery leaves

SERVES 10 TO 12

Season the cubed beef with the salt and pepper and pat dry with paper towels.

Heat the oil in a large soup pot until almost smoking. Add the beef, stirring until it browns on all sides. Remove the browned meat from the pot and reserve.

Add the onions, carrots, celery, potatoes, turnips, and garlic to the pot and sprinkle lightly with salt and pepper. Stirring constantly, sauté over medium heat until the onions are translucent and wilted. Add the tomatoes, thyme, and rosemary and stir to combine well. Sauté for 5 minutes more. Add the red wine and Worcestershire, stirring to loosen any caramelized bits that are stuck to the bottom of the pot. Stir in the stock, bring to a simmer, and cook for 30 minutes. Season the stew to taste with salt and pepper.

About 10 minutes before you are ready to serve, stir in the pasta and simmer until tender. Add the parsley and celery leaves and serve immediately.

Me and Mom ca. 1998.

ROASTED ACORN SQUASH BISQUE

I was tasked with making soup from acorn squash one Friday afternoon at Crook's Corner by then *chef de cuisine* Fred Meuller. He was on his way out of town for vacation, and blew by the restaurant with two brown paper grocery bags of these things I had never glimpsed before. He gave me a 15-second run-through on how to treat them and was gone. It is critical that you remember how much I resented soup at this point. I summoned everything in me and went to work. I turned out something similar to this, though we have tweaked it over the last quarter century. It is splendid with some quickly sautéed shrimp and a crumble of *cotija* cheese.

"Mother Popcorn" —James Brown

ingredients

Preheat the oven to 375°F. Cut the squash in half, remove the seeds, rub the cut sides with the oil, and sprinkle with the salt and white pepper. Place the squash halves, cut side down, on a parchment paper–lined sheet pan and roast for 45 minutes, or until the flesh is tender and easily pierced with a knife. Remove from the oven and set aside to cool.

While the squash is roasting, in a soup pot, melt the butter and sauté the onions, celery, and garlic until tender and beginning to brown. With a large spoon, scrape the squash flesh into the vegetables and stir well. Stir in the curry powder and Garam Masala until warm through. Add the Cognac and brown sugar and combine well. Add the chicken and shrimp stocks and bring to a boil over high heat. Lower the heat to maintain a low simmer for 45 minutes.

Blend with an immersion blender (or let cool and puree in batches in a countertop blender). Stir in the cream and cilantro. Return to the stove and stir just until heated through. Season to taste with salt and white pepper.

4 to 5 pounds acorn squash
(2 or 3 whole vegetables)

¼ **cup pure olive oil**

2 **teaspoons salt**

2½ **teaspoons freshly ground white pepper**

½ **cup unsalted butter**

1½ **cups small-dice yellow onions**

1 **cup small-dice celery**

2 **tablespoons finely minced garlic**

1½ **teaspoons Madras curry powder**

4 **teaspoons Garam Masala** *(page 157)*

¾ **cup Cognac**

1 **tablespoon dark brown sugar**

4 **cups Dark Chicken Stock** *(page 31)*

4 **cups Shrimp Stock** *(page 34)*

¾ **cup heavy cream**

½ **cup packed fresh cilantro**

SERVES 8 TO 10

GUMBO Z'HERBES

There is absolutely no better way to make use of an abundance of greens than this recipe. Traditional recipes call for as many as 15 different greens, but the makeup really doesn't amount to a tremendous difference in the final product. Use whatever you have or can get your hands on. Just have fun with it.

The finest time and place to eat this dish is at Dooky Chase on Holy Thursday (the Thursday before Easter). Holy Thursday marks the day of the Last Supper and the beginning of the intense run of Catholic masses leading up to Easter Sunday. There are few places, to me, closer to holy than next to Leah Chase, wherever she may be. She prepares her version of Gumbo Z'Herbes with no effort whatsoever and with the grace and beauty of a ballerina. Leah, please forgive my ham-fisted, Uptown version of your classic, but it's just far too wonderful not to take a stab at it. I love mine with a creamy, cool dollop of German potato salad right in the middle of it.

"Eight Miles High" —Hüsker Dü

ingredients

Wash all the greens thoroughly and set aside to drain in a colander.

In a large cast-iron skillet, brown the pork sausage and tasso in the olive oil over medium heat, transfer to a plate with a slotted spoon, and reserve. In the same skillet over medium heat, combine the butter and flour. Whisk constantly and cook until you have a medium-brown roux (see note on page 43). Stir in the onions, celery, and garlic and sauté until tender. Be careful not to burn the roux. Set aside.

In a separate pot, briefly wilt the cabbage in the bacon fat over medium-low heat, while stirring constantly. Stir in the greens and cook until wilted. Add the stock, bring to a simmer, and cook until the greens are completely tender.

With a ladle, remove about 4 cups of the liquid from the greens and add to the roux-vegetable mix. Whisk to combine and return the skillet to the stovetop over medium heat. Warm briefly and, using a rubber spatula, scrape all of the roux mixture into the greens. Bring to a simmer and stir in the reserved sausage and tasso, the thyme, tarragon, bay leaves, and cayenne and simmer for 20 minutes. Blend with an immersion blender (or let cool and puree in batches in a countertop blender) until smooth. Return the soup to a simmer. Stir the filé with 2 tablespoons water in a small bowl until smooth and add it to the gumbo. Simmer for another 20 minutes and then season with the salt and black pepper.

Note:

Filé powder, or gumbo filé, is ground dried leaves from the sassafras tree. It is used as seasoning and for thickening in certain gumbos from south Louisiana. Filé powder illustrates a significant point in American culinary history, which is the interaction of the Acadian settlers from Canada and the Native American Indians living along the Gulf Coast. As sassafras is indigenous to the southeastern United States, it had to have been introduced to European settlers by the Indians, who allegedly used it both for cooking and for medicinal remedies. It is said to have been used for thickening when okra was not in season, but since okra arrived along with the slave ships from western Africa, the original gumbos would likely have used the powder mostly for its seasoning properties. Filé has a very slight eucalyptus flavor, which perfumes seafood gumbo and greens gumbo very nicely. You should be able to find it in the spice aisle at your grocery store.

1 bunch collard greens, roughly chopped
1 bunch mustard greens, roughly chopped
1 bunch turnip greens, roughly chopped
2 bunches carrot greens, roughly chopped
1 bunch fresh flat-leaf parsley, roughly chopped
1 bunch kale, roughly chopped
6 cups spinach, roughly chopped
¾ pound smoked pork sausage, cut into small dice
½ pound tasso ham, cut into small dice
2 tablespoons pure olive oil
½ cup unsalted butter
½ cup all-purpose flour
1½ cups small-dice yellow onions
1 cup small-dice celery
2 tablespoons finely minced garlic
½ head green cabbage, roughly chopped
2 tablespoons bacon fat
10 cups Dark Chicken Stock *(page 31)*
5 teaspoons fresh thyme leaves
5 teaspoons chopped fresh tarragon
4 fresh bay leaves *(or 2 dried)*
1 teaspoon cayenne
1 tablespoon filé powder *(see Note)*
2½ teaspoons salt
3½ teaspoons freshly ground black pepper

SERVES 10 TO 12

RED BEANS AND RICE "GUMBO"

I remember when Cochon opened in New Orleans in those hazy, booze-fueled months after Hurricane Katrina. A magnificent black-eyed pea gumbo was on the opening menu. I loved that it was adventurous and stretched the boundary of what gumbo was. My friend and NOLA stalwart Lolis Elie and I crossed swords about it, and in a way that tells a story about how territorial we all got after the storm. Lolis is a traditionalist, yet one of the most forward-thinking people I know. To his mind, while the concoction was unarguably delicious, it did not meet his definition of gumbo. I, on the other hand, am a cavalier enough hack and look at gumbo as being an ambiguous enough term these days that if Donald Link says it's *gumbo*, who's to argue?

Well, Lolis, I'm gonna make it even worse. This is our mashup of *gumbo* and red beans and rice. I'm ready for my tongue lashing, but I hope the quotation marks in the title will give me slightly more leeway.

ingredients

"You're Still Standing There" —Steve Earle with Lucinda Williams

½ **pound dried red kidney beans, preferably Camellia brand** *(see Notes)*

½ **pound medium-dice andouille sausage** *(see Notes)*

2 **tablespoons vegetable oil**

1 **cup medium-dice yellow onions**

1 **tablespoon finely minced garlic**

¾ **cup medium-dice celery**

½ **cup medium-dice green bell peppers**

½ **pound okra, sliced ½ inch thick**

1 **teaspoon salt**

1 **teaspoon freshly ground black pepper**

1 **tablespoon Creole Seasoning** *(page xxvi)*

1 **tablespoon fresh thyme leaves**

4 **fresh bay leaves** *(or 2 dried)*

8 **cups Ham Stock** *(page 33)*

2 **tablespoons Steen's cane syrup** *(see page 180)* **or dark brown sugar**

1 **tablespoon filé powder** *(see Note, page 41)*

2 **teaspoons Tabasco hot sauce**

Rice Pilaf *(recipe follows)*

Thinly sliced green onions, for garnish

SERVES 4 TO 6

Soak the red beans, covered by 3 inches of cold water, overnight in the refrigerator. When ready to cook, discard the water and reserve the beans.

In a soup pot over medium heat, brown the andouille in the vegetable oil. Remove with a slotted spoon and reserve.

In the same pot, sauté the onions and garlic over medium heat until transparent. Add the celery, bell peppers, and okra and sauté for an additional 3 minutes. Add the salt and black pepper, and then stir in the spice blend, thyme, and bay leaves. Stir in the beans and warm through. Add the stock and cane syrup and bring to a boil. Lower the heat to maintain a low simmer for 1 hour, or until the beans are tender. Add the reserved andouille to the pot and return to a simmer.

Stir the filé with 2 tablespoons cold water in a small bowl until smooth. Add it to the pot and simmer for another 5 to 7 minutes. Stir in the Tabasco and season to taste with salt and pepper.

Serve over the rice pilaf and garnish with the green onions.

Notes:

This recipe calls for Camellia red kidney beans. They are available regionally around the South, and nothing substitutes for them. If you must use something else, the recipe will turn out, but perhaps not as well, because nothing makes a pot of red beans like Camellia. Walmart carries them regionally these days, but you can also find them at camelliabrand.com.

Spend the money and get a good-quality andouille sausage. I prefer Jacob's from LaPlace, Louisiana, available by mail order, though we are happy to mail you some of our own brand from Big Bad Breakfast if you call and place an order.

RICE PILAF

2 tablespoons unsalted butter
¼ cup small-dice yellow onions
3 tablespoons finely diced celery stalk
2 teaspoons finely minced garlic
1½ cups long-grain white rice
½ cup dry white wine
3¼ cups Dark Chicken Stock *(page 31)*
2 fresh bay leaves or 1 dried
1¼ teaspoons salt
3 tablespoons finely chopped fresh
flat-leaf parsley

In a small saucepan, melt the butter over medium heat. Add the onions, celery, and garlic and cook, stirring constantly, until the vegetables are transparent. Add the rice and stir to coat fully with the butter and sautéed vegetables. Stir in the wine and reduce for about 1 minute. Pour in the stock and add the bay leaves and salt. Once the rice comes to a boil, turn the heat to low, cover, and cook for precisely 20 minutes. *Do not stir the rice while cooking*, no matter how badly you want to. At the end of 20 minutes, the rice should have absorbed all the liquid and be cooked perfectly. Fluff with a fork, stir in the parsley, and serve immediately.

A NOTE ON MAKING ROUX

Opinions on how to make roux and what ingredients to use vary greatly. This is particularly ironic, as it is comprised of only two ingredients (fat and flour). You might wonder exactly how much debate might arise over something so simple, but trust me, in south Louisiana that discussion can heat up like a prison dice game in about half a second.

Creoles (heavily influenced by traditional French cooking), who were the backbone of the kitchens in the nineteenth and early twentieth centuries in New Orleans, made their roux with butter. Their dishes were more refined and "lighter" and employed roux mostly for thickening and a tiny bit of flavor. Roux made in this tradition were typically blond, or golden. They rarely got darker than that.

Cajuns, on the other hand, used roux heavily for flavor, color, and thickening. Cajuns use vegetable oil almost exclusively for their roux, which are frequently cooked to a deep chocolate brown to add a depth of flavor, likely to help mask the gaminess of some of the bayou protein used to make those gumbos. Butter is unsuitable for this because of its makeup, being comprised of three parts: 1) butterfat; 2) milk solids; and 3) water. When you melt butter, the white stuff that foams up and then sinks to the bottom of the pot (and is the thing that burns so quickly) is the milk solids. This happens at a relatively low temperature, so a long cooking time for butter in a dark roux is recipe for failure. Vegetable oil has a higher smoke point, is without solids, and can take a greater amount of abuse.

Cast iron is not the *only* choice for cooking roux, but because of its excellent heat retention properties, it is an excellent vehicle for this process. Once you have warmed the pan to its ideal temperature, cast iron tends to hold a steady temperature throughout the entire cooking surface and sides. Aluminum pans, Calphalon pans, and Calphalon-esque pans (to a lesser degree) offer less in the way of consistent surface temperature and can more easily lend a hand to a failed roux.

All this being said, making roux is about attention and love. You have to love that roux and give it constant attention (stirring, whisking) in order for it to turn out properly. It's a little like a houseplant . . . talk to it, love on it, and it will thrive. Ignore it and it dies. Be patient. It will take some time and concentration to cook a good dark roux, but you will be rewarded in the end.

A final tip: No matter how good it looks and smells, never stick your finger in for a taste. Roux is like hot lava and delivers the same results to the tip of the finger as you may imagine. Take it from the pointy finger on my left hand, which made that mistake once.

SPINACH-RICOTTA GNUDI

1 pound whole-milk ricotta cheese
1 large egg
½ cup finely grated Parmesan cheese
¾ cup all-purpose flour, plus more for dusting
2 teaspoons salt
1 tablespoon freshly ground black pepper
¼ teaspoon freshly grated nutmeg
Pinch of cayenne
¾ cup wilted spinach, squeezed very dry and very finely chopped
3 tablespoons unsalted butter

SERVES 6 TO 8

Drain the ricotta in a fine-mesh strainer suspended over a bowl for 30 minutes. In a stand mixer fitted with the paddle attachment, blend the egg, Parmesan, flour, salt, pepper, nutmeg, and cayenne until fully combined. Blend in the ricotta and spinach and mix again until smooth. Scoop out 2-teaspoon portions, dust them with flour until fully coated, and refrigerate until ready to cook. These can be made a day ahead, if you like.

In a medium sauté pan, melt the butter over medium heat. Add the *gnudi* and sear them until lightly browned all over, 3 to 4 minutes.

LEMON-DILL BABY CARROTS

¼ cup plus ¼ teaspoon salt
2 bunches baby carrots
4 tablespoons unsalted butter
½ teaspoon freshly ground white pepper
Finely grated zest and juice of 1 lemon
1 tablespoon finely minced fresh dill

SERVES 6 TO 8

Bring 4 quarts water and the ¼ cup salt to a boil in a large soup pot. Trim the carrots of their green tops, leaving ½ inch of stem. Place the carrots in a metal strainer or colander and lower the strainer into the water. When the water returns to a boil, simmer the carrots for 1½ minutes. Remove and immediately plunge into cold water to stop the cooking.

In a medium sauté pan over medium heat, melt the butter. Add the carrots, season with the remaining ¼ teaspoon salt and the white pepper, turn up the heat to medium-high, and sauté, stirring every 30 seconds, for 3 minutes. Add the lemon juice and stir until the pan is almost dry, another minute or so. Remove from the heat, stir in the zest and dill, and combine well. Serve immediately.

TOP-SHELF CHICKEN AND DUMPLINGS

My buddy Chris Hastings totally changed the way I looked at chicken and dumplings in the fall of 2011 at the Southern Foodways Alliance Symposium. He raised the bar on a humble Southern classic in the way that guys like Keller and Achatz do within the vernacular they work. It is something I have always loved, and as much as Southern is my sandbox, chicken and dumplings has stayed largely in my home kitchen. For our version at City Grocery, we do a velvety, tarragon-scented chicken velouté with spinach-ricotta gnudi and lemon-dill baby carrots. It is "chicken and dumpling" in concept and ingredients only. It's absolutely killer. Thanks, Chris, for the inspiration. For a quicker version, you can substitute miniature Herbed Biscuits (page 127) for the *gnudi*.

"Unsatisfied" —The Replacements

ingredients

Place the chicken, onions, minced garlic, roughly chopped carrots, roughly chopped celery, black peppercorns, bay leaves, tarragon (chopped and sprigs), and thyme sprigs in a soup pot and cover with water. Bring to a boil over high heat, decrease the heat to low, cover, and simmer for 45 minutes. Remove from the heat and let cool briefly. Strain the stock through a fine-mesh sieve and reserve both the stock and the solids. Separate the chicken from the remaining debris, and discard the skin and vegetable solids. Pick the chicken meat from the bones, discard the bones, and chop the meat somewhat finely.

In a heavy soup pot over low heat, melt the butter. Whisk in the flour and stir and cook to make a blond roux (see page 43). As soon as it begins to smell nutty, add the diced onion, the 2 teaspoons finely minced garlic, the diced celery, and fennel. Increase the heat to medium and cook, stirring constantly, until the vegetables begin to get tender. Add the chicken and stir until well combined. Stir in the vermouth, thyme leaves, and parsley. Add 6 cups of the reserved chicken stock and bring to a simmer. After a minute or two, the sauce will begin to thicken. Continue adding stock, ½ cup at a time, until the desired consistency is reached. It should be thick enough to nicely coat the back of a spoon. Season with the salt and black pepper. Ladle the stew over the top of the sautéed *gnudi* and garnish with chopped tarragon and pecan pieces. Serve with the baby carrots.

1 (3- to 4-pound) whole free-range chicken

¾ cup roughly chopped yellow onions, plus ½ cup small-dice yellow onions

1 teaspoon minced garlic, plus 2 teaspoons finely minced garlic

1 cup peeled, roughly chopped carrots

1 cup roughly chopped celery, plus 1 cup small-dice celery

2 teaspoon black peppercorns

2 dried bay leaves

8 sprigs fresh tarragon, plus ¼ cup chopped fresh tarragon, plus more for garnish

4 sprigs fresh thyme, plus 2 tablespoons fresh thyme leaves

½ cup unsalted butter

½ cup all-purpose flour

¼ cup small-dice fennel bulb

3 tablespoons dry vermouth

¼ cup finely chopped fresh flat-leaf parsley

2 teaspoons salt

2½ teaspoons freshly ground black pepper

Spinach-Ricotta Gnudi *(page 44)*

¼ cup toasted pecan pieces

Lemon-Dill Baby Carrots *(page 44)*

SERVES 6 TO 8

CELERY HEART VELOUTÉ

Chefs go in and out of fascination with ingredients. Celery is one I didn't give a whole lot of thought to until about 10 years ago. It hit me like a lightning bolt. I have always loved what celery brings to so many things raw and cooked. I use different parts for different things: The leaves go beautifully in a crab salad or to finish an asparagus risotto, the diced stalk lends crunch in potato salad, but there's nothing better than the tender hearts to make this subtle, silky gem. With some marinated jumbo lump crabmeat, this is tough to beat and very easy to make.

ingredients

"Volare/On an Evening in Roma" —Dean Martin

½ cup plus 4 tablespoons unsalted butter

½ cup all-purpose flour

1½ cups chopped yellow onions

2 teaspoons minced garlic

8 cups chopped celery hearts *(see Note)*

2 tablespoons fresh thyme leaves

2 dried bay leaves

1 cup dry white wine

8 cups Dark Chicken Stock *(page 31)*

2 teaspoons salt

2 teaspoons freshly ground white pepper

SERVES 8 TO 10

In a small cast-iron or other heavy pan over low heat, melt the ½ cup butter. Whisk in the flour and cook, while whisking, until the roux just barely begins to change color and gives off a sweet aroma (see page 43). Remove from the heat and cool in the pan. Reserve.

Melt the remaining 4 tablespoons butter in a soup pot over medium heat and sauté the onions and garlic until transparent. Stir in the celery, thyme, and bay leaves and sauté until the celery is tender. Stir in the white wine, bring to a simmer, and reduce by half. Stir in the stock, and bring to a boil, then simmer over medium heat for 30 minutes.

Take 2 cups of the cooking liquid from the soup pot and whisk it into the cooled roux until smooth. With a rubber spatula, scrape the roux into the soup pot and bring back to a boil. Simmer for 15 minutes over medium heat. Blend with an immersion blender (or let cool and puree in batches in a countertop blender) until smooth. Season with the salt and white pepper.

Note:

You can use full celery bunches to make this recipe and it will be excellent. Using the hearts yields a slightly sweeter and more refined finished product.

SPICY SUMMER PEA SOUP

Summer peas have a very short window. I never seem to be able to get enough of them for the three or so weeks in the summer when they are ripe. In the South, when we talk of peas, we are speaking of the black-eyed, crowder, cow, Sea Island red, Lady cream, and so forth, not English green peas. They are a magnificent genus and packed with flavor whether eaten fresh or dried and reconstituted. Few things take pork flavor more honestly and subtly and little else loves a little fresh pepper heat or a splash of vinegar like summer peas. One of my favorite memories was my granddad pulling out his Case knife to slice fresh "garden" pepper on top of his peas after a long day's work. This one is for him. It was next to him at the supper table that I fell in love with summer peas.

"Unattainable" —Little Joy

ingredients

Heat the butter and bacon fat in a soup pot over medium heat and sauté the ham until browned on all sides, 5 to 7 minutes. Remove from pot with a slotted spoon and set aside. Sauté the onions, celery, carrots, jalapeño, bell peppers, and garlic until just barely tender. Add the peas, ham hock, stock, parsley, savory, red pepper flakes, and bay leaves and bring to a boil over medium heat. Lower the heat to medium and simmer for 1 hour. Season with the salt and pepper. Serve with cornbread and a splash of vinegar pepper sauce.

Notes:

You can use dried summer peas, but it will just take a little more liquid than fresh will.

For a vinegar-pepper sauce, I like Trappey's, but any of the "sport" pepper sauces, which are typically white vinegar with spicy little green peppers in the bottle, will do. It is really just a dash of vinegar with the slightest bit of heat that does the trick with peas.

1 tablespoon unsalted butter
1 tablespoon bacon fat
1½ cups small-dice smoked ham
¾ cup small-dice yellow onions
½ cup small-dice celery
½ cup small-dice carrots
3 tablespoons finely minced jalapeño pepper
½ cup small-dice green bell peppers
2 teaspoons finely minced garlic
1 pound fresh or frozen summer peas
(choose any variety; see Notes)
1 smoked ham hock or 2 smoked turkey necks
8 cups Dark Chicken Stock *(page 31)*
½ cup chopped fresh flat-leaf parsley
2 tablespoons roughly chopped fresh summer savory
2 teaspoons red pepper flakes
3 fresh bay leaves *(or 2 dried)*
2¼ teaspoons salt
1 tablespoon freshly ground black pepper
Cracklin' Cornbread *(page 225)*
Vinegar-pepper sauce *(see Notes)*

SERVES 8 TO 10

CREAM OF ROASTED SALSIFY SOUP

Salsify is also known as oyster root, though I've never really noticed any more similarity to oysters than portobello mushrooms have to steak. I love it nonetheless, though I don't feel obliged to compartmentalize it. Salsify has a wonderful texture and a nice mellow flavor that needs little more than green herbs and a touch of aromatic vegetables. It is a root vegetable that doesn't possess the bitterness or mineral flavor associated with some of the other roots. Salsify is a good source of fiber and vitamins C and B_2. It's a little hard to find, but if you come across it, grab it immediately. You'll love it.

ingredients

"Treat Her Like a Lady" —Cornelius Brothers and Sister Rose

1 tablespoon herbes de Provence *(see Notes)*

2 teaspoons black peppercorns

1 dried bay leaf

8 sprigs fresh thyme

4 sprigs fresh flat-leaf parsley

2 tablespoons chopped fresh chives

3 pounds salsify, peeled *(see Notes)*

¼ cup pure olive oil

1 teaspoon salt

2 teaspoons freshly ground white pepper

4 tablespoons unsalted butter

1¼ cups small-dice yellow onions

1 cup small-dice celery

1 tablespoon finely minced garlic

2 medium baking potatoes, peeled and diced into ¾-inch cubes

8 cups Dark Chicken Stock *(page 31)*

¾ cup heavy cream

SERVES 8 TO 10

Preheat the oven to 400°F. In a piece of cheesecloth or a coffee filter, combine the *herbes de Provence*, peppercorns, bay leaf, thyme, parsley, and chives and secure with a piece of butcher's string. Set aside.

Toss the salsify with the olive oil and sprinkle with ½ teaspoon of the salt and 1 teaspoon of the white pepper. Spread in a single layer on a parchment paper–lined baking sheet and roast for 15 minutes (or until pierced easily with a knife). Remove and set aside.

In a soup pot over medium heat, melt the butter and sauté the onions, celery, and garlic until soft. Add the potatoes, sprinkle with the remaining ½ teaspoon salt and 1 teaspoon white pepper, and sauté for 5 to 7 minutes. Toss in the salsify and stir until well combined. Add the sachet of herbs and spices and the stock. Bring to a boil, lower the heat to medium, and simmer until the potatoes are tender.

Remove the sachet and discard. Blend the soup with an immersion blender (or let cool and puree in batches in a countertop blender) until smooth. Stir in the cream and bring to a simmer for 5 to 7 minutes. Season to taste with salt and white pepper.

Garnish with quickly sautéed shrimp and a drizzle of chive oil (see Notes).

Notes:

Treat salsify like potato. It oxidizes when it is peeled, so keep it in plain water once it is peeled.

Herbes de Provence is, today, a blend of dried herbs indigenous to that area of France. It typically is comprised of the most abundant herbs there: lavender, savory, fennel, and thyme. These blends are available at specialty food stores and larger grocery stores, and frequently come in spiffy little ceramic pots that will make your kitchen look super sophisticated.

For chive oil, substitute dried chives for bay leaves in the flavored oil recipe on page 172.

A NOTE ON OYSTERS

My best friend from high school and I used to sneak off campus at lunch to eat raw oysters and drink Dixie beer at a little neighborhood joint called Joe Petrossi's. Petrossi's was as quintessential a New Orleans neighborhood seafood restaurant as ever existed. The front room (bar/oyster bar) was mosaic tile—floor, walls, and bar top. The shuckers would harvest your oysters, toss them on the bar, and work until you stopped eating. They'd count the shells and we'd pay a dime per piece. This is my ground zero for oyster memories. I remember eating them everywhere I've been and enjoying them more than any other foodstuff on those travels. I've eaten briny little ones overlooking the Mediterranean in France and Italy, and comfortably at the bar at Grand Central Station in New York City. I have enjoyed them at oyster roasts on the Chesapeake Bay and everywhere up and down the Atlantic along the Gulf Coast. My most transformative experience was sitting on the dock at Buddy Ward and Sons 13 Mile Seafood in Apalachicola, Florida. I spent the day on one of their boats, hand-harvesting oysters from the bottom of the bay with giant oyster tongs and loading them into the boat. When we returned, I was given an oyster knife and a bottle of Tabasco. I sat there for hours shucking, slurping, and drinking beer with my buddy Tory McPhail from Commander's Palace. They were perfectly salty and creamier than any oysters I had ever tasted. It was about as perfect a moment as I can remember (other than my daughter being born), and it delivered me the source for the finest oysters I have ever had. They pack. They ship. I recommend you go the extra "13 Mile." You'll be glad you did. Otherwise, try to find an oyster that is meaty and not too salty. And whatever you do, wait until the very last moment to add them to your stew so they do not overcook.

NOLA OYSTER STEW

This is another one of those dishes that could not be any simpler, so much so that you don't even have to make a stock to put it together. This one is about good oysters and perfect seasoning. If you like the flavor the fennel adds, add more of it. The same goes for the celery, onion, lemon, and so on. Make this one your own. Just don't overcook the oysters.

"The High Road" —The Feelies

ingredients

Bring a large pot filled with 4 quarts water and the ¼ cup salt to a boil over high heat. Place the potatoes in a metal strainer or colander and lower it into the water. Cook until just tender. Remove from the water and set aside.

In a soup pot, melt the butter and bacon fat over medium heat. Add the shallots and garlic and sauté until transparent. Stir in the celery and fennel and sauté until transparent, 3 to 5 minutes. Stir in the white wine and sherry, bring to a simmer, and reduce the liquid by half, about 5 minutes.

Mash the potatoes with the back of a fork and add to the pot with the vegetables. Add the oyster liquor, stock, cream, milk, thyme, tarragon, parsley, Worcestershire, and lemon zest and juice, bring to a boil, and then simmer over low heat for 15 minutes. Add the pepper.

Place the oysters in a metal strainer or colander, lower them into the simmering soup, and swirl them gently until their edges just begin to curl. Remove and divide the oysters among warm soup plates. Taste the soup for seasoning once more and adjust with salt and pepper to taste. Ladle the soup over the oysters. Garnish each plate with a scattering of the chopped fresh herbs.

¼ cup salt

1 cup peeled and diced baking potatoes

2 tablespoons unsalted butter

1 tablespoon bacon fat

1 cup finely minced shallots

2 teaspoons finely minced garlic

1 cup small-dice celery

½ cup small-dice fennel bulb

¾ cup dry white wine

2 tablespoons dry sherry

1 cup oyster liquor
(if you have to stretch what you have available with a little chicken stock, you can, but dilute it by no more than 25%)

3 cups Dark Chicken Stock *(page 31)*

½ cup heavy cream

½ cup whole milk

2 teaspoons fresh thyme leaves

2 teaspoons finely chopped fresh tarragon

2 teaspoons finely chopped fresh flat-leaf parsley

1½ teaspoons Worcestershire Sauce *(page 97)* or store bought

Finely grated zest and juice of 1 lemon

2½ teaspoons freshly ground black pepper

48 fresh oysters, shucked

Chopped fresh herbs, such as thyme, chives, tarragon, and basil, for garnish

SERVES 8 TO 10

FRENCH VIDALIA ONION SOUP

This recipe lives or dies by three things: 1) patience while caramelizing the onions; 2) good veal stock; and 3) salt. If you aren't prepared to stand over the pot and stir the onions for the 30 minutes it will take to slowly coax the natural sugars from them, walk away now. And while I'll tell you that you can never get the same result from store-bought beef broth, you certainly can make a nice version of French onion soup with it. This soup is the testament to the beauty of simplicity. While it is more of a light winter dish, Vidalia onions, because of their high content of natural sugars (which make their appearance in the late spring and early summer), make a really nice twist to the finished soup instead of traditional yellow onions.

"La Vie En Rose" —Edith Piaf

ingredients

¾ cup unsalted butter

3 tablespoons thinly sliced garlic

12 cups thinly sliced Vidalia onions
(about 1 pound; slice them root to tip)

2 tablespoons dark brown sugar

2 tablespoons fresh thyme leaves

5 fresh bay leaves *(or 3 dried)*

2 teaspoons salt

1 tablespoon freshly ground black pepper

1⅓ cups white wine

8 cups Veal Stock *(page 30)*

1½ cups Dark Chicken Stock *(page 31)*

2 tablespoons Worcestershire Sauce
(page 97) **or store bought**

Toasted sourdough bread cubes, for serving

Shredded Gruyère cheese, for serving

SERVES 8 TO 10

Melt the butter in a soup pot over low heat and lightly sauté the garlic until fragrant. Stir in the onions and sugar. Cook while stirring constantly. The onions will first wilt and then slowly begin to brown. Remain vigilant, because the onions will want to burn. Remember, you want to caramelize and milk as much sweetness as possible from the onions but not burn them. If you turn that corner toward burned, the onions will go from sweet to bitter very quickly. Taste them constantly. As soon as you are pleased with your work, move on to the next step.

Add the thyme, bay leaves, salt, and pepper and sauté briefly. Stir in the white wine and reduce by half. Add both stocks and the Worcestershire and simmer for 30 minutes over medium heat. Season to taste with additional salt and pepper.

When ready to serve, preheat the broiler. Ladle the soup into ovenproof cups and top with toasted bread cubes and shredded cheese. Place under the broiler until the cheese has melted and browned. Serve immediately.

STEWED OKRA AND TOMATOES

This is a dish I remember eating at my maternal grandmother's table. I learned to cook from Bill Neal, but came to love the kitchen at City Grocery. Few dishes make me as happy or transport me to a better place than this one.

Oxford and the surrounding counties explode with tomatoes and okra in the summertime. This recipe can be made and eaten immediately, or cooked in a large batch and canned for later use. It is excellent served alone as a side, or with some sautéed shrimp or fish on top. Layer some white rice underneath it and substitute olive oil for the bacon fat and it's as good a Southern vegetarian dish as there is.

"Sacred Love" —Bad Brains

In a medium saucepan over medium heat, heat the bacon fat and garlic oil, and sauté the garlic and onion until transparent, about 3 minutes. Add the okra, season with half of the salt and black pepper, and sauté, stirring an additional 7 minutes. Decrease the heat to low, stir in the tomatoes, and continue stirring until the tomatoes begin to break down and loose their shape. Add the thyme, oregano, red pepper flakes, wine, Tabasco, and chicken stock and simmer over low heat, stirring occasionally, until the okra is completely tender, 20 to 25 minutes. If the stew begins to dry up, add water as needed to maintain a thick consistency while cooking. Serve immediately or follow the instructions on page 82 to preserve.

ingredients

2 tablespoons bacon fat
(substitute olive oil for a vegetarian option)
2 tablespoons Garlic Olive Oil *(see page xxvi)*
1 tablespoon finely minced garlic
1 cup small-dice yellow onions
6 cups fresh okra, sliced ½ inch thick
1 teaspoon salt
2 teaspoons freshly ground black pepper
6 cups seeded small-dice tomatoes
1 tablespoon fresh thyme leaves
2 teaspoons fresh oregano, chopped
1½ teaspoons red pepper flakes
¼ cup white wine
1½ teaspoons Tabasco hot sauce
1½ cups Dark Chicken Stock *(page 31, substitute vegetable stock for vegetarian alternative)*

SERVES 8

Chapter 3

PICKLING & CANNING

SPICY PICKLED OKRA — 61
PICKLED SWEET POTATOES — 62
KENTUCKY SOY-COLLARD KIMCHI — 63
SOY-PICKLED SHIITAKES — 64
PICKLED DUCK LEGS (ESCABECHE) — 66
PICKLED SHRIMP — 67
PICKLED PIG'S EARS — 68
ROSEMARY-PICKLED LAMB HEARTS — 69
DEVILED PICKLED EGGS WITH SUNBURST TROUT ROE — 71
PICKLED GRAPES — 72
PICKLED PEACHES — 76
DILL SLICES — 78
BREAD-AND-BUTTER PICKLES — 79
PICKLED SWEET CORN — 81
LEMON-PICKLED HONEYCRISP APPLES — 82
ROASTED CHERRY TOMATO MARINARA — 85
SPICY PEPPER JELLY — 86
PICKLED WATERMELON RIND — 87

Chapter 3

PICKLING & CANNING

PICKLING & CANNING

There is precious little that passes through our kitchens that isn't subjected to some sort of salting, vinegar soaking, or can processing. We do this as much in the interest of "preserving" summer's bounty as we do in the interest of simply creating these crispy, bright, enormously delicious morsels. The guys in our kitchens purloin these in much the same way they do fresh-baked cookies. The pickle is a very easy "grab and go" snack.

Pickling and fermenting have been practiced, quite literally, for thousands of years. Earthen jars that were used for pickling have been excavated from Pharaohs' tombs in Egypt, Cleopatra purportedly ate pickles because she thought they made her skin more beautiful (I can attest to this—you should see my skin), and in China, fermented pickles were part of the steady diet of the laborers who built the Great Wall. And though your mind may immediately drift to the ubiquitous cucumber when you hear the word *pickle*, I offer here an array of fruits and vegetables that can be thrown into vinegar or brine for preservation.

Today, pickles are as Southern as cast iron, sweet tea, caramel cake, and Coca-Cola. Oddly, it seems that pickles are somewhat passed over by chefs outside the South. However, there are chefs who are toying with them. The first time I ate at the original Momofuku Noodle Bar in New York City, I was completely transfixed by David Chang's pickle plate. Cucumber, radish, cabbage, and other vegetables were blended with vinegars and flavors that were totally surprising and refreshing. Considering how easy the process is, it's surprising more people don't dabble.

On top of being delicious, pickles are one of the healthier snacks you can consume. Though they can be high in sodium, vegetable pickles are remarkably low in calories and carbohydrates, and have zero fat. The fermentation process both preserves nutrients in vegetables and, in some cases, enhances them.

Fermenting is the process of packing vegetables in salt and seasonings and allowing the natural sugars in the vegetables to convert to pickles. Once you have a recipe and the simplest of ingredients, you heat, blend, steep, and age; the result is your pickle.

Canning is a little more complicated. It requires some special equipment, a commitment of time, and an understanding of some basic scientific principles. In short, you have to be a bit dedicated to the process to can anything, but pickles don't have to be "canned" if you keep them in the refrigerator. Only if you are trying to process and can in order to store items at room temperature or in a cool basement do you need to worry about proper canning technique. Otherwise you can simply pop your pickles in a jar and put them up in the refrigerator and they will keep for months. How's that for one thing no one tells you?

SPICY PICKLED OKRA

Perhaps the most common of Southern pickle recipes, this bears inclusion because of the proliferation of this pod in the height of summer. We pickle, literally, hundreds of pounds of okra each summer because there is so much of it, and we try to make use of as much of it as we can. When canned in a water bath, it keeps for about 8 months, so it carries our Bloody Mary garnish from growing season to growing season.

"Last Nite" —The Detroit Cobras

Place the okra in a medium stainless-steel bowl. In a medium nonreactive saucepan, combine 1 cup water with the red pepper flakes, dill, vinegar, white wine, shallots, garlic, salt, sugar, mustard seeds, peppercorns, and thyme over medium heat and bring to a simmer. Remove from the heat, let cool for 3 minutes, and pour over the okra. Let stand for 30 to 45 minutes.

Pack the okra into quart-size glass jars and pour the liquid over, filling to the bottom of the neck of each jar and covering the okra completely. When cooled to room temperature, screw the lids onto the jars. Chill thoroughly for 3 or 4 days before serving. They will keep for up to 12 months refrigerated.

Alternatively, to prepare the okra to store at room temperature, fill a water-bath canner or large pot with a lid with water and bring to a boil over high heat. (If you have a rack that fits the canner, use it, or simply line the bottom with a kitchen towel to prevent the jars from banging around during canning.) Carefully place the empty jars, lids, and rings in the water, filling the jars with the water to submerge them. Boil for 10 minutes. Carefully remove the jars and lids with canning tongs from the bath, dumping the water back into the bath. Briefly drain the jars on a clean kitchen towel. Fill the jars first with the okra, and then pour their pickling liquid over them, filling to just below the neck of the jars. Wipe the rims clean, place the lids on top, and screw the rings onto the jars just finger-tight. Return the jars to the canning bath, making sure the water covers the jars by at least 1 inch. Once the water returns to a boil, simmer for 45 minutes. Remove the jars from the bath and let cool to room temperature. Canned this way, the okra will keep for up to 8 months. Before opening a can of room temperature–stored food product, always check to make sure the seal is still good. With mason-type jars, the lid should be indented and not "pop" when pushed on. If it appears the seal is not good, discard the contents of the jar.

ingredients

3 pounds small okra pods (1½ to 2 inches), trimmed just under the cap

3 tablespoons red pepper flakes

1 tablespoon dried dill weed

4 cups apple cider vinegar

2 cups white wine

2 large shallots, thinly sliced

10 cloves garlic, thinly sliced

3 tablespoons salt

¼ cup sugar

3 tablespoons yellow mustard seeds

2 tablespoons black peppercorns

12 sprigs fresh thyme

MAKES 3 QUARTS

PICKLED SWEET POTATOES

These often surprise folks, as sweet potato is not the first thing you think of when you think of pickles. But these are bright and crisp; the key is to not overcook the sweet potatoes. They are nice to just snack on or to use as an interesting addition to a vinegar coleslaw.

"My Sweet Potato" —Booker T and the M.G.'s

ingredients

½ cup sweet white wine

1 cup champagne vinegar

Finely grated zest and juice of 1 lemon

Finely grated zest and juice of 1 medium orange

½ cup light brown sugar

1 teaspoon salt

2 tablespoons peeled and chopped fresh ginger

1 whole star anise

2 teaspoons black peppercorns

1 medium shallot, sliced

2 cloves garlic, thinly sliced

1 dried bay leaf

1 teaspoon red pepper flakes

3 whole cloves

4 cups peeled sweet potatoes in matchstick-size pieces

SERVES 6 TO 8 AS A SNACK

In a nonreactive saucepan, combine 1½ cups water, the white wine, vinegar, lemon zest and juice, orange zest and juice, sugar, and salt and bring to a simmer over medium heat. Wrap the ginger, star anise, black peppercorns, shallot, garlic, bay leaf, red pepper flakes, and cloves in cheesecloth or a coffee filter and tie up tightly with butcher's string. Place the sachet in the simmering liquid and simmer, uncovered, for 10 minutes.

Stir in the sweet potatoes and simmer for an additional 3 minutes. Remove from the heat, discard the sachet, and allow the sweet potatoes to cool in the liquid to room temperature.

Pack the potatoes into glass jars and pour the liquid over, filling to the bottom of the neck of each jar and covering the potatoes completely. When cooled to room temperature, screw the lids onto the jars. Chill thoroughly. They will keep for up to 8 months refrigerated.

Alternatively, to prepare the potatoes to store at room temperature, fill a water-bath canner or large pot with a lid with water and bring to a boil over high heat. (If you have a rack that fits the canner, use it, or simply line the bottom with a kitchen towel to prevent the jars from banging around during canning.) Carefully place the empty jars, lids, and rings in the water, filling the jars with the water to submerge them. Boil for 10 minutes. Carefully remove the jars and lids with canning tongs from the bath, dumping the water back into the bath. Briefly drain the jars on a clean kitchen towel. Fill the jars first with the potatoes, and then pour their pickling liquid over them, filling to just below the neck of the jars. Wipe the rims clean, place the lids on, and screw the rings onto the jars just finger-tight. Return the jars to the canning bath, making sure the water covers the jars by at least 1 inch. Once the water returns to a boil, simmer for 45 minutes. Remove the jars from the bath and let cool to room temperature. Canned this way, the potatoes will keep for up to 1 year. Before opening a can of room temperature–stored food product, always check to make sure the seal is still good. With mason-type jars, the lid should be indented and not "pop" when pushed on. If it appears that the seal is not good, discard the contents of the jar.

KENTUCKY SOY-COLLARD KIMCHI

I thank my buddies David Chang and Sean Brock for spurring my interest in vegetable fermentation. At first blush, the concept may sound a little off-putting, but the results are sublime. My first real experiences with fresh-made kimchi were with Dave during very blurry, late-night hours at Ssäm Bar. I had tried loads of jarred kimchis in the past, but nothing had registered for me at all. I remember my first mouthful of Dave's with some roasted pork shoulder. The flavors sliced through the copious amounts of bourbon and pork fat, and lit a spark. Sean and I had, in that same time, an extended conversation about applying foreign technique to local ingredients as a result of recognizing comfort qualities in ethnic food like Dave's. Bo Ssäm was an exotic dish, to us, but couldn't have been any more of a family dinner staple to Chang and his family. The spark ignited.

I immediately returned home and began experimenting. My immediate thought was, if napa cabbage is good for kimchi, how good would collards be? The answer was, tremendous. My friend Matt Jamie, in Louisville, Kentucky, makes a delicious American soy sauce from local, organic soybeans. When I visited his plant very late one night with Ed Lee and Mike Lata, I was knocked over by the flavor of the fermented soybean solids that were left over after pressing the soy sauce out. Matt sent me a bag of his residual product, and adding it to the kimchi seemed obvious. This goes amazingly well with Steen's Syrup-Braised Pork Belly (page 180) or with spicy mustard on a brat.

"Big Pimpin'" —Jay Z and UGK

ingredients

Toss the collards, sugar, and salt together in a stainless-steel bowl, cover, and place in the refrigerator overnight. After 24 hours, remove the bowl from the refrigerator and drain off all the liquid, reserving both the collards and the liquid.

In a separate bowl, combine the soybean paste, ginger, garlic, chili powder, fish sauce, red onions, and carrots and blend well. Stir in ¾ cup of the reserved collard liquid and mix well. Toss this mixture with the reserved collards and cilantro until well combined. Cover and refrigerate in the same container. The kimchi will be tasty after sitting for a couple of days, but is best after about 10 days. You can, at this point, transfer to individual jars or leave in the original container. It should remain refrigerated and will keep for 2 months.

With Matt Jamie and Mike Lata.

1 large bunch collard greens

⅔ cup plus ½ cup sugar

2 tablespoons salt

⅓ cup fermented soybean paste, or ¼ cup soy sauce

2 tablespoons peeled and minced fresh ginger

1 tablespoon minced garlic

⅓ cup Korean chili powder *(or paste)*

1 tablespoon fish sauce

¾ cup slivered red onions

¾ cup coarsely shredded carrots *(use the large holes on a box grater)*

½ cup chopped fresh cilantro

MAKES 2 QUARTS

SOY-PICKLED SHIITAKES

I wrote this recipe based entirely on a hunch. I didn't have any idea whether it would actually work or whether it would be a complete bust. It was the result of a really outstanding beef and broccoli dish I had at a Chinese restaurant in New York. The addition of mushrooms to the dish gave it a unique texture that I could not get out of my head.

There is little that smells better to me than the aroma of shiitakes roasting, so my thought was that we could combine those two things and come up with a crazy-cool pickle. The experiment worked, and the result is one of the most highly prized pickles in our pantry.

"Wave of Mutilation" —Pixies

ingredients

30 to 35 medium shiitake mushrooms, stemmed

⅓ cup pure olive oil

3½ teaspoons salt

2 teaspoons freshly ground black pepper

½ cup sugar

2 cups rice wine vinegar

¾ cup apple cider vinegar

1½ cups soy sauce

1 medium jalapeño pepper, halved, deseeded, and minced

3 tablespoons peeled and minced fresh ginger

2 tablespoons mustard seeds

2 tablespoons coriander seeds

⅔ cup chopped fresh cilantro

MAKES 2 PINTS

Preheat the oven to 425°F. In a stainless-steel bowl, toss the shiitakes with the olive oil, 1½ teaspoons of the salt, and the black pepper until well coated. Place the mushrooms, gill side down, on a baking sheet lined with parchment paper or coated with nonstick spray. Roast the mushrooms for 15 to 17 minutes, until their edges just begin to crisp. Transfer the mushrooms to a large bowl and let cool.

In a nonreactive saucepan, combine the sugar, wine and cider vinegars, soy sauce, jalapeño pepper, ginger, the remaining 2 teaspoons salt, the mustard seeds, and coriander seeds and bring to a boil over medium-high heat. Immediately remove from the heat and let cool for 5 minutes. Pour the liquid over the shiitakes. Let cool to room temperature. Stir in the cilantro and pack into pint-size glass jars. Seal the jars and refrigerate. These will keep in the refrigerator for 6 to 8 months.

Alternatively, to prepare the mushrooms to store at room temperature, fill a water-bath canner or large pot with a lid with water and bring to a boil over high heat. (If you have a rack that fits the canner, use it, or simply line the bottom with a kitchen towel to prevent the jars from banging around during canning.) Carefully place the empty jars, lids, and rings in the water, filling the jars with the water to submerge them. Boil for 10 minutes. Carefully remove the jars and lids with canning tongs from the bath, dumping the water back into the bath. Briefly drain the jars on a clean kitchen towel. Fill the jars first with the mushrooms, and then pour their pickling liquid over them, filling to just below the neck of the jars. Wipe the rims clean, place the lids on top, and screw the rings onto the jars just finger-tight. Return the jars to the canning bath, making sure the water covers the jars by at least 1 inch. Once the water returns to a boil, simmer for 45 minutes. Remove the jars from the bath and let cool to room temperature. Canned this way, the mushrooms will keep for up to 1 year. Before opening a can of room temperature–stored food product, always check to make sure the seal is still good. With mason-type jars, the lid should be indented and not "pop" when pushed on. If it appears the seal is not good, discard the contents of the jar.

PICKLED DUCK LEGS (ESCABECHE)

In Miami for the 2010 Super Bowl (or the Saints game, as we called it), my best drinking buddy, Wright Thompson, took me to lunch at a super old-line Uruguayan restaurant in Little Havana called Zuperpollo. Escabeche, basically pickled meat, in this case chicken, was one of the things they were known for. We ordered a plate, and out came an anemic, gelatinous pile of something almost indistinguishable. On first blush I was entirely put off by its appearance, but I tried it, knowing my mother would slap the shit out of me if she were there and I didn't. It was amazing. The flavor of the chicken came through wonderfully and the vinegar brightened everything the way hot sauce does fried chicken. My mind went to work immediately, and I was pickling every kind of meat imaginable in my head. We use duck here, but you can just as easily substitute chicken, if you like. Thanks, Zuperpollo!

ingredients

"Evil Woman" —Electric Light Orchestra

2 teaspoons salt

2 teaspoons freshly ground black pepper

1 tablespoon garlic powder

2 teaspoons onion powder

2 teaspoons fresh thyme leaves

4 whole duck leg quarters
(about 8 ounces each, bone in)

1 cup red wine vinegar

1 cup apple cider vinegar

¾ cup white wine

¾ cup Dark Chicken Stock *(page 31)*

4 cloves garlic, thinly sliced

¾ cup thinly sliced red onions *(cut root to tip)*

2 teaspoons black peppercorns

2 dried bay leaves

SERVES 4

Combine the salt, pepper, garlic powder, onion powder, and thyme in a bowl and blend well. Rub the duck legs liberally with this mixture, place in a shallow baking dish, cover tightly, and refrigerate overnight.

Combine the wine and cider vinegars, wine, stock, garlic, onions, peppercorns, and bay leaves in a large nonreactive saucepan. Remove the duck legs from the refrigerator and place in the liquid. Bring the pot to a boil over medium heat, decrease the heat to low, and simmer for 40 minutes. Remove the pot from the heat and let cool for 10 minutes.

Carefully remove one of the legs from the mixture and check for doneness. The meat should almost fall away from the bone. Return the leg to the liquid and place the entire pot, covered, in the refrigerator to chill (the meat will firm up slightly and the legs will be easier to handle).

The pickled legs can be shredded over salad or tossed right in as is. They can be sautéed in olive oil and served as a center-plate item or simply put out on a platter for folks to pick at cold. The legs will keep, refrigerated, for 2 weeks as long as they remain in their liquid.

TOMATO ASPIC

1 pound fresh heirloom tomatoes, cored, deseeded, and roughly chopped

2 tablespoons finely minced shallots

¼ cup finely minced celery

2 teaspoons minced garlic

1 teaspoon salt

1 dried bay leaf or 2 fresh

2 sprigs fresh thyme

½ teaspoon sugar

1 (¼-ounce) package powdered gelatin

1 tablespoon Worcestershire Sauce *(page 97)* or store bought

1 teaspoon freshly squeezed lemon juice

1 tablespoon freshly grated horseradish

Combine the tomatoes, shallots, celery, garlic, salt, bay leaf, thyme, and sugar with 4 cups water in a large saucepan and bring to a boil over medium heat. Decrease the heat to low and simmer for 10 minutes. Remove the bay leaf and puree with an immersion blender, or transfer the contents to an upright blender and puree. Force the puree through a fine-mesh sieve and return to the saucepan over low heat. Discard the solids remaining in the sieve.

Dissolve the gelatin in ½ cup cold water and set aside.

Stir the Worcestershire, lemon juice, and horseradish into the warm tomato liquid.

Whisk in the gelatin and stir to combine. Divide equally among 4 soup cups and refrigerate to set. When set, turn out onto individual plates and serve with the pickled shrimp (page 67).

PICKLED SHRIMP

Pickled shrimp is quintessentially Southern, yet it gets little consideration. When executed properly, these little gems are the perfect preservation victim. They hold color and texture like few other things. When plucked from their vinegary brine, they are as crisp and bright as freshly boiled shrimp. There is little I remember Bill Neal being more excited or passionate about in the kitchen than this.

The keys to this dish are 1) precision in cooking the shrimp (or just barely undercooking them), and 2) using fresh shrimp. Overcooked shrimp get rubbery, and frozen shrimp always end up with a mealier texture. Serve with Homemade "Duke's" Mayonnaise (page 93) over Tomato Aspic if you like, or add to the top of a simple green salad.

"Almost Blue" —Diana Krall

ingredients

Peel the shrimp, and then cut a shallow line down the back of each one, exposing its dorsal vein. Remove the vein and discard.

Prepare a large bowl of ice water for an ice bath. Bring the liquid shrimp boil to a boil in a large pot with 3 quarts water and 3 tablespoons of the salt. Place the shrimp in a metal strainer or colander that fits easily inside the pot. Lower the strainer into the boiling liquid. Swirl the strainer and shrimp so they cook evenly. Continue to gently swirl and cook just until the liquid begins to bubble again. The minute it does, immediately remove the shrimp and examine one. If you pinch it, it should be firm to the touch. If it is still a little soft, return the shrimp to the boil and stir for another 30 seconds. As soon as the shrimp feel firm, plunge them into the ice bath to cool them as quickly as possible. Set aside.

Combine the remaining ½ teaspoon salt, the onions, garlic, lemon, peppercorns, pepper flakes, mustard seeds, vinegar, ½ cup water, lemon juice, sugar, Tabasco, ginger, and bay leaves in a nonreactive saucepan and bring to a simmer over medium heat. Remove from the heat and let cool for 10 minutes. Remove and discard the bay leaves.

Pack the shrimp into glass jars and pour the liquid over, filling to the bottom of the neck of the jar and covering the shrimp completely. When cooled to room temperature, screw the lids onto the jars. Chill thoroughly. You can use them as soon as they are cold, or store them in the refrigerator for up to 1 month. I don't recommend hot-process canning here, as it tends to overcook the shrimp. Serve with the aspic.

Note:

Shrimp are graded by the number per pound. "16 to 20" means that there are an average of 16 to 20 shrimp to the pound. These are about the size of a grown man's index finger. Fresh shrimp lend themselves better to this process because texture is such a key element to this pickle. Fresh shrimp produce a crispier pickle than their frozen counterpart because no matter how carefully they are frozen, the act of freezing ruptures cell walls and causes water loss, making for a chewier cooked shrimp.

1½ pounds fresh, shell-on shrimp *(16 to 20 count; see Note)*

¼ cup liquid shrimp boil or liquid crab boil

3 tablespoons plus ½ teaspoon salt

¾ cup thinly sliced yellow onions

2 cloves garlic, thinly sliced

1 lemon, thinly sliced *(peel included)*

1 teaspoon black peppercorns

½ teaspoon red pepper flakes

1 teaspoon mustard seeds

1½ cups apple cider vinegar

2 tablespoons freshly squeezed lemon juice

2 teaspoons dark brown sugar

1 teaspoon Tabasco hot sauce

1 tablespoon peeled and grated fresh ginger

2 dried bay leaves

Tomato Aspic *(page 66)*

SERVES 4 AS AN APPETIZER

PICKLED PIG'S EARS

My college roommate and all-around swell guy Coyt Bailey dragged me, blisteringly hung over, to a place called the Big Apple Inn (or Red's, depending on who you talk to) on Farrish Street in Jackson, Mississippi, on a painfully warm Thanksgiving in 1985. On the menu were hot dogs, tamales, and "pig ears." The pig ear, it turns out, was actually a little sandwich on a small bun of pressure-boiled pig's ear and a vinegar–hot sauce slaw. *They were amazing.* Even in my hung-over state, they registered as remarkable.

They have been there making those sandwiches since 1939, and they are just as good today as they were when I had them for the first time almost 30 years ago. They lit a fire for me early in my cooking career, but I have found that going heavier on the vinegar and making more of a pickle makes a better product. These are amazing when thinly sliced, then lightly battered and fried.

ingredients

"Skankin' to the Beat" —Fishbone

2⅓ cups apple cider vinegar
4 teaspoons light brown sugar
2 teaspoons black peppercorns
2 teaspoons red pepper flakes
2 teaspoons mustard seeds
1½ teaspoons salt
2 whole cloves
1 dried bay leaf
4 cloves garlic, thinly sliced
¾ cup thinly sliced yellow onions
Finely grated zest and juice of 1 lemon
1 tablespoon tomato paste
1 to 1½ pounds fresh pig's ears
(2 to 2½ ounces each)

**MAKES ENOUGH FOR ABOUT
12 SMALL SANDWICHES**

Combine the vinegar, 3½ cups water, the brown sugar, peppercorns, red pepper flakes, mustard seeds, salt, cloves, bay leaf, garlic, onions, lemon zest and juice, and tomato paste in a pressure cooker and bring to a boil. Decrease the heat to low and simmer for 5 minutes. Add the pig's ears and lock the lid onto the pot. Bring the pressure cooker back to a boil over high heat. When it reaches high pressure, regulate the heat to keep the pressure steady for 20 minutes. Turn off the heat and allow the pressure to fall naturally, 30 to 45 minutes. Remove the lid; it will release easily once the pressure has fallen to normal.

Remove the pig's ears and slice into ¼- to ½-inch-thick strips and pack them into quart-size glass jars. Pour the pickling liquid over the ears, submerging them completely and filling the jars to just below the necks. Let cool to room temperature, and screw the lids onto the jars. Refrigerate until cold. Store in the refrigerator for 2 weeks.

ROSEMARY-PICKLED LAMB HEARTS

This was a follow-up to my experience with the pickled chicken in Miami (see page 66). My friend Craig Rogers raises the finest lamb I have ever had the pleasure of eating at his farm, Border Springs, in western-central Virginia. It is precious cargo and, as a result, I spent a lot of time shopping bargains from him (that is, items that don't move as well or as quickly and come at a better price point).

Hearts was one he sold me on early. The minute I tasted Craig's lamb hearts, I was hooked. Marinated in salt, black pepper, and olive oil, they grill up like the finest sirloin you have ever tasted. Knowing that I would likely have trouble selling them as such, though, I started playing with them in a number of dishes. Sliced over some creamy rosemary white beans, these are spectacular. Pickled, sliced, and served on their own, they are an excellent and surprising addition to any charcuterie board.

"The Choice Is Yours" —Black Sheep

ingredients

Combine 2 teaspoons of the salt, the ground black pepper, dried rosemary, and onion powder in a bowl and blend together well. Season the lamb hearts liberally with the seasoning mix, and let sit, covered, in the refrigerator overnight.

In a nonreactive saucepan, combine the garlic, red onions, black peppercorns, the remaining 1½ teaspoons salt, cider and wine vinegars, white wine, bay leaves, and ¼ cup of the fresh rosemary. Place the pan on the stove over medium heat. When the liquid begins to simmer, carefully add the lamb hearts and simmer, covered, over low heat for 45 minutes (add water as needed to keep the hearts covered with liquid).

Remove the pan from the stove and chill for 30 minutes. Stir in the remaining ¼ cup fresh rosemary, pack into a quart-size glass jar, seal with the lid, and refrigerate. These will keep very well, refrigerated, for up to 3 weeks.

3½ teaspoons salt

2 teaspoons freshly ground black pepper

2½ teaspoons dried rosemary

1½ teaspoons onion powder

4 medium lamb hearts *(5 to 6 ounces each)*

8 cloves garlic, thinly sliced

¾ cup thinly sliced red onions

2 teaspoons black peppercorns

2 cups apple cider vinegar

¾ cup red wine vinegar

¾ cup white wine

2 dried bay leaves

½ cup fresh rosemary

SERVES 8 AS A SNACK

DEVILED PICKLED EGGS

12 pickled eggs

2 tablespoons Homemade "Duke's" Mayonnaise *(page 93)*

1 teaspoon finely minced shallots

½ teaspoon finely minced garlic

2 teaspoons Dijon mustard

½ teaspoon Tabasco hot sauce

2 teaspoons freshly ground black pepper

½ teaspoon salt

½ teaspoon smoked paprika

2 large pinches of Madras curry powder

1 teaspoon sugar

2 teaspoons chopped fresh flat-leaf parsley

2 teaspoons chopped celery leaves

2 ounces Sunburst Trout Farm trout roe *(see Note)*

¼ cup finely minced red onions

Freshly ground white pepper, for garnish

¼ cup crème fraîche *(you can substitute lightly salted sour cream)*, for garnish

24 DEVILED EGG HALVES

Cut the pickled eggs in half and gently scoop out the yolks into the bowl of a stand mixer fitted with the paddle attachment. Blend in the mayonnaise, shallots, garlic, mustard, Tabasco, black pepper, salt, paprika, curry powder, sugar, parsley, and celery leaves and blend until fully combined and smooth. Scoop the yolk mixture into a small ziplock plastic bag and force the mixture toward a corner of the bag. Squeeze out as much of the air as possible and seal the top of the bag. Using scissors, clip a small corner off the bag and pipe the mixture into the egg halves.

Garnish with the roe, red onions, white pepper, and crème fraîche.

Note:

The folks at Sunburst Trout Farm, in western North Carolina, raise the finest trout I have ever cooked with. Because it is available, we occasionally get a delivery of their roe, which is equally good. It is a beautiful orange color and has a nice "pop" on the tongue. They ship everything from fresh trout fillets to roe to smoked trout dip. Visit them at sunbursttrout.com.

DEVILED PICKLED EGGS WITH SUNBURST TROUT ROE

Pickled eggs were unwelcome in our house as a youngster. My dad always made jokes about them, but my mother was never amused. Apparently, they had some catastrophically negative effect on my dad's lower GI tract, so we didn't ever speak of them. It wasn't until I started hunting and fishing with my dad and we were afforded uninterrupted time together that I experienced the mystery for myself. Combined with beer, the pickled egg had lethal effects on my dad and all of his hunting buddies.

Pickled eggs, in my childhood mind, didn't register as a memorable flavor. The jars at convenience stores had little character and held little more than boiled eggs in briny white vinegar. So, when we started pickling things in earnest, eggs were among the first non-vegetable items I squared off with. Pickled eggs, it turned out, were delicious, so the deviled pickled egg was an obvious next step. The trout roe is a wonderful, lightly salty exclamation point. Add a touch of crème fraîche and some minced onion, and you are looking at the classic caviar accompaniments.

"Suspicious Minds" —Fine Young Cannibals

To make the pickled eggs: Place the eggs in a large saucepan, cover with water, and add ¼ cup of the cider vinegar. Bring to a boil over high heat. From the moment they begin to boil, let them cook for 8 minutes. Meanwhile, prepare a bowl of ice water. Immediately remove the eggs from the boiling water and plunge them into the ice water to cool rapidly. Peel the eggs.

Combine the remaining ½ cup apple cider vinegar, the red wine vinegar, white wine, shallots, garlic, peppercorns, allspice, red pepper flakes, smoked paprika, bay leaves, and cloves in a nonreactive saucepan and bring to a boil. Decrease the heat to medium-low and simmer for 5 minutes. Place the cooled eggs in a nonreactive container, pour the hot liquid over them, and let cool. Stir in the green onions. Pack the eggs into 3 quart-size glass jars, cover with the pickling liquid, submerging them completely and filling the jars to just below the necks of the jars, screw on the lids, and refrigerate. The eggs will keep, refrigerated, for 4 to 5 months.

Alternatively, to prepare the eggs to store at room temperature, fill a water-bath canner or large pot with a lid with water and bring to a boil over high heat. (If you have a rack that fits the canner, use it, or simply line the bottom with a kitchen towel to prevent the jars from banging around during canning.) Carefully place the empty jars, lids, and rings in the water, filling the jars with the water to submerge them. Boil for 10 minutes. Carefully remove the jars and lids with canning tongs from the bath, dumping the water back into the bath. Briefly drain the jars on a clean kitchen towel. Fill the jars first with the eggs, and then pour their pickling liquid over them, filling to just below the neck of the jars. Wipe the rims clean, place the lids on top, and screw the rings onto the jars just finger-tight. Return the jars to the canning bath, making sure the water covers the jars by at least 1 inch. Once the water returns to a boil, simmer for 45 minutes. Remove the jars from the bath and let cool to room temperature. Canned this way, the eggs will keep for up to 1 year. Before opening a can of room temperature–stored food product, always check to make sure the seal is still good. With mason-type jars, the lid should be indented and not "pop" when pushed on. If it appears the seal is not good, discard the contents of the jar.

ingredients

12 large farm eggs
¾ cup apple cider vinegar
2½ cups red wine vinegar
¾ cup white wine
2 medium shallots, sliced
4 cloves garlic, thinly sliced
2 teaspoons black peppercorns
1 teaspoon whole allspice berries
1 tablespoon red pepper flakes
2 teaspoons smoked paprika
3 dried bay leaves
2 whole cloves
½ cup finely chopped green onions

MAKES 1½ QUARTS PICKLED EGGS

PICKLED GRAPES

I was designing a lamb shoulder dish and trying to think of something sweet and tart to finish it. For some reason, I remembered my grandmother's pickled plums, and it occurred to me that perhaps grapes would work just as well. These were a smash hit and are one of my favorites. They retain all of their natural flavor and pick up the bite of the vinegar. Unassuming in appearance, they are extremely surprising when you pop them in your mouth.

"Photograph" —Camper Van Beethoven

ingredients

6 cups mixed red and green seedless grapes

¾ cup granulated sugar

¼ cup light brown sugar

2½ cups apple cider vinegar

¾ cup white wine

2 tablespoons coriander seeds, crushed

2 tablespoons mustard seeds, toasted

1 tablespoon ground cinnamon

7 whole cloves

1 teaspoon salt

2 tablespoons peeled and thinly sliced fresh ginger

2 jalapeño peppers, finely diced, seeds included

MAKES 2 QUARTS, ENOUGH FOR 12 PEOPLE TO SNACK ON

Remove the stems from the grapes and barely slice off the top of each grape with a sharp paring knife.

Combine the granulated and brown sugars, vinegar, wine, coriander and mustard seeds, cinnamon, cloves, salt, ginger, and jalepeños in a large nonreactive saucepan and bring to a boil over medium heat. Decrease the heat to maintain a simmer for 5 minutes and then remove from the heat.

Place the grapes in pint- or quart-size jars, and pour the liquid over them to cover the grapes completely. The jars should be filled to just below the necks of the jars. Let cool to room temperature and screw on the lids. Refrigerate. These will keep, refrigerated, for 5 to 6 months.

Alternatively, to prepare the grapes to store at room temperature, fill a water-bath canner or large pot with a lid with water and bring to a boil over high heat. (If you have a rack that fits the canner, use it, or simply line the bottom with a kitchen towel to prevent the jars from banging around during canning.) Carefully place the empty jars, lids, and rings in the water, filling the jars with the water to submerge them. Boil for 10 minutes. Carefully remove the jars and lids with canning tongs from the bath, dumping the water back into the bath. Briefly drain the jars on a clean kitchen towel. Fill the jars first with the grapes, and then pour their pickling liquid over them, filling to just below the neck of the jars. Wipe the rims clean, place the lids on top, and screw the rings onto the jars just finger-tight. Return the jars to the canning bath, making sure the water covers the jars by at least 1 inch. Once the water returns to a boil, simmer for 45 minutes. Remove the jars from the bath and let cool to room temperature. Canned this way, the grapes will keep for up to 1 year. Before opening a can of room temperature–stored food product, always check to make sure the seal is still good. With mason-type jars, the lid should be indented and not "pop" when pushed on. If it appears the seal is not good, discard the contents of the jar.

HOW DO I LOVE THEE, PICKLE?
LET ME COUNT THE WAYS . . .

I'm not entirely sure that pickles are not somehow part of my DNA. I have loved them from my earliest possible memory. That being said, and before my brother, Richard, goes public with statements discrediting my claim, I was a sweet-pickle lover as a youngster. Richard and my dad shared a beautiful bond over the sour pickle, but my mother and I loved the sweet ones. These were most definitely delineated sides, and though we did not fully understand the others' fascinations, we most certainly met in the middle at the kosher dill.

My maternal grandparents exposed me first to the wider array of things pickled. As a city boy, I was most familiar with the cucumber and glimpsed the occasional pickled egg and pig's foot on the way to hunting or fishing camp in south Louisiana, but these things were infamous for their effects on the digestive system, so they were eyed with reverence and suspicion. I never experimented with them in the company of my mother, for fear of indiscretion.

My grandparents pickled to preserve the precious summer vegetables through the lean growing months of the year. They turned okra into delicate little whole pickles, corn into piccalilli, hot peppers into sport sauce, and green tomatoes into chowchow, to mention a few items. The basement of their house was like a cathedral to me. It was filled with things mysterious that had been long forgotten, and makeshift shelves of salvaged weatherboards sagged under the weigh of mason jars filled with my grandmother's pickles. The afternoon sun illuminated those jars like primitive stained glass and hypnotized me every time I was down there.

It was on one of those afternoons that I spied a jar of peaches just out of my reach. I was a lover of the Del Monte variety, which my dad would frequently feed us, allowing us to slurp the syrup straight from the can. My greedy little brain went to work . . . nobody would ever know if I made just one of those hundreds of jars my very own. I was a kid let loose in a candy shop. I stacked boxes and climbed to where I could reach my prize, and in a fit of glutinous stupidity, I tried to wrestle the top from the Kryptonite-sealed vessel while still perched atop my fragile pyramid. In doing so, I managed to bring down my mountain of moron along with an entire shelf and dozens of jars.

In the puddle of vinegar and syrup I lay, stunned but unhurt. My grandmother waddled in as I began to rise out of the muck, jar of peaches still in hand, intact. Understanding my plight, she effortlessly wrung the top free and popped a slice into my mouth. A new world of pickled possibility opened to me in that moment, and, for a hot second, I forgot I would probably get my butt torn up for the damage I had done.

We pickle everything now, from shiitakes to sweet potato, from chicken to chayote. Some are added to salads, others to sauces. Some are simple garnishes, while others are main components. Whatever the case may be, they can all stand alone and are some of the most prized snacks in the kitchen.

PICKLED PEACHES

These are simply the gold standard of fruit pickles and get eaten as quickly as they are preserved in our kitchens. There are so many uses for them that it is futile to even try to list them. Try these with everything, but whatever you do, make the Pickled Peach Relish (page 118). It is just amazing.

(page 118)

ingredients

"Beat Surrender" —The Jam

10 ripe summer peaches
¾ cup granulated sugar
½ cup dark brown sugar
1½ cups champagne vinegar
1 cup apple cider vinegar
1 tablespoon mustard seeds
2 dried bay leaves
2 teaspoons black peppercorns
1 teaspoon red pepper flakes
¾ teaspoon salt
3 cinnamon sticks
10 whole cloves

MAKES ABOUT 3 QUARTS

Place a medium soup pot on the stove over high heat. With a sharp paring knife, cut an "X" through the skin on the non–stem end of each peach. Prepare an ice-water bath in a large bowl. When the water comes to a boil, dunk the peaches into the boiling water, in batches, for 30 to 45 seconds. Transfer the peaches immediately to the ice bath to cool rapidly. Peel the peaches; once cooled, the skins should slip off easily.

With a sharp paring knife, slice the peaches from root to tip around the pit into 6 to 8 wedges each. Place the peach slices in a nonreactive bowl.

Combine both sugars, both vinegars, ¾ cup water, the mustard seeds, bay leaves, black peppercorns, red pepper flakes, salt, cinnamon sticks, and cloves in a small nonreactive saucepan and bring to a boil over medium heat. Decrease the heat to maintain a simmer for 5 minutes. Pour the hot liquid over the peaches and cool to room temperature.

Pack the peaches into quart-size glass jars. Make sure the peaches are completely submerged in the liquid and fill the jars to just under their necks. Screw on the lids. These will keep, refrigerated, for 8 to 10 months.

Alternatively, to prepare the peaches to store at room temperature, fill a water-bath canner or large pot with a lid with water and bring to a boil over high heat. (If you have a rack that fits the canner, use it, or simply line the bottom with a kitchen towel to prevent the jars from banging around during canning.) Carefully place the empty jars, lids, and rings in the water, filling the jars with the water to submerge them. Boil for 10 minutes. Carefully remove the jars and lids with canning tongs from the bath, dumping the water back into the bath. Briefly drain the jars on a clean kitchen towel. Fill the jars first with the peaches, and then pour their pickling liquid over them, filling to just below the neck of the jars. Wipe the rims clean, place the lids on top, and screw the rims onto the jars just finger-tight. Return the jars to the canning bath, making sure the water covers the jars by at least 1 inch. Once the water returns to a boil, simmer for 45 minutes. Remove the jars from the bath and let cool to room temperature. Canned this way, the peaches will keep for up to 1 year. Before opening a can of room temperature–stored food product, always check to make sure the seal is still good. With mason-type jars, the lid should be indented and not "pop" when pushed on. If it appears the seal is not good, discard the contents of the jar.

DILL SLICES

We had our sights set on opening an all-from-scratch, fast-food burger concept for a short while. When we went to work on it, I bought a jar each of Duke's mayonnaise, Hunt's tomato ketchup, French's yellow mustard, and dill pickle chips. The charge was to re-create those flavors and textures from local, garden-fresh ingredients. When the work was done, I could not have been more proud. We had the toughest time with the pickles, but the final version was one we couldn't have been much happier with.

ingredients

"*Cat People*" —David Bowie

3 pounds seedless cucumbers, sliced ⅛ inch thick

5 teaspoons pickling salt

3½ cups apple cider vinegar

1 tablespoon chopped garlic

1 tablespoon salt

1 tablespoon mustard seeds

2 teaspoons dried dill weed

2 teaspoons sugar

1 teaspoon dill seeds

6 dried bay leaves

MAKES 3 TO 4 PINTS

Salt the cucumber slices with the pickling salt in a large stainless-steel or plastic bowl. Cover the cucumber slices with water, cover the bowl well, and refrigerate overnight. When ready to continue with the recipe, drain the cucumbers well and pat dry.

Combine 1 cup water, the vinegar, garlic, salt, mustard seeds, dried dill weed, sugar, dill seeds, and bay leaves in a large nonreactive pot and bring to a simmer. Pour the pickling liquid over the drained cucumber slices and let stand until cooled.

Pack into pint-size glass jars, cover with pickling liquid, covering the cucumbers completely to just below the necks of the jars, screw on the lids, and refrigerate. These will keep, refrigerated, for 6 to 8 months.

Alternatively, to prepare the pickles to store at room temperature, fill a water-bath canner or large pot with a lid with water and bring to a boil over high heat. (If you have a rack that fits the canner, use it, or simply line the bottom with a kitchen towel to prevent the jars from banging around during canning.) Carefully place the empty jars, lids, and rings in the water, filling the jars with the water to submerge them. Boil for 10 minutes. Carefully remove the jars and lids with canning tongs from the bath, dumping the water back into the bath. Briefly drain the jars on a clean kitchen towel. Fill the jars first with the pickles, and then pour their pickling liquid over them, filling to just below the neck of the jars. Wipe the rims clean, place the lids on top, and screw the rings onto the jars just finger-tight. Return the jars to the canning bath, making sure the water covers the jars by at least 1 inch. Once the water returns to a boil, simmer for 45 minutes. Remove the jars from the bath and let cool to room temperature. Canned this way, the pickles will keep for up to 1 year. Before opening a can of room temperature–stored food product, always check to make sure the seal is still good. With mason-type jars, the lid should be indented and not "pop" when pushed on. If it appears the seal is not good, discard the contents of the jar.

BREAD-AND-BUTTER PICKLES

Growing up, we were a house divided. My dad and brother loved sour pickles, and my mother and I loved sweet ones. There were always loads around, but I remember tasting bread-and-butter pickles for the very first time and realizing that I could easily slide toward the dill and even ultimately align myself with my dad and brother. I would become a pickle double agent.

Bread-and-butter pickles are very similar to traditional sweet pickles but use onion, garlic, turmeric, and mustard seed in the pickling liquid and an overnight salt brine to give a slightly more savory bent to these delicious little babies.

"Grow Old with Me" —The Postal Service

Combine the salt, pickling lime, and 1½ cups water in a nonreactive bowl and stir to dissolve. Add the cucumbers, cover well, and refrigerate in the brine overnight. When ready to continue with the recipe, drain and rinse the cucumber slices in fresh water three times.

In a large nonreactive saucepan, combine ¾ cup water with the vinegar, shallot, garlic, sugar, mustard seeds, red pepper flakes, celery seeds, turmeric, and black pepper. Place over medium heat and bring to a boil. Add the cucumbers and bring back to a simmer; cook for 4 to 5 minutes. Remove from the heat and cool in the liquid.

Ladle the pickles into a quart-size jar and cover completely with the liquid, filling the jar to just below the neck. The pickles will keep, refrigerated, for 10 to 12 months.

Alternatively, to prepare the pickles to store at room temperature, fill a water-bath canner or large pot with a lid with water and bring to a boil over high heat. (If you have a rack that fits the canner, use it, or simply line the bottom with a kitchen towel to prevent the jars from banging around during canning.) Carefully place the empty jars, lids, and rings in the water, filling the jars with the water to submerge them. Boil for 10 minutes. Carefully remove the jars and lids with canning tongs from the bath, dumping the water back into the bath. Briefly drain the jars on a clean kitchen towel. Fill the jars first with the pickles, and then pour their pickling liquid over them, filling to just below the neck of the jars. Wipe the rims clean, place the lids on top, and screw the rings onto the jars just finger-tight. Return the jars to the canning bath, making sure the water covers the jars by at least 1 inch. Once the water returns to a boil, simmer for 45 minutes. Remove the jars from the bath and let cool to room temperature. Canned this way, the pickles will keep for up to 1 year. Before opening a can of room temperature–stored food product, always check to make sure the seal is still good. With mason-type jars, the lid should be indented and not "pop" when pushed on. If it appears the seal is not good, discard the contents of the jar.

Notes:
The pickling lime can be omitted. It just yields a crisper pickle.

You can use English seedless cucumbers or traditional American pickling cucumbers and achieve the same results.

ingredients

2 tablespoons salt

1 tablespoon pickling lime *(see Notes)*

4 cups Japanese cucumbers, sliced ½ inch thick *(see Notes)*

2½ cups apple cider vinegar

1 medium shallot, thinly sliced

3 cloves garlic, thinly sliced

2 cups sugar

2 teaspoons mustard seeds

1½ teaspoons red pepper flakes

½ teaspoon celery seeds

2 teaspoons ground turmeric

2 teaspoons freshly ground black pepper

MAKES 1 QUART

PICKLED SWEET CORN

Corn is one of the things I most hate to see go in the summer, and its time usually passes first. As each year rolls by, good sweet corn seems harder to come by, so we try to snap up every bit there is whenever it's available. We treat that corn several ways to preserve it. Some is quickly frozen after a quick blanch or roasting and removed from the ears, some is put up as creamed corn, and some is pickled for salads, relishes, and garnishes. This version, though, is hard not to eat as quickly as it is made.

"I Felt Like a Gringo" —Minutemen

Combine the sugar, mustard seeds, salt, pepper, vinegar, and ¾ cup water in a medium saucepan and bring to a simmer over medium heat. Simmer for 10 minutes and then remove from the heat.

Mix together the corn, shallots, and garlic in a bowl, and then divide the mixture evenly between 2 quart-size jars. Pour the hot pickling liquid over the corn, submerging it completely and filling the jars to just under the necks. Cool to room temperature, screw on the lids, and refrigerate. These will keep, refrigerated, for 8 to 10 months.

Alternatively, to prepare the corn to store at room temperature, fill a water-bath canner or large pot with a lid with water and bring to a boil over high heat. (If you have a rack that fits the canner, use it, or simply line the bottom with a kitchen towel to prevent the jars from banging around during canning.) Carefully place the empty jars, lids, and rings in the water, filling the jars with the water to submerge them. Boil for 10 minutes. Carefully remove the jars and lids with canning tongs from the bath, dumping the water back into the bath. Briefly drain the jars on a clean kitchen towel. Fill the jars first with the corn, and then pour their pickling liquid over them, filling to just below the neck of the jars. Wipe the rims clean, place the lids on top, and screw the rings onto the jars just finger-tight. Return the jars to the canning bath, making sure the water covers the jars by at least 1 inch. Once the water returns to a boil, simmer for 45 minutes. Remove the jars from the bath and let cool to room temperature. Canned this way, the corn will keep for up to 1 year. Before opening a can of room temperature–stored food product, always check to make sure the seal is still good. With mason-type jars, the lid should be indented and not "pop" when pushed on. If it appears the seal is not good, discard the contents of the jar.

ingredients

2 tablespoons sugar

2 tablespoons mustard seeds

1 tablespoon salt

5 teaspoons freshly ground black pepper

3½ cups apple cider vinegar

7 cups sweet corn kernels

¾ cup minced shallots

1 tablespoon minced garlic

MAKES 2 QUARTS

LEMON-PICKLED HONEYCRISP APPLES

Apples have always been my favorite fruit. I can still drink an entire kindergarten class under the table when it comes to apple juice, and I can't think of a simple snack I like better than a sliced Fuji or Honeycrisp. So it was only a matter of time before I started pickling them, and our salads took on a completely different face. If you thought apples, walnuts, and blue cheese were a great combination before, spread these out for your friends next time and wait for the accolades. There is little more to this than peeling the apples and pouring warm pickling liquid over them. This recipe is for more savory applications, but you can easily leave out most of the salt and add sugar and spices and come out with a sweet pickle that tastes just like apple pie. This is one of the great recipes to mess around with because no matter what you do, these will not stay around long, and apples are plentiful and inexpensive for further experimentation.

ingredients

"Don't Go Away" —The Primitons

6 Honeycrisp apples, peeled, cored, and sliced into 12 wedges each

1 cup sliced yellow onions

Finely grated zest and juice of 2 lemons

2 cups apple cider vinegar

2 tablespoons honey

2 dried bay leaves

4 whole cloves

1½ teaspoons salt

1 teaspoon freshly ground black pepper

⅛ teaspoon cayenne

MAKES 2 QUARTS

In a large stainless-steel bowl, toss together the apples, onions, and lemon zest and juice until combined. Pack into 2 quart-size jars.

Combine the vinegar, honey, ½ cup water, the bay leaves, cloves, salt, black pepper, and cayenne in a nonreactive saucepan and bring to a simmer. Remove from the heat and cool briefly. Pour the pickling liquid over the apples, submerging them completely and filling the jars to just below the necks. Let cool to room temperature and screw on the lids. The apples will keep, refrigerated, for 4 months.

A NOTE ON CANNING

Canning is a process that is daunting to people, based on conversations I continue to have. Granted, it requires some special equipment, and a canning bath can look a little hulking in size. However, if you have space in your pantry to store it away and are willing to spend a few bucks on the tools you need, it really isn't too complicated or expensive to try. And if you consider what you can do, as far as preserving the best of the seasons, the cost and space is next to nothing.

That being said, it is serious business, and with ingredients that have lower acidity, like green beans or squash, the topic of botulism definitely becomes unavoidable. The addition of some lemon juice or citric acid can bring the pH level down enough to be nonthreatening. With the right equipment the process can be simple: Sterilize your jars, pack them with your product, cover with pickling liquid, screw on the lids, and return them to the canning bath to process for a certain amount of time. Check to make sure the seal is good after the jars have cooled completely. If the seal is good, the vacuum inside

the jar will draw the lid down and it will be taut. If the seal is bad, the center will "pop" up and down. (If you have a bad seal, simply place the jar immediately in the refrigerator, where the contents will keep for about 2 weeks. For additional information, I recommend a primer like *Ball's Complete Book of Home Preserving*. It gives a great overview of canning and pressure canning and has a pile of recipes to work from.

Generations of our foremothers and forefathers canned, and it is a practice that is slowly dying. What is unfortunate is that most people don't get to taste a jar of summer tomatoes in mid-January next to a can of factory-processed tomatoes to see how astounding the difference is. Afforded this opportunity, most dedicated cooks will go flying to the store to buy basic canning equipment. It is nothing short of amazing how much of summer's flavors and textures can be preserved under a vacuum in a little glass jar.

ROASTED CHERRY TOMATO MARINARA

At farmers' markets in the summer, cherry tomatoes are frequently so prolific that farmers almost give them away rather than let them go bad. This is a windfall I shamelessly take advantage of. Cherry tomatoes make a great marinara that is extremely easy to prepare and store for whenever you need it. This recipe is somewhat neutral in flavor, so you can pull the marinara out of the pantry and use it however you want. I've also included instructions for water-bath canning; however, if you aren't interested in that method, it's just as easy to store the jars in the refrigerator without processing.

"Dial Tone" —The Pressure Boys

Preheat the oven to 325°F. In a stainless-steel bowl, toss together the tomatoes, extra-virgin olive oil, salt, and pepper. Line two baking sheets with parchment paper and spread the tomatoes, cut side up, in a single layer on the baking sheets. Roast for 30 to 45 minutes, until the tomatoes just begin to shrivel but don't completely dry out. Remove from the oven and let cool. Working in batches, pulse the tomatoes in a food processor until chopped but not pureed.

In a medium soup pot, heat the pure olive oil over medium heat until the surface just begins to shimmer. Stir in the onions and garlic and sauté until transparent. Add the chopped tomatoes and bring to a simmer. Stir in the basil and red pepper flakes and blend together well. Stir in the lemon juice and citric acid and combine well. Remove from the heat.

Pour the marinara into 4 quart-size jars, filling to just below the necks of the jars. Screw on the lids until finger-tight and refrigerate. The marinara will keep refrigerated for 10 days.

Alternatively, to prepare the marinara to store at room temperature, fill a water-bath canner or large pot with water, cover, and bring to a boil over high heat. (Use a rack that fits the canner if you have one, or simply line the bottom with a kitchen towel to prevent the jars from banging around during canning.) Carefully place the empty jars, lids, and rings in the water, filling the jars with the water to submerge them. Boil for 10 minutes. Using canning tongs, carefully remove the jars, lids, and rings from the bath, dumping the water back into the bath. Fill the jars with the hot marinara to just below the neck of the jars. Wipe the rims clean, place the lids on top, and screw the rings onto the jars until finger-tight. Return the jars to the canning bath, making sure the water covers the jars by at least 1 inch. Once the water returns to a boil, simmer for 45 minutes. Remove the jars from the bath and let cool to room temperature. Canned this way, the marinara will keep for up to 1 year. Before opening a can of room temperature–stored food product, always check to make sure the seal is still good. With mason-type jars, the lid should be indented and not "pop" when pushed on. If it appears the seal is not good, discard the contents of the jar.

Notes:

Chiffonade describes a classic French cut for larger leafy herbs and lettuce. Stack a dozen or so basil leaves, roll them up like a cigarette, and cut into thin strips across the roll. When unrolled, you will have tight little threads.

The lemon juice and citric acid can be omitted if you plan to store your marinara in the refrigerator.

5 quarts cherry tomatoes, halved
5 tablespoons extra-virgin olive oil
2 teaspoons salt
1 tablespoon freshly ground black pepper
3 tablespoons pure olive oil
2 cups minced yellow onions
3 tablespoons minced garlic
¾ cup fresh basil, cut into chiffonade *(see Notes)*
2 teaspoons red pepper flakes
¼ cup freshly squeezed lemon juice *(optional; see Notes)*
1 tablespoon citric acid *(optional; see Notes)*

MAKES 4 QUARTS

SPICY PEPPER JELLY

Pepper jelly is one of the great utility players on the gridiron of Southern food items. It is outstanding over most grilled meats because it has that sweet, spicy, salty trifecta that has an almost universal appeal. But one of my absolute favorite uses is simply spooning it over a block of cream cheese and spreading on crackers (Triscuits, to be specific). Topped with some toasted pecans, this is the perfect quick snack for dinner guests to nibble on over drinks. Substitute pepper jelly for "sweet and sour sauce" if you love that end of the Chinese food spectrum; this is an outstanding improv ingredient.

ingredients

2½ cups sugar

1 cup apple cider vinegar

2 tablespoons freshly squeezed lemon juice

2 teaspoons red pepper flakes

2 cups small-dice red bell peppers

1¼ cups small-dice green bell peppers

4 jalapeño peppers, deseeded and cut into small dice

6 ounces liquid pectin

MAKES 2 PINTS

"In the Aeroplane over the Sea" —Neutral Milk Hotel

In a medium nonreactive saucepan, combine the sugar, vinegar, lemon juice, and red pepper flakes and bring the mixture to a boil over medium heat, stirring until the sugar has dissolved. Add the red and green bell peppers and jalapeño and simmer for 7 to 8 minutes. Stir in the pectin and boil the mixture over moderately high heat, stirring, until it reaches the jelly stage (222°F on a candy thermometer). Remove from the heat and cool to room temperature, unless you will be canning to store at room temperature.

Divide the jelly between 2 pint-size glass jars, seal with the lids, and refrigerate. It will keep, refrigerated, for up to 4 months.

Alternatively, to prepare the jelly to store at room temperature, fill a water-bath canner or large pot with a lid with water and bring to a boil over high heat. (If you have a rack that fits the canner, use it, or simply line the bottom with a kitchen towel to prevent the jars from banging around during canning.) Carefully place the empty jars, lids, and rings in the water, filling the jars with the water to submerge them. Boil for 10 minutes. Carefully remove the jars and lids with canning tongs from the bath, dumping the water back into the bath. Briefly drain the jars on a clean kitchen towel. Fill the jars with the hot jelly, filling to just below the neck of the jars. Wipe the rims clean, place the lids on top, and screw the rings onto the jars just finger-tight. Return the jars to the canning bath, making sure the water covers the jars by at least 1 inch. Once the water returns to a boil, simmer for 45 minutes. Remove the jars from the bath and let cool to room temperature. Canned this way, the jelly will keep for up to 1 year. Before opening a can of room temperature–stored food product, always check to make sure the seal is still good. With mason-type jars, the lid should be indented and not "pop" when pushed on. If it appears the seal is not good, discard the contents of the jar.

PICKLED WATERMELON RIND

I remember eating watermelon rind pickles for the first time off of a relish tray at one of those restaurants in Colonial Williamsburg where everyone wears period costumes and talks funny to try to make you feel like you have gone back in time. One glance around the room and an eyeball full of "I'm With Stupid" T-shirts and Chuck Taylor high-tops and it is hard to forget where you actually are and that the servers are just giving everything funny names for the sake of the shtick.

So when I started into this delicious little pot of watermelon rind pickles put in front of me, there was no reason for my eighth-grade brain to believe that they were actually made from watermelon rinds. They are, of course, and they're a staple of summer in the South. The pickles themselves are made from the hard flesh between the green rind and the edible sweet pink flesh. (The most tedious part of this process is trimming the "pith" out to make the pickles.) I spike ours with a little red pepper for some heat and to separate them from the traditional sweet pickle treatment. They are highly addictive . . . I warn you now. And you can feel good about making them because you are making use of a part of a plant usually just discarded. Congratulations—you are practically a hippie.

"Straight Outta Compton" —N.W.A.

ingredients

Mix together the salt and 4 cups water in a large bowl. Add the watermelon rind and refrigerate, covered, overnight. When you are ready to continue with the recipe, drain the rind.

Combine the sugar, vinegar, mustard seeds, red pepper flakes, and 1 cup water in a large nonreactive stockpot and bring to a simmer over medium heat. Decrease the heat to low. Wrap the lemon slices, cloves, cinnamon stick, and black peppercorns in cheesecloth (or a coffee filter) and tie with butcher's string. Place in the pot of syrup and simmer for 15 minutes. Add the watermelon rind, bring back to a boil, and simmer for 15 minutes. Let cool briefly in the liquid.

Ladle the rind into a quart-size glass jar. Make sure the syrup covers the pieces of rind completely, and fill the jars to just below the necks. Let cool to room temperature and then screw on the lids. Refrigerate. The rind will keep, refrigerated, for 6 to 8 months.

Alternatively, to prepare the watermelon rind to store at room temperature, fill a water-bath canner or large pot with a lid with water and bring to a boil over high heat. (If you have a rack that fits the canner, use it, or simply line the bottom with a kitchen towel to prevent the jars from banging around during canning.) Carefully place the empty jars, lids, and rings in the water, filling the jars with the water to submerge them. Boil for 10 minutes. Carefully remove the jars and lids with canning tongs from the bath, dumping the water back into the bath. Briefly drain the jars on a clean kitchen towel. Fill the jars first with the rinds, and then pour their pickling liquid over them, filling to just below the neck of the jars. Wipe the rims clean, place the lids on top, and screw the rings onto the jars just finger-tight. Return the jars to the canning bath, making sure the water covers the jars by at least 1 inch. Once the water returns to a boil, simmer for 45 minutes. Remove the jars from the bath and let cool to room temperature. Canned this way, the pickles will keep for up to 1 year. Before opening a can of room temperature–stored food product, always check to make sure the seal is still good. With mason-type jars, the lid should be indented and not "pop" when pushed on. If it appears the seal is not good, discard the contents of the jar.

3 tablespoons salt

4 cups watermelon rind, cut into ¾-inch cubes

2 cups sugar

1½ cups apple cider vinegar

2 teaspoons mustard seeds

1½ teaspoons red pepper flakes

6 (¼-inch-thick) lemon slices *(including the rind)*

1 teaspoon whole cloves

1 cinnamon stick, crushed

1 teaspoon black peppercorns

MAKES 1 QUART

Chapter 4

SLATHERING, SQUIRTING & SMEARING

HOMEMADE "DUKE'S" MAYONNAISE 93
YELLOW MUSTARD 93
WHOLE-GRAIN GUINNESS MUSTARD 94
GRAINY MUSTARD 94
ROASTED RED PEPPER HARISSA 96
WORCESTERSHIRE SAUCE 97
CHIMICHURRI (SMOOTH) 98
CHIMICHURRI (RUSTIC) 98
CORN AND RED PEPPER CHOWCHOW 101
JALAPEÑO HOT SAUCE 102
TOMATO JAM 105
NEW ORLEANS–STYLE RÉMOULADE 106
FRESH HERB TARTAR SAUCE 107

Chapter 4

SLATHERING, SQUIRTING & SMEARING

SLATHERING, SQUIRTING & SMEARING

Condiments are one of my favorite pastimes. I come by my obsession with them very honestly. On a particularly bleary Sunday afternoon in college, I was lying around my parents' house and a group of my buddies and I were watching football and nursing our "consumption" with roast beef po'boys and ice-cold Miller High Life. The process of assembling the aforementioned sandwiches was interrupted as two of my closest friends began pulling my mother's condiment cabinet apart in order to find a suitable mustard. By the time they were done, they had identified no less than 37 different brands of mustard, and you could barely tell they had been in the cabinet. I knew my interest was profound when this number of mustards, which would seem obscene to some, didn't even register as remotely odd to me.

It was in this moment that I realized exactly how specific my interest was in each of these products individually. I don't see them as simply ketchup, mayonnaise, or mustard. To me there are very specific uses for each one. Yellow mustard goes on fried bologna or boudin, and nothing but a good grainy mustard can go with roast beef. Tabasco goes in my seafood gumbo, but nothing is better than Crystal on red beans and rice. Heinz ketchup goes on a grilled burger, while Hunt's definitely goes on a griddled one and the accompanying fries. This is, as it turns out, precisely how I establish my order to the universe . . . through condiment pairings.

Naturally, my own cabinet closely resembles my mother's now, but my fascination for the past 20 years has turned from curating a huge variety of things to trying to isolate the parts of each of these products that are appealing and duplicate them in our own kitchen. We make dozens of things now I would have never dreamed of making when I first started cooking, but the process could not be more fun.

These make great and very personal gifts or are just handy to have around your table for conversation when folks come over. An afternoon of good music or a football game in the kitchen with this chapter and you can check off most of your Christmas list *and* look like a total stud. Go online, select some weird, cool bottles from somewhere like specialtybottle.com, and get to work on a couple of these. You can thank me later.

ROASTED RED PEPPER HARISSA

Vishwesh Bhatt, our chef at Snackbar, is one of the most talented chefs I've encountered as well as one of the finer gentlemen I have ever had the opportunity to know. He is a native of Gujarat, India, and has lived in the United States for almost 30 years. His love for French food is remarkable, but what is exceptional is the deft hand he has in preparing the food his mother and family taught him to make. From the blends of aromatic spices he toasts and grinds to the soulful braises and stews they frequently become, the kitchen is alive with the exotic, wherever he is.

One night about 15 years ago, he whipped up a harissa to go along with a grilled fish dish we were serving. I remember those flavors exploding in my mouth for the first time. It was stunning, and in a moment I was imagining the mountain of different things I wanted to try it with. This is a great condiment to keep around to dip fresh vegetables in, spread on a sandwich, or spoon over the top of absolutely anything cooked on a grill.

ingredients

"Cast Iron" —Superchunk

3 red bell peppers, roasted, peeled, and deseeded

2 teaspoons ground cumin

1 teaspoon ground cardamom

1 teaspoon ground coriander

4 teaspoons sriracha hot sauce

1 tablespoon minced garlic

3 tablespoons Garlic Olive Oil *(page xxvi)*

Salt and freshly ground black pepper

MAKES 4 CUPS

Combine the roasted peppers, cumin, cardamom, coriander, hot sauce, garlic, and garlic oil in a blender and blend well. Season to taste with salt and black pepper. Transfer to a glass or plastic container and refrigerate for up to 3 months.

CORN AND RED PEPPER CHOWCHOW

The dry goods storage area at Crooks Corner was a little added-on, cinder block room outside the back door to the kitchen. I loved it because it was always tidy—Bill would not have it any other way. Nestled among peanut oil cans and apple cider vinegar jugs were stacks of jars of Bill's chowchow and piccalilli. The colors, even in the dark shadows of that little windowless room, were vibrant and clear, and on an occasion we opened one for a special or to spoon alongside pickled shrimp. The flavors were as bright as the colors suggested. This one is outstanding for dabbing on top of fresh black-eyed peas. The sweet and spicy flavor cuts the slight bitterness that the peas have initially.

"Burning Down the House" —Tom Jones and the Cardigans

ingredients

Preheat the oven to 350°F. Place the corn on a baking sheet and roast in the oven for 25 minutes. Remove from the oven, cool, shuck, and carefully remove the kernels from the cobs and reserve. Discard the husks and cobs.

Combine the shallots, bell peppers, mustard, molasses, vinegar, red pepper flakes, celery seeds, thyme, salt, and black pepper in a medium nonreactive saucepan and bring to a simmer over medium heat. Decrease the heat to low and simmer for 5 minutes. Remove from the heat and stir in the corn kernels. Let cool and then pack into glass jars. This will keep, refrigerated, for 4 months.

Note:

If you would like to can the chowchow, ladle it into sterilized jars, seal, and process in a boiling-water bath canner for 30 minutes. The chowchow will then keep for 1 year at room temperature. If canning, add 1 tablespoon lemon juice to each quart before packing chowchow into jars. See page 82 for further instructions.

8 ears fresh sweet corn in the husks

½ cup minced shallots

¾ cup small-dice red bell peppers

2 tablespoons plus 2 teaspoons Yellow Mustard *(page 93)*

¼ cup molasses

3 tablespoons apple cider vinegar

1 teaspoon red pepper flakes

½ teaspoon celery seeds

2 teaspoons fresh thyme leaves

2 teaspoons salt

2 teaspoons freshly ground black pepper

MAKES 4 CUPS

JALAPEÑO HOT SAUCE

I am a huge fan of the McIlhenny Company and everything Tabasco does. Their dedication to quality, integrity, and flavor is absolutely unparalleled in the hot sauce world. They also happen to be headquartered in, what I think is, one of the most beautiful places on the planet: Avery Island, Louisiana. It is a wonder of wildlife and lush vegetation that the family has, for five or more generations, done everything to help promote and propagate.

I am fascinated with their lengthy fermentation process for the original flavor hot sauce: They ferment the crushed Tabasco peppers for three years before making their famous sauce . . . and eight years for the family reserve! This process creates a mellow yet bright profile and delivers a wonderful representation of the actual flavor of the pepper without all of its original heat. Being the curious and adventurous type I am, we decided we would take on the process with locally grown jalapeños ourselves. The result is remarkable, and this is great to dash on fresh field peas and rice or fried chicken. It takes fried fish to a whole other level.

ingredients

"You're Gonna Get Yours" —Public Enemy

1 pound jalapeño peppers *(see Notes)*
2 tablespoons minced garlic
¼ cup salt
4 teaspoons sugar
2½ cups champagne vinegar
½ teaspoon xanthan gum *(see Notes)*

MAKES ABOUT 3 CUPS

Puree the peppers, garlic, salt, and sugar in a food processor until well chopped. Transfer the puree to a food-grade, 2-quart plastic bucket or a medium stainless-steel or glass bowl, cover with cheesecloth, and secure with a string or rubber band. Allow the mixture to sit at room temperature for 2 days, and then place in the refrigerator for 1 month.

Remove from the refrigerator and whisk in the vinegar. Transfer the mixture to a heavy-duty blender and blend in the xanthan gum. Puree on high speed for 3 minutes. Divide among 4- to 6-ounce sauce bottles, seal, and store for another month at room temperature. (You can use the hot sauce right away, but the flavors will develop much more over time.) This will keep for 1 year in the refrigerator and for a couple of months at room temperature before discoloring. It will still be fine to eat, but it will lose its bright color.

Notes:

You can substitute any hot pepper you like. Jalapeños make a milder version. Serrano peppers have a little more citric quality. Cayenne and Tabasco peppers get hotter, and Scotch bonnets are about the hottest of the readily available peppers. The fermentation process mellows some of the heat, but not much. What it does do, though, is enhance the natural flavors of all those peppers. Use the whole peppers—stems, seeds, and all. Seeds bring heat to the sauce, and the stems kick-start the fermentation.

Xanthan gum is a naturally occurring polysaccharide food additive used for thickening and stabilizing (emulsification) food products. In this recipe, it helps prevent the hot sauce from separating into a layer of pepper solids and a layer of vinegar. Xanthan is available in the health food section of most grocery stores. Look for the Bob's Red Mill brand.

Paul McIlhenny, late CEO of Tabasco.

DUCK PROSCIUTTO — 113

PORK BELLY RILLONS WITH SPICED APPLE BUTTER — 114

POLISH SMOKED SAUSAGE — 115

BROWN SUGAR–BLACK PEPPER BACON — 116

DUCK CONFIT WITH PEACH RELISH — 118

TASSO HAM — 119

GARLIC-DUCK SAUSAGE WITH COLLARD "CHOUCROUTE GARNI" — 121

JAMBALAYA "BOUDIN" — 122

COUNTRY-STYLE PORK PÂTÉ WITH CHESTNUTS — 125

PORK RILLETTES — 126

CONFIT OF CHICKEN GIZZARDS WITH HERBED BUTTERMILK BISCUITS AND GRAINY MUSTARD — 127

SPICY HILL COUNTRY MEAT PIES WITH SRIRACHA MAYONNAISE — 128

Chapter 5

CURING, PRESERVING & STUFFING

CURING, PRESERVING & STUFFING

So before Internet detractors light up the switchboard, I am well aware that pickling and smoking are preservation techniques, but this chapter is dedicated to protein exclusively and outlines a number of preservation techniques for non-vegetable items. It was the only way to pull the proteins out distinctly, so here goes.

Preservation of food dates back to the dawn of civilization. It was a matter of survival until a hundred years ago and is only currently undergoing a reexamination by chefs looking backward to better understand the roots and origins of our food and the way it was handled traditionally. Evidence suggests that pigs, which receive the greatest amount of attention when it comes to these techniques, were being raised captive as long as 2,000 years ago from China to Italy. So it only makes sense that there are long, storied traditions of preservation through those areas and beyond. However, pigs would not have reached the United States until the 1500s, with the earliest Western European settlers.

Though the South doesn't necessarily consume much (if any more) pork than any other part of the country, this particular protein plays a significant role in our food. Pigs pack a tremendous punch for their dollar value. Almost the entire animal is edible, from "the rooter to the tooter," as is said. Pigs, even free-ranging ones, can grow to a good "kill weight" in a matter of months, and the amount of room they need is significantly less than cattle.

Hams hanging in the tobacco barn at my great-grandfather's house never really struck me as curious when I was a child. But they hung there for a reason, and it's one I love and appreciate today more than ever. Those hams represent—along with the community of hog butchering, blood sausage, smoked ham hocks, boudin, and spicy breakfast sausage that I grew up with—total product utilization, not for economics' sake, but out of both absolute necessity and respect for the animal. While cattle certainly see significant usage of the overall carcass, a significant portion is not used for human consumption. Killing a cow for its tenderloin and a few other pieces here and there is philosophically tantamount to slaughtering buffalo for the hide or elephants for their ivory. The pig, on the other hand, resides in the place of the proverbial culinary reverence in the South.

Like everything else about Southern cooking, these techniques have a direct and obvious tie to European tradition, brought to America by the immigrants who settled these areas. Some recipes, such as the Country-Style Pork Pâté with Chestnuts, are personal direct interpretations of their European cousins, made with local ingredients, while others are twists on originals with a New World touch, for example the Jambalaya "Boudin." Some of these take some time, patience, and dedication, but the end result is something to be massively proud of and connected to. This is the food that stories are made of.

DUCK PROSCIUTTO

Duck "prosciutto" is something I don't hold in very high regard normally. In my experience, this has been the charcuterie hack's easy go-to, the "hey-look-at-me-I'm-doing-charcuterie" item. More often than not it is dry, rubbery, and overseasoned, and it is rarely if ever remarkable, so when we started our *charcuterie* program in the mid-2000s, this was one of the first things I wanted to tackle and do right. Our *charcutier*, Kirk Lovejoy, who has all the drive of a freight train, wanted to devour all the knowledge he possibly could on his path to greatness and was completely on board with this challenge.

We worked on texture first, measuring precisely the ratios of salt and sugar to the ounces of breast meat. Once we had a "ham" we could hang our hats on, we tackled the flavor profile. Clove with the slightest hint of heat was our favorite. I love rolling this out because most of the chefs and food lovers I know feel very much the same way about this item as I do, and ours is one I couldn't be more proud of. It is easy to pull off at home, if you have the patience to wait a couple of weeks for the breasts to cure.

"A Hold of You" —Lambchop

ingredients

In a small bowl, blend together the salt, pepper, bay leaf, coriander seeds, red pepper flakes, garlic powder, cinnamon, curing salt, and brown sugar. Place the duck breasts in a glass baking dish and evenly sprinkle half of the curing spice blend over them, then flip them over and sprinkle the other half on that side. Place a plate on top of the breasts, weight it with a large can of olive oil or a gallon of milk, and refrigerate for 24 hours.

At the end of the 24-hour cure, remove the breasts from the pan, wipe off all the excess curing spice, and pat dry with paper towels. Wrap the breasts in two layers of cheesecloth and secure with a string. Hang the breasts in the refrigerator (or if you have a large humidor, hang them there). Be sure to place a pan underneath the breasts to catch any drips. Allow the breasts to hang for 3 weeks.

Cold-smoke the breasts for 4 hours (see Note). Unwrap, thinly slice, and serve.

Note:

Cold smoking is done in an outdoor pit that usually has a separate but attached firebox where the fire is set. The fire produces smoke that is channeled into a smoking chamber where the meat rests. Temperatures for cold smoking rarely get above 120° to 150°F because the heat is isolated from the smoking chamber. You can achieve the same result with a stovetop smoking rig, but it takes a certain amount of diligence because the wood chips or sawdust needs to be replenished every so often.

3 tablespoons salt

2 teaspoons freshly ground black pepper

1 dried bay leaf, crumbled

2 teaspoons coriander seeds, toasted and crushed

1 teaspoon red pepper flakes

½ teaspoon garlic powder

⅛ teaspoon ground cinnamon

⅛ teaspoon pink curing salt
(available with canning supplies)

2 tablespoons dark brown sugar

3 whole skin-on duck breasts
(7 to 9 ounces each)

**MAKES 3 BREASTS
(ENOUGH TO SERVE 20 TO 25)**

PORK BELLY RILLONS WITH SPICED APPLE BUTTER

Rillons are not given much consideration or attention, but for me they strike a very similar chord to duck confit . . . just made with pig. What's not to like, I ask? This specialty of the Loire Valley is basically a cubed, cured, fried confit of pork belly. It is fatty, so I don't endorse regular full meals of it, but it is an exceptional first course or single bite.

These crispy, porky little devils are wonderful with a fresh fall apple butter and some spiced pecans, along with a pungent blue cheese.

ingredients

"*Click, Click, Click, Click*" —Bishop Allen

1 pound pork belly, cut into 1½-inch cubes
2 teaspoons salt
2 teaspoons freshly ground black pepper
5 tablespoons lard *(see page 136)*
10 sprigs fresh thyme
8 cloves garlic, very thinly sliced
2 dried bay leaves
1 cup dry red wine
Spiced Apple Butter *(recipe follows)*

SERVES 4

In a small stainless-steel or glass bowl, toss the pork belly with the salt and pepper. Cover with plastic wrap and refrigerate for at least 2 hours and preferably overnight.

Preheat the oven to 300°F. Melt 3 tablespoons of the lard in a large sauté pan over medium heat. Add the pork belly and brown on all sides, about 3 minutes. Dump the pork and fat into a medium ovenproof saucepan and add the thyme, garlic, bay leaves, and wine. Cover and place in the oven for 3 hours, or until the belly is extremely tender. Remove from the oven and let cool in the saucepan. Remove the rillons from the pan and set aside on a plate.

Heat the remaining 2 tablespoons lard in a sauté pan and brown the rillon pieces until just crispy. Drain on paper towels, and serve immediately with the apple butter.

SPICED APPLE BUTTER

5 pounds (about 10 large) apples, preferably a mix of sweet and tart varieties, peeled and cut into 1-inch chunks
2 cups apple cider
1 cup granulated sugar
½ cup dark brown sugar
¼ cup applejack or Calvados
¼ cup apple cider vinegar
Finely grated zest and juice of ½ large lemon
1 teaspoon vanilla extract
1 teaspoon ground cinnamon
½ teaspoon salt
¼ teaspoon freshly grated nutmeg
¼ teaspoon ground ginger
⅛ teaspoon ground cloves
⅛ teaspoon ground allspice

MAKES ABOUT 4 CUPS

Preheat the oven to 400°F. Spread the apple chunks in a single layer on a baking sheet lined with parchment paper and roast until they have softened but not browned very much, about 20 minutes. Transfer the apples and any juices they've released to a medium soup pot. Add the cider, granulated and brown sugars, applejack, vinegar, lemon zest and juice, vanilla, cinnamon, salt, nutmeg, ginger, cloves, and allspice and stir to combine. Bring the apples to a simmer over medium heat. Lower the heat to low and cook, stirring occasionally to prevent scorching, for about 4 hours. (Alternatively, everything can be transferred to a slow cooker and cooked with almost no attention given to it.) The apple butter should turn a nice shade of light brown. The longer it cooks, the thicker it will get.

Scrape the apple butter into a blender and puree thoroughly. Return to the soup pot and bring back to a simmer for another 45 minutes over medium-low heat. Stir constantly. Pack into glass jars and refrigerate for up to 1 month.

POLISH SMOKED SAUSAGE

My buddies Stephen Stryjewski and Donald Link make some the best sausages, hams, and salamis I have ever had. I love what they do and am not ashamed to say that when we embark on creating a new item, I frequently use them and their approval as a measuring stick of success. They are both notoriously stoic, so when I saw each one of them smile after trying this sausage for the first time at our Memphis in May gathering, I knew we had hit on something exceptional . . . that, or we were all already too deep into the "spirit" of the event for me to know any different.

There is a series of semi-complicated steps to this recipe, all crucial to the texture of the sausage, which will make or break the success of the recipe. Follow this closely and you will make an exceptional smoked sausage that can be either dropped in a bun with mustard and caramelized onions or be sliced for pick-up snacks. We sell thousands of pounds of this at Bouré every year on our Mississippi Sausage and Cheese Plate.

"Pretend We're Dead" —L7

In a stainless-steel bowl, combine the pork butt, milk powder, garlic, marjoram, salt, sugar, mustard seeds, white pepper, Cure #1, and ice and blend well. Set a meat grinder up with the small-hole die (3⁄16 inch, ideally). Grind the pork mixture and immediately place in the bowl of a stand mixer fitted with the paddle attachment. Beat on low speed until the mixture reaches 55°F. When it does, spread it on a baking sheet and refrigerate until the mixture reaches 40°F.

In the meantime, grind the bacon to the same size. Fold it into the chilled pork mixture until evenly blended.

Set up your sausage stuffing machine according to the manufacturer's directions and load the sausage meat into it. Stuff the pork mixture into the casings. As you go, coil the sausage into a single layer. If you want a finished product that appears more like a "link," you can tie off the sausage at "bun lengths" with butcher's string. We typically do not do that with this sausage, preferring to cut it to length after it is smoked.

Build a fire in your smoker and hot-smoke the sausage at 200°F until it reaches an internal temperature of 155°F.

Notes:
Cure #1 is a blend of salt and sodium nitrite that eliminates the threat of botulism in alkaline protein curing. It is available online and at most sausage-making operations. Do not confuse it with Cure #2. The two are similar but are not interchangeable.

When buying sausage casings, there are a number of options. The only catch is that, no matter what you choose, you will end up with more than you need, unless you plan to make tons of sausage. Fortunately, sausages are 1) inexpensive and 2) store well. Casings come in either "natural," which are actual washed intestine from any number of animals, or "artificial," which are usually manufactured with collagen. When cooked, the artificial ones make an acceptable casing, though I *always* prefer natural casings. Collagen casings have a shelf life of a couple of years. Natural casings come either packed in salt, which keep refrigerated for 3 to 4 months, or vacuum sealed and fresh, which can easily be frozen for 4 to 6 months. Visit thesausagemaker.com for an excellent source for everything you may want or need to make almost any kind of sausage.

ingredients

- 3 pounds pork butt, cut into 1-inch cubes
- 3⁄4 cup dried milk powder
- 1 tablespoon minced garlic
- 1 tablespoon chopped fresh marjoram
- 1 tablespoon salt
- 1½ teaspoons sugar
- 1 teaspoon mustard seeds, crushed
- 1 teaspoon freshly ground white pepper
- 1⁄8 teaspoon Cure #1 *(see Notes)*
- 3⁄4 cup crushed ice
- 1 pound thick-cut bacon
- Beef sausage casings *(1½ inch diameter; see Notes)*

MAKES 4 POUNDS (SERVES 10)

BROWN SUGAR–BLACK PEPPER BACON

I was getting on a plane for Argentina when I got the call from a property owner saying that the space where the original Big Bad Breakfast now sits was open if I wanted it. However, he had to have an immediate answer because there were a half dozen people lined up to take it. Unfortunately I could not get my sweet wife on the phone to discuss it before the plane door closed. With no idea what concept we would develop exactly, I agreed to lease the space and then immediately left the country. It was monumentally stupid.

On that trip, I began to sketch the design for a super-local and entirely-from-scratch breakfast concept. We are told our entire lives that this is the most important meal of the day, so the nagging question to me was, why don't we give it the same consideration as we do dinner, or even lunch? One of the first things I addressed was bacon. If we were going to open this place I wanted to make everything from scratch, including the bacon. It would be sourced from the best pigs we could identify, and I had very definite ideas about the flavor profile. I wanted to play sweet against salty and add some spice, and thus began our adventure in creating the Tabasco and Brown Sugar Bacon that is served today at Big Bad Breakfast.

This a version of that bacon with black pepper, as the Tabasco mash we use to make the bacon for BBB is no longer available to the general public. It takes 7 to 10 days to cure and smoke. Get some whole belly and you will soon be the Baron of Breakfast.

ingredients

"Calling Dr. Love" —Kiss

3 cups salt

3 cups dark brown sugar

½ cup freshly ground black pepper

1 teaspoon ground cinnamon

½ teaspoon ground cloves

Scant ⅛ teaspoon Cure #1 *(see Note, page 115; optional, but it helps preserve a nicer color)*

1 whole side pork belly *(about 10 pounds)*

MAKES ABOUT 8 POUNDS

Combine the salt, sugar, pepper, cinnamon, cloves, and Cure #1 in a large stainless-steel bowl and blend well. Place the pork belly in a perforated pan, such as a broiler pan, to catch drips, sprinkle half of the curing mixture over one side, and rub in well. Flip the belly over and repeat on the second side. Cover the belly with a kitchen towel and place in the refrigerator for 10 days.

In a cooker equipped with a separate firebox, build a wood fire and get it burning nicely. Remove the cured belly from the refrigerator and brush off as much of the curing spice as possible. Lay the belly on the grill grate and cold-smoke at 95° to 105°F for 12 to 16 hours. Remove from the smoker and refrigerate.

Portion the smoked pork belly into 1-pound blocks for easy slicing, packaging, and/or freezing. The best way to package this for freezing is with a vacuum sealer. Plastic wrap will work fine in the freezer for up to a couple weeks and it is fine for storing in the refrigerator. The bacon will keep for 10 days in the refrigerator and 6 to 8 months in the freezer.

DUCK CONFIT WITH PEACH RELISH

As with pork rillettes, I remember the very first moment that a bite of duck confit passed my lips. It was at Gautreau's in the summer of 1988. I had moved home from Chapel Hill, where I had fallen into the industry, to take a job as Larkin Selman's sous chef. Larkin was fresh off of time with Alfred Portale and Jonathan Waxman in New York and was armed to do battle, with their inspiration, in our hometown of New Orleans. Duck confit with marinated lentils and red onion marmalade was one of the first dishes Larkin rolled out, and a bite during lineup the night it premiered blew me away.

Properly prepared confit is a perfect balance of saltiness. It is "cured" for about 24 hours before it is cooked with a heavy hand of salt and other seasonings. Too much and the final result is too salty to eat, but not enough and it is anemic and bland. The cooking time on this is a little long, but it is something that you can stick in the oven and then go play golf, and when you return, it'll be just done. It is a total crowd-pleaser.

A touch of almost anything sweet dances beautifully with the saltiness of the duck. Here I pair it with Pickled Peach Relish, but you can just as easily drizzle it with honey or hit it with a touch of fig preserves, Spicy Pepper Jelly (page 86), mango chutney, or sweet Thai chili sauce.

ingredients

"Mama Said Knock You Out" —LL Cool J

8 whole duck leg quarters
3 tablespoons salt
1 tablespoon freshly ground white pepper
1 tablespoon garlic powder
1 tablespoon onion powder
8 cloves garlic, thinly sliced
20 sprigs fresh thyme
4 dried bay leaves
1 tablespoon black peppercorns
6 cups rendered duck fat *(see Note)*
2 cups lard *(see page 136)*; or pure olive oil
Pickled Peach Relish *(recipe follows)*

SERVES 8

Lay the duck legs on a baking sheet, skin side down. In a small bowl, combine the salt, white pepper, garlic powder, and onion powder and liberally sprinkle half of it over the duck flesh. Sandwich the legs together, flesh on flesh, and season the skin on both sides with the remaining salt mix. Cover with plastic wrap and refrigerate overnight.

Preheat the oven to 225°F. Remove the duck legs from the refrigerator and separate them. Scatter the garlic slices and thyme sprigs evenly over the duck and place the legs, flesh side down, in a braising pan. Scatter the bay leaves and peppercorns evenly over the duck legs.

In a large saucepan, warm the duck fat over low heat until just melted and stir in the lard until melted. Pour the fat over the duck legs in the braising pan and cover the pan with aluminum foil. Bake for 5 to 6 hours, until the meat easily pulls away from the bone. Remove from the oven and let cool thoroughly in the fat at room temperature. Cover and refrigerate for up to 3 months.

When ready to serve, preheat the oven to 400°F. Heat a large cast-iron skillet over high heat for 2 minutes. Carefully remove the legs from the fat. Decrease the heat to medium. Spoon 4 tablespoons of the duck fat into the pan and swirl until it has melted. Place 4 of the legs in the pan, skin side down, and brown for about 2 minutes. Flip them over and brown the second side. Transfer the first 4 legs to a baking sheet and repeat with the remaining 4 leg quarters. When they have browned, place all 8 on the center rack of the oven and warm them through for about 7 minutes. Serve with the peach relish (left).

Note:

Rendered duck fat is available in specialty food stores or from D'artagnan (dartagnan.com) along with *tons* of other delicious stuff.

PICKLED PEACH RELISH

1½ cups Pickled Peaches *(page 76)*, cut into very small dice
1 tablespoon minced shallots
1 teaspoon minced garlic
1 tablespoon deseeded and minced jalapeño pepper
1 tablespoon pure olive oil
4 teaspoons Yellow Mustard *(page 93)*
1 tablespoon chopped fresh flat-leaf parsley
½ teaspoon salt
¾ teaspoon freshly ground black pepper

SERVES 8

Blend the peaches, shallots, garlic, jalapeño, olive oil, mustard, parsley, salt, and pepper in a stainless-steel bowl. Let stand at room temperature for 30 minutes to allow the flavors to develop and blend.

TASSO HAM

Simply referred to as "tasso" in Louisiana, this is the unsung hero of a pot of dried beans and is a great addition to jambalaya, braised greens, or scrambled eggs. Tasso is extremely easy to make but rarely listed as an ingredient in mainstream recipes. It is also a great extra ingredient for quiche, grilled pimento cheese, or vegetable soup. It also makes a good slice-and-eat charcuterie board item.

The finished product has similar texture to a wet-cured capocollo but is typically cut from the shoulder into 3- to 4-ounce pieces and coated heavily with a Creole spice cure before smoking. As an alternative (and one that makes a more tender final product), I like to use pork cheeks, as the intramuscular marbling of fat lends itself to a better finished product.

Tasso freezes nicely for up to 6 months, so you can buy a whole shoulder, cure it, smoke it, vacuum-seal it, and freeze however much you like.

"Friendly Ghost" —Harlem

ingredients

In a small stainless-steel bowl, combine the paprika, cayenne, onion and garlic powders, sage, cloves, brown sugar, and salt. Coat the pork cheeks evenly with the spice cure mix. Wrap the meat in 3- or 4-piece batches tightly in plastic wrap and refrigerate for 5 days.

In a smoker with a separate firebox, build a hot wood fire (we use oak, which burns a little bit hotter than other local hardwoods). When ready to smoke, remove the pork cheeks from the plastic wrap and hot-smoke at 200°F until the tasso reaches an internal temperature of 155°F. Remove from the smoker and store in the refrigerator, wrapped in plastic, for up to 10 days. Alternatively, this can be vacuum-sealed and frozen for up to 4 months.

5 tablespoons smoked paprika
2 tablespoons cayenne
2 tablespoons onion powder
5 teaspoons garlic powder
1 tablespoon dried sage
¾ teaspoon ground cloves
2 tablespoons dark brown sugar
¼ cup salt
5 pounds pork cheeks *(trimmed of fat)* or pork butt, cut into 4-ounce pieces

MAKES 5 POUNDS

The Big Bad Smokehouse, Oxford, Mississippi.

COLLARD "CHOUCROUTE GARNI"

2 tablespoons olive oil

2 pounds Garlic Duck Sausage *(page 121)*

½ pound smoked bacon, sliced into thin strips

3 cups thinly sliced yellow onions

3 tablespoons thinly sliced garlic cloves

2 bunches collard greens, stems removed and thinly sliced

¾ cup white wine

4 Granny Smith apples, unpeeled, cored, and sliced medium thick *(alternatively, use Pickled Peaches, page 76, but only use half the amount of peaches, and stir in at the very end of the cooking process)*

¼ cup apple cider vinegar

2 teaspoons salt

1 tablespoon freshly ground black pepper

3 fresh bay leaves *(or 2 dried)*

2 teaspoons red pepper flakes

½ teaspoon ground allspice

Preheat the oven to 350°F. In a large cast-iron skillet over medium heat, brown 2 pounds of the sausage on two sides in the olive oil, then remove from the heat and set aside.

In a medium ovenproof braising pan over medium heat, cook the bacon until almost crispy, stirring constantly, 4 to 5 minutes. Remove the bacon and reserve. Add the onions and garlic to the pan and sauté until wilted and transparent. Stir in the collards and white wine and cook until the collards begin to wilt. Stir in the apples, vinegar, salt, pepper, bay leaves, red pepper flakes, allspice, and the reserved bacon. Decrease the heat to low, cover, and let simmer for 15 minutes. Place the reserved sausage into the pan with the choucroute, burying the sausage slightly. Place the pan, covered, in the oven for 15 minutes. Serve immediately.

GARLIC-DUCK SAUSAGE
WITH COLLARD "CHOUCROUTE GARNI"

Sometimes the best things in the world are the absolute simplest. This recipe is a testament to that fact. I was doing a winter James Beard Foundation dinner for my friend Jeff Black a few years ago and decided that I wanted to make the most crushing Southern version of cassoulet that had ever been done.

Cassoulet is a French "casserole," for lack of a better term, with shredded duck confit, sausage, flageolet beans, and bread crumbs. It is a difficult dish to pull off well. As a matter of fact, it can be challenging to find a well-executed version in France these days. Because of the absorbency of the beans and bread crumbs, the final product can be dry and unpleasant. So everything must be perfect for it to work . . . especially the sausage and confit.

I wrote this recipe thinking we would need to tweak it with a few things to get it right, but on the first pull, it was perfect. Here we serve it like traditional Alsatian choucroute, but instead of sauerkraut and apples, ours uses collards and pickled peaches. This is awesome for a meal in front of the fire.

This duck sausage is great for smoking. If you decide that you want to cold-smoke it, thoroughly mix ⅛ teaspoon of Cure #1 into the duck and seasonings before grinding; otherwise, the sausage should be fully cooked or frozen within 24 hours of making it. Browning in a pan on the stove or cooking over a hot grill is how I recommend cooking this sausage if serving it alone.

"Cashing In" —Minor Threat

ingredients

To make the sausage: Combine the duck meat, bacon, salt, pepper, peppercorns, *quatre épices*, cayenne, brandy, and garlic in a stainless-steel bowl and chill in the refrigerator for 30 minutes.

In a meat grinder with the small die in place, grind the mixture. Set up your sausage stuffing machine according to the manufacturer's directions and load the sausage meat into it. Stuff the duck mixture into the casing, tying the sausage off every 5 inches or so with butcher's string. Vacuum-seal and freeze or cook immediately (within 24 hours).

Note:

Quatre épices is a French spice blend available in specialty food stores. It typically combines equal amounts of white pepper, cloves, nutmeg, and ginger, though slight variations to this equation occur from brand to brand. If you have the ingredients on hand, this is just as easily and equally good stirred together at home as it is purchased.

3½ pounds duck meat, untrimmed of fat (preferably legs), cut into ¾-inch cubes

¾ pound thick-sliced bacon

2 teaspoons salt

½ teaspoon freshly ground black pepper

1 teaspoon black peppercorns

½ teaspoon quatre épices spice mix *(see Note)*

⅛ teaspoon cayenne

1½ teaspoons brandy

1½ teaspoons minced garlic

Lamb sausage casing
(¾ inch diameter; see Note, page 115)

**MAKES 5 POUNDS OF SAUSAGE
(USE 2 POUNDS TO FEED 4 PEOPLE
AND FREEZE THE REMAINDER)**

JAMBALAYA "BOUDIN"

Boudin is the very first thing I remember connecting with a place. Simply put, boudin is south Louisiana. It is about using all of the pig and stretching it with an inexpensive grain (much in the same way of Scottish haggis) in order to manufacture a greater volume of sustenance. Boudin is traditionally served with saltine crackers and cheap yellow mustard, which completely connects with the white trash part of me. It also speaks directly to the democratic nature of my experience in the Louisiana swamplands, the mantra being "nothing extravagant . . . nothing wasted."

Though boudin is cased and presented like a traditional link sausage, when served, the casing is typically pierced and the sausage spread on saltines, rather than sliced. It is truly "a food of the people." I would estimate that about 85 percent of the boudin I have consumed in south Louisiana has, more often than not, been busted open with a plastic knife and served on a paper plate. If Donald Link had not come along with his white linen version at Cochon, which I also can't say no to, that percentage would be much closer to 100.

I have made thousands of pounds of boudin in various incarnations in the last twentysomething years. I like each of them individually, like my own children. This is one I like because it marries things I love. Jambalaya is, arguably, unstuffed boudin, minus liver, plus seafood. So why not turn this Louisiana classic into a grillable sausage?

ingredients

"Jambalaya (On the Bayou)" —Hank Williams

3 tablespoons unsalted butter

½ cup small-dice yellow onions

¼ cup minced celery

¼ cup minced red bell peppers

1 tablespoon minced garlic

¾ pound shelled crawfish tails, chopped

¾ pound shelled shrimp, chopped
(26 to 30 count)

½ cup chopped chicken livers *(optional)*

1¼ teaspoons salt

2 teaspoons freshly ground black pepper

2 tablespoons Creole Seasoning *(page xxvi)*

5 tablespoons heavy cream

2½ cups cooked long-grain white rice

2 teaspoons freshly squeezed lemon juice

1 teaspoon finely grated lemon zest

½ cup chopped green onions

3 tablespoons fresh flat-leaf parsley

Large hog casings
(1-inch diameter; see Note, page 115)

SERVES 10

In a large sauté pan over medium heat, melt the butter. Stir in the onions, celery, bell peppers, and garlic and sauté until the vegetables just begin to wilt, about 3 minutes. Stir in the crawfish, shrimp, chicken livers, salt, pepper, and Creole seasoning and stir until the shrimp begins to turn pink. Blend in the cream and immediately remove from the heat and let cool briefly.

Place the seafood mixture in a food processor and pulse 2 or 3 times, until it is roughly chopped. Dump the mixture into a bowl and stir together with the cooked rice until evenly blended. Add the lemon juice and zest, green onions, and parsley and combine well.

Set up your sausage-stuffing machine according to the manufacturer's directions and load the jambalaya mixture into it. Stuff the mixture into the hog casings, tying links off every 5 inches with butcher's string.

From here, the sausage can be treated in a number of ways. Since the contents are completely cooked before the sausage is stuffed, all you need to do is rewarm the sausage to serve it: for instance, in a 375°F oven for 8 to 10 minutes. Or poach them in crab boil or beer for 8 to 10 minutes, or cook them over a hot fire in the barbecue pit for 6 to 8 minutes.

Note:
These do not freeze well and should be consumed within a day or two of making them.

COUNTRY-STYLE PORK PÂTÉ WITH CHESTNUTS

As much as I hate employing clichés, one of my favorites addresses the Eastern Seaboard's historic proliferation of chestnut trees. It is said that there were once so many that a squirrel could jump from one tree to the next going from Mississippi to Maine without feet ever touching the ground. Prized for the quality of its lumber more so than for its nut production, the chestnut was harvested to the brink of extinction in our corner of the country. A good specimen can live hundreds of years and grow to 100 feet high and 10 feet in diameter at its base. Its fruit is one of my favorite seasonal ingredients for both the final potential of its fruit and the dedication to proliferation it shows in its evolution. Fresh from the tree, the chestnuts are encased in a spiny casing that requires a glove just to lift them from the ground. So they are much less likely to fall prey to scavengers and more likely to survive to germinate.

My dear friend Dr. Dee Canale from Memphis owns a beautiful piece of hardwood-studded property not far from where I live in the country. One of my favorite fall activities is to spend a late afternoon with him and his wife (and usually a very good bottle of red wine) in his grove of 300 or so chestnut trees, picking up and harvesting chestnuts. My prep cooks hate me at this time of year, because once harvested, they have to be split, roasted, and shelled. It is tedious work, but the final product is spectacular and can be used whole, pureed, milled into flour, and so on.

"Sugarfoot" —Black Joe Lewis and the Honeybears

Combine the pork, ¾ pound of the bacon, the livers, celery leaves, onions, parsley, garlic, salt, black pepper, cayenne, nutmeg, cinnamon, cardamom, and cloves in a medium stainless-steel bowl. Feed this mixture through a meat grinder fitted with a medium die. Place in a bowl, cover with plastic wrap, and refrigerate until thoroughly cold.

Preheat the oven to 300°F. In a stainless-steel bowl, whisk together the cream, eggs, flour, and bourbon.

Place the chilled meat in the bowl of a stand mixer fitted with the paddle attachment and blend in the reserved egg mixture. Stir in the chestnuts by hand.

Take a small spoonful of the mixture and sear it in a small nonstick sauté pan with a touch of neutral oil, like peanut oil, for about 2 minutes, or until brown on both sides. Taste it to check for seasoning and adjust the rest of the mix, if needed, with salt and black pepper.

Line an 8-inch pâté mold with plastic wrap, letting a border wide enough to later cover the top of the mold hang over the edges. Line the bottom and sides of the mold with the remaining bacon strips. Let the bacon hang over the sides to wrap over the top of the pâté. Pack the mold with the chestnut mixture. Wrap the bacon over the top and then seal with the plastic. Place the pâté mold in a larger pan, such as a roasting pan, and set it on the oven rack. Bring a kettle full of water to a boil and carefully pour it around the mold until the level reaches most of the way up the side of the mold. Bake to an internal temperature of 160°F, about 2 hours.

Remove from the oven, remove from the water bath, and remove the top of the pâté mold. Wrap a brick, a small can of olive oil, or anything weighty in aluminum foil and place the weight on top of the pâté. Let cool to room temperature.

Remove the weight from the top of the pâté and place the mold in the refrigerator to chill. Once chilled, remove from the mold, remove the plastic wrap, and serve with a selection of mustards and pickles.

ingredients

2 pounds pork butt, cut into 1-inch cubes   *1*
1¼ pounds thick-cut bacon   *3/4*
½ pound chicken livers   *1/4*
¾ cup celery leaves   *6 oz 1/4*
½ cup small-dice yellow onions   *1/4*
⅓ cup chopped fresh flat-leaf parsley   *2 TBS + 2 tsp*
2 tablespoons finely minced garlic   *1*
1 tablespoon salt   *1/2*
2 teaspoons freshly ground black pepper   *1*
1½ teaspoons cayenne   *3/4 + sp*
1 teaspoon freshly grated nutmeg   *1/2*
½ teaspoon ground cinnamon   *1/4*
½ teaspoon ground cardamom   *1/4*
¼ teaspoon ground cloves   *1/8*
½ cup heavy cream   *1/4*
2 large eggs, lightly beaten   *1*
3 tablespoons all-purpose flour   *1 ½ T*
¼ cup bourbon   *2 TBS*
1½ cups roasted chestnuts, quartered   *3/4*
Selection of mustards and pickles, for serving

SERVES 8 TO 10

PORK RILLETTES

Arguably the forefather of Hormel's "potted meat," rillettes are significantly more refined, in that the process is more deliberate and the protein used is more select than what most people speculate goes into American potted meat. My first rillettes were not in a roadside bistro in the French countryside, but from the hand of my friend Frank Stitt. I remember Frank scooping a dollop from a small ceramic crock and spreading it roughly on some hot crusty bread just off the grill. I watched momentarily as the heat from the bread began to turn the congealed mass into a warm, gooey, fatty mouthful of deliciousness. This examination could only last so long before my first bite that started a love affair in my mouth. In the years since, there has been very little, from shrimp to rabbit and boar to tomatoes, that we have not turned into "rillettes."

The process involves little more than simmering a meat in its fat until it falls apart, shredding it roughly, and packing it in a nonreactive (traditionally ceramic) container and using a layer of the strained fat to seal the container, in which it will keep for 3 to 4 months.

ingredients

"When the Levee Breaks" —Led Zeppelin

1 pound pork shoulder

½ pound pork belly
(you can substitute a fatty piece of pork butt)

1 tablespoon salt

5 teaspoons freshly ground black pepper

½ pound slab bacon

1 cup Dark Chicken Stock *(page 31)*

1 tablespoon chopped fresh thyme

1 tablespoon chopped fresh rosemary

4 cloves garlic, minced

½ cup medium-dice red onions

¼ cup medium-dice celery

¼ cup peeled, small-dice carrots

3 dried bay leaves

2 teaspoons red pepper flakes

¼ cup Cognac or other brandy

SERVES 8

Cut the pork shoulder and pork belly into ½-inch cubes and toss with the salt and pepper in a large bowl. Let stand for 1 hour.

Cut the bacon into similar sized cubes. Heat a medium saucepan over medium heat and add the diced bacon. As soon as the bacon has begun to render its fat, add the pork and pork belly, the stock, thyme, rosemary, garlic, onions, celery, carrots, bay leaves, and red pepper flakes and bring to a boil. Decrease the heat to low and let simmer, stirring occasionally, for 1½ hours or until the pork is completely tender and falling apart.

Strain the liquid into a glass bowl, skim off the fat with a ladle or large spoon into another bowl, and reserve the broth and fat separately. Transfer the meat and vegetables to a food processor, discard the bay leaves, and pulse until the meat is roughly chopped. Add 4 tablespoons of the reserved broth and the Cognac and pulse briefly to combine.

Pack the rillettes into 8 half-pint canning jars and pour ⅓ inch of the reserved fat over the top to seal. Screw on the lids and refrigerate. Store chilled for 2 months. When ready to serve, let come to room temperature before serving and offer with warm, crusty bread.

CONFIT OF CHICKEN GIZZARDS WITH HERBED BUTTERMILK BISCUITS AND GRAINY MUSTARD

Gas stations in the South serve lots of food. It never struck me as odd until friends from outside the South visited Oxford and remarked on the strangeness of this custom. My thought (and perhaps it says something about me) was not immediately that we were gluttonous because we could not pump a tank of gas without a fried chicken tender on a stick, burrito, or pizza roll, but rather how unfortunate it was that everyone else didn't enjoy the same privilege.

One of the more prolific items under the heat lamp, protected from my grasp by greasy glass, is fried chicken gizzards. They are similar in flavor to livers (though a little less gamey) but have a completely different texture. Eaten alone or with a dash of vinegary hot sauce, these are one of my go-to gas station snacks.

As a variation, we cook them confit style in duck fat. We like to thinly slice them after they are cooked and use them to top a light, crunchy biscuit with a touch of mustard; it's our version of the cocktail party country ham biscuits I grew up with.

"Fried Chicken and Gasoline" —Southern Culture on the Skids

Toss the gizzards, garlic, thyme, bay leaves, salt, black pepper, sugar, and cayenne together in a stainless-steel bowl until well combined. Cover and refrigerate overnight.

Preheat the oven to 325°F. Transfer the gizzards and their marinade to a heavy baking dish large enough to hold them in a single layer. Add enough of the melted duck fat to cover the gizzards. Cover the pan with aluminum foil and bake for 2½ hours.

Lift the gizzards from the fat with a slotted spoon and drain them well on paper towels. Slice the gizzards, split the biscuits, and use the gizzards as filling, adding a touch of mustard. The drained gizzards will keep, refrigerated, for up to 4 days. If left in the duck fat and refrigerated, they will keep for up to 2 months.

ingredients

1 pound chicken gizzards
2 tablespoons plus 2 teaspoons minced garlic
3 tablespoons fresh thyme leaves
3 dried bay leaves
1 tablespoon salt
2 tablespoons freshly ground black pepper
2 teaspoons sugar
½ teaspoon cayenne
6 cups warm melted duck fat
Herbed Buttermilk Biscuits *(recipe follows)*
Grainy Mustard *(page 94)*

SERVES 8 TO 10

HERBED BUTTERMILK BISCUITS

2 cups all-purpose flour
1 teaspoon salt
1½ teaspoons sugar
2 teaspoons baking powder
½ teaspoon baking soda
3 tablespoons chopped mixed fresh herbs (any mix will do)
3 tablespoons chilled butter, cubed plus additional for brushing
3 tablespoons chilled lard
¾ cup chilled buttermilk

Preheat the oven to 400°F. Combine the flour, salt, sugar, baking powder, baking soda, and herbs in the food processor and pulse to combine. Add the butter and lard and pulse several times until the flour mixture resembles a course meal. Turn the flour mixture out into a mixing bowl and stir the buttermilk in with a fork until the dough begins to come together. Sprinkle the dough with flour. Flour your hands and knead the dough briefly until it comes together completely. Turn the dough out onto a floured work surface and knead for 4 to 5 turns, or until the dough begins to look smooth. Roll out to ½ inch and cut the dough into 2-inch rounds. Brush with butter and bake for 20 minutes or until golden brown.

SPICY HILL COUNTRY MEAT PIES WITH SRIRACHA MAYONNAISE

During the 18 months or so after Katrina, while working on rebuilding Willie Mae's Scotch House, I made friends with one of the funniest, most thoughtful, and most talented people I have ever known, Joe York. Joe shoots almost all of the documentary footage for the Southern Foodways Alliance and chronicled that rebuilding project. He and I spent a tremendous amount of time together down in New Orleans in those months, much of which involved late nights medicating the pain that came along with seeing my hometown crippled and flailing.

Some of my favorite memories involved "second dinner" at or around 2 A.M. at Cooter Brown's, sharing a plate of bite-size meat pies. It occurred to me that meat pies actually had their origin in Natchitoches, Louisiana, and that due to its geography, some would make the argument that the meat pie is as much Arkansas or Mississippi as it is Louisiana. I am certain that there is an entire population of that fair city that would love to string me up for saying that, but my point is that due to its terroir, the meat pie is subject to interpretation. So the idea of fusing the meat pie with the traditional Indian samosa seemed obvious and easy with a few ingredients plentiful in north Mississippi. Besides the mayo, these are also great with a touch of Yellow Mustard (page 93).

"99" —Sonny Boy Williamson

ingredients

To make the filling: Warm the olive oil over medium heat in a large cast-iron skillet. Crumble in the pork and sprinkle with the salt and pepper. Brown the pork, stirring constantly, until cooked through, about 5 minutes. Transfer with a slotted spoon to a small bowl.

Add the onions, red and green bell peppers, celery, and garlic to the skillet. Sauté over medium heat until they begin to wilt. Blend in the Creole seasoning, sweet potatoes, and peas and warm through. Add the ground pork and combine thoroughly. While stirring, sprinkle the flour over the mixture and combine well. Stir in the cane syrup, bourbon, and stock and bring to a simmer, stirring constantly. As soon as the liquid thickens, remove from the heat and stir in the green onions. Set aside to cool.

2 tablespoons olive oil
1 pound ground pork *(about 80% lean)*
1½ teaspoons salt
1½ teaspoons freshly ground black pepper
½ cup small-dice yellow onions
⅓ cup minced red bell peppers
⅓ cup minced green bell peppers
¼ cup minced celery
1 tablespoon finely minced garlic
½ tablespoon Creole Seasoning *(page xxvi)*
½ cup small-dice sweet potatoes, blanched in salted water for 1 minute
½ cup cooked crowder or field peas
1 tablespoon all-purpose flour
1 tablespoon cane syrup
2 tablespoons bourbon
¼ cup Ham Stock *(page 33)*
¼ cup thinly sliced green onions

MAKES ENOUGH FOR 8 LARGE PIES OR 16 SMALLER PIES

SRIRACHA MAYONNAISE

1 cup Homemade "Duke's" Mayonnaise *(page 93)*
2 tablespoons sriracha hot sauce
2 tablespoons apple cider vinegar
½ teaspoon salt
½ teaspoon sugar

MAKES 1¼ CUPS

Blend the mayonnaise, hot sauce, vinegar, salt, and sugar together well in a stainless-steel bowl. Transfer the mayonnaise to a glass or plastic container, cover, and refrigerate until needed. It will keep for up to 3 weeks.

PIE DOUGH

4 tablespoons cold unsalted butter
4 tablespoons cold lard *(see page 136)*
2½ cups all-purpose flour, plus ½ cup for rolling
½ teaspoon baking powder
1½ teaspoons salt
4 teaspoons fresh thyme leaves
5 tablespoons whole milk
1 whole egg

Dice the butter and place on a saucer with the lard in the freezer for 30 minutes. Meanwhile, combine the flour, baking powder, salt, and thyme in a food processor and pulse together. Scatter the frozen butter into the flour, and break the lard into 3 or 4 pieces (it does not freeze hard) and add it to the flour. Pulse the mixture until it resembles a coarse meal.

Blend the milk and egg together and set aside. Dump the flour mix into a stainless-steel bowl and, with a fork, slowly blend in the milk and egg mix until the dough just barely begins to come together. Flour your hands and the dough slightly and gather the dough together in the bowl, kneading lightly until all of the dough just comes together. Turn the dough out onto a floured work surface and knead with the palms of your hands, folding the dough over several times, until it just begins to look homogenous. Wrap in plastic wrap and refrigerate to let relax for 30 minutes.

Return the dough to the floured work surface and roll it out to just over ⅛ inch thick. Cut it into 4-inch circles (2½-inch circles for smaller pies).

FRYING AND SERVING

1¼ cups peanut oil
1¼ cups lard *(see page 136)*
1 large egg, lightly beaten
Sriracha Mayonnaise *(left)*

In a medium cast-iron skillet over medium heat, warm the oil and lard to 375°F. Lower the heat to hold the fat at that temperature. Alternatively, the pies can just as easily be baked at 350°F for 12 to 15 minutes, until golden.

Place 2½ to 3 tablespoons of filling on one half of a large pie dough circle. (For smaller pies, place about 1½ tablespoons filling on one half of each circle.) Brush the edges of the pie dough with the beaten egg and fold the dough over, crimping with the tines of a fork to seal. Brush the top of the pie with the egg. Repeat this with all the dough circles.

Gently place the meat pies in the hot oil, 5 or 6 at a time, turning them over occasionally until they become golden brown on both sides, 3 to 5 minutes (a bit shorter for smaller pies). Transfer with a slotted spoon to paper towels to drain. Serve immediately with the Sriracha Mayonnaise.

Chapter 6

FRYING (PAN & DEEP)

QUAIL AND WAFFLES — 134

COCA-COLA BRINED FRIED CHICKEN THIGHS — 137

FRIED CHICKEN LIVER PÂTÉ SALAD — 138

CORNMEAL-FRIED OYSTERS WITH BLACK PEPPER BUTTERMILK RANCH — 139

CHICKEN-FRIED DUCK WITH CARAMELIZED ONION GRAVY — 140

PAN-FRIED DUCK RILLETTES — 141

OKRA AND GREEN ONION HUSH PUPPIES — 143

PAN-FRIED CATFISH WITH ROASTED JALAPEÑO TARTAR SAUCE — 144

GARLIC-FRIED FROG'S LEGS SAUCE PIQUANT — 145

DEEP SOUTH "RAMEN" WITH FRIED POACHED EGGS — 146

SHRIMP AND LOBSTER CORN DOGS — 149

CRISPY PIG'S EAR "FRITES" WITH COMEBACK SAUCE — 150

PIMENTO CHEESE FRITTERS — 151

Chapter 6

FRYING (PAN & DEEP)

FRYING (PAN & DEEP)

Dear nervous eaters, health nuts, and fry haters,

Because it is fried, that does not necessarily mean that it is "terrible" for you. Are boiled potatoes less fattening than French fries? No doubt, every freaking time, but by the time you are done loading those boiled potatoes with butter, sour cream, and bacon bits, they are arguably just as bad for you as the fries, if not worse. (News flash: From a caloric standpoint, the corn syrup–laced ketchup you are dipping those fries in is much worse for you than the fries themselves.)

Here's the real secret: Healthful living is not about cutting out fried chicken or hush puppies entirely. It is, on the other hand, about having those things in greater moderation. Not that I expect anyone to be able to control themselves after cooking our Coca-Cola fried chicken, or our Crispy Pig's Ear "Frites" with Comeback Sauce, but there's the challenge. The beautiful thing about *not* eating all the fried chicken for supper is that then there's leftover cold fried chicken to eat later. And it is, without exception, the *only* fried thing worth half a damn eating when it is cold.

My mom didn't fry very much when we were growing up, and we literally begged for fried chicken. As much as I resent the fact that she refused, I give her reasoning the greatest credibility for steering clear of it. Mom didn't want to fry because of the cleanup afterward. Make no mistake about it—frying does make a mess of the stove. Is fried chicken worth the extra 10 minutes you will take to pull the grates off your stove and clean up the spattered grease? To me, you're damn right it is . . . but to my mom, absolutely not.

I recommend you treat yourself to a fried something or the other (and maybe a smaller portion of it) from time to time. Get comfortable with the fact that, if you cook it, you will have to do some cleanup, but the risk is *definitely* worth the reward.

For those of you who weren't going to buy into this from the inception, enjoy your salad. For the rest of you: Enjoy!

Warmest regards,
Johnny Snack

QUAIL AND WAFFLES

Roscoe's Chicken and Waffle gets credited for the beginning of this plate of culinary genius, though I am certain there are plenty of folks out there who will line up to dispute the legacy. Whatever the case, this combination of sweet and salty, playing against the crispy fry and the pillowy soft waffle, is just excellent.

In our twist, we use a hot sauce and buttermilk marinade and drizzle the quail with black pepper–infused Steen's cane syrup. Dig it.

ingredients

"Tear Stained Eye" —Son Volt

QUAIL
4 semi-boneless quail *(3 to 4 ounces each)*
½ teaspoon salt
1 teaspoon freshly ground black pepper
1 cup buttermilk
3 tablespoons Crystal Hot Sauce

WAFFLE BATTER
½ cup all-purpose flour
½ teaspoon baking soda
¼ teaspoon salt
1 teaspoon fresh cracked black pepper
2 tablespoons minced green onions
1 teaspoon fresh thyme leaves
2 teaspoons chopped fresh flat-leaf parsley
1 large egg, separated
½ cup whole milk
½ cup buttermilk
2 tablespoons and 2 teaspoons unsalted butter, melted
¼ teaspoon cream of tartar

SERVES 4

To marinate the quail: Season the quail inside and out with the salt and black pepper and let sit for 30 minutes. Meanwhile, blend together the buttermilk and hot sauce in a nonreactive container. After 30 minutes, place the quail in the buttermilk to marinate overnight, covered and refrigerated.

To make the waffle batter: Preheat a waffle maker and spray with nonstick cooking spray, just to make sure the waffles don't stick. (Even with nonstick waffle makers, the high sugar content makes them stick a little at times.) Mix the flour, baking soda, salt, pepper, green onions, thyme, and parsley together in a medium bowl and set aside. In a separate bowl, whisk together the egg yolk, milk, buttermilk, and butter. Stir the wet ingredients into the dry, blending well.

Whip the egg white with the cream of tartar to stiff peaks with an electric handheld mixer. Fold the egg white gently into the batter until evenly incorporated.

Spray the waffle maker with nonstick spray again. Ladle about one-quarter of the waffle batter into the waffle maker and cook according to the manufacturer's directions until golden brown. Repeat to make 4 waffles. Keep warm in a low oven.

TIPS FOR FRYING

Take the items you are frying out of the refrigerator a little beforehand, to let them come up to room temperature a bit. The less you are changing the temperature of that item with the heat of the oil, the less spatter there will be.

Pat your items dry. Water is what causes oil to spit and spatter. The drier your items are, the less the oil will roil and the better the batter will stick to the item being fried.

Choose a good-quality oil (peanut, grapeseed, some folks advocate extra-virgin olive). I *love* to fry in lard.

Fry at 350° to 375°F. Lower temperatures result in greasier food.

BLACK PEPPER STEEN'S CANE SYRUP

½ cup Steen's cane syrup *(see page 180)*
1½ teaspoons freshly ground black pepper
1 tablespoon minced shallots
1 teaspoon chopped fresh rosemary
Pinch of salt

Combine the Steen's, pepper, shallots, rosemary, and salt in a small saucepan. Bring to a boil over medium heat. Remove from the heat and let cool to room temperature.

FRYING AND SERVING

3 cups peanut oil
1 cup lard *(see page 136)*
3 cups Seasoned Flour *(page xxvii)*
Unsweetened whipped cream

Heat the oil and lard together in a 10- or 12-inch cast-iron skillet over medium heat to 375°F. Use a candy or frying thermometer to monitor the temperature. Lower the heat to low.

Working quickly, remove the quail from the buttermilk one by one. Allow most of the buttermilk to drain off, and toss the quail in the seasoned flour. Knock off any excess flour and gently place the quail in the hot oil. Cook for 2 minutes and then flip. Fry for another 2 minutes, and then begin turning every 30 seconds until the quail is golden brown on both sides. Transfer to a plate lined with paper towels to drain.

To serve, place a waffle on each warm serving plate. Place a quail on top and drizzle with the flavored syrup. Garnish with unsweetened whipped cream and serve immediately.

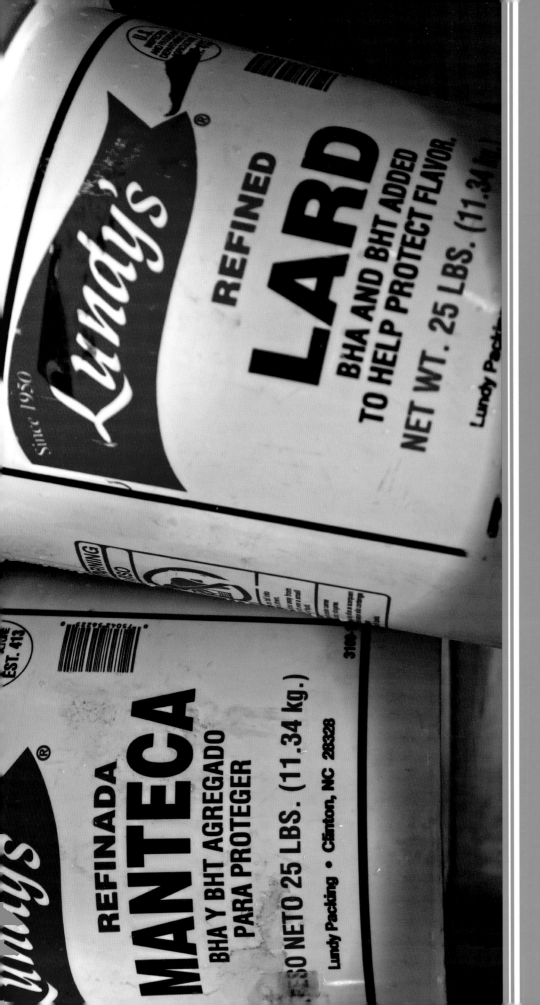

A WORD ON LARD

Lard gets a bad rap, but in the right proportions adds a delicious layer of flavor and texture. Bill Neal once told me, "I am not saying 'you shouldn't'—I'm saying *'don't ever'* make biscuits or piecrust without lard. It's just a waste of time." The irony here is that lard really began its trip into ingredient obscurity about 40 years ago with the misconceptions passed around that pork was bad or unhealthy. It became a victim of the marketing of the hydrogenated vegetable shortenings, like Crisco, that allegedly lowered the risk of heart disease. Science has proven in recent years how incorrect and, actually, opposite that is. So while the pig is exalted, lard still languishes in disdain on the culinary blacklist.

Natural lard is a completely naturally occurring fat and has fewer calories and a cleaner fat content than butter, containing less nonfat solids. Do not confuse with shelf-stable lard, which is not terrible, but not as good for you as natural lard, which must be refrigerated. There are no trans fats in lard since it is a natural fat, and it is very high in omega 3 fatty acids. Studies indicate that it is no more responsible for raising LDL cholesterol than any other fat and will actually help raise HDL ("good" cholesterol) levels.

So get with the program, get over the stigma, and buy a little bucket of lard next time you are at the store. You'll be happy you did, and your stuff will start tasting a lot more "like your grandmother used to make it."

COCA-COLA BRINED FRIED CHICKEN THIGHS

There is no better piece of the chicken to eat than the thigh. I don't give a damn what anyone else thinks. Dark meat has more flavor, it has better texture, it takes seasoning better, and it's extremely easy to gnaw on.

Brining is a practice I firmly advocate with all birds. It adds moisture and is a vehicle for adding flavor to your protein. For this particular brine, we use Coca-Cola because of the sweetness the Coke imparts; and the carbonic, phosphoric, and citric acids present help in mildly tenderizing the chicken flesh.

Finally, this is a wet batter chicken. Wet batter is rarely used in frying chicken in the South, Willie Mae's Scotch House in New Orleans being one of the few exceptions to that rule. I spent almost two years at Willie Mae's with a bunch of folks rebuilding after Katrina, and while I will never fry chicken as good as they make on the corner of Saint Ann and North Tonti, this is my tribute. It rocks.

"A Girl Like You" —The Smithereens

ingredients

To make the brine: Blend the cola, salt, thyme, garlic, and hot sauce together in a large stainless-steel bowl until the salt has dissolved. Add the chicken thighs, cover, and refrigerate for 4 to 5 hours.

To make the spice blend: Mix the salt, paprika, cayenne, sage, rosemary, and onion and garlic powders together in a bowl. Pack into a sealed plastic or glass container and store in a cool, dry place for up to 1 year.

To make the batter: Blend together the flour, baking soda, salt, black pepper, cayenne, and onion and garlic powders in a large bowl. Whisk in 3¼ cups water and the oil until fully incorporated. When mixing wet and dry ingredients, always add the wet to the dry; it keeps your batter from clumping. Taste for seasoning and add salt, if needed.

To fry the chicken: Warm the peanut oil and lard in a large cast-iron Dutch oven over medium heat to 375°F. Decrease the heat to low and monitor the temperature using a candy or frying thermometer, adjusting the heat to maintain the temperature right at 375°F.

Drain the chicken thighs and pat dry with paper towels. Sprinkle both sides liberally with the spice blend and pat dry again. One by one, dip the chicken thighs into the batter and let the excess batter run off a bit. Carefully and slowly lower the thighs into the hot oil. Fry just a few at a time, if necessary. The chicken will quickly lower the temperature of the oil, so increase the heat to high to return the oil to 375°F as quickly as possible. Cold oil makes for greasy chicken. The quicker you seal the batter to the surface of the chicken, the less oil will permeate the meat. As soon as the oil returns to temperature, lower the heat back to medium-low. After 3 minutes, turn the chicken. If you let the pieces rest on the bottom of the Dutch oven too long, they can overbrown. Allow the thighs to cook for another 3 minutes before turning again to cook for a final 2 minutes.

Remove one of the thighs to drain on a brown-paper grocery bag (nothing else will do). Pierce the thigh at the thickest point with a small knife and press on the meat with the side of the blade. If the juice comes out clear, remove the rest of the pieces from the oil and allow to drain briefly, until you can no longer wait to bite into one. Mild hot sauce is awesome on fried chicken. Go get a bottle of Texas Pete, Crystal, or Valentina. They are mostly vinegar and add an excellent brightness to the meat.

BRINE

5 cups Coca-Cola

1 tablespoon salt

10 sprigs fresh thyme

4 cloves garlic, sliced

4 teaspoons Crystal Hot Sauce

8 small chicken thighs, preferably free-range *(about 4 ounces each)*

SPICE BLEND

3 teaspoons salt

2 teaspoons smoked hot paprika

1 teaspoon cayenne

1½ teaspoons ground dried sage

½ teaspoon ground dried rosemary

1 teaspoon onion powder

1 teaspoon garlic powder

BATTER

2 cups all-purpose flour

3 teaspoons baking soda

4 teaspoons salt

2 teaspoons freshly ground black pepper

2½ teaspoons cayenne

1½ teaspoons onion powder

1½ teaspoons garlic powder

¾ cup peanut oil or vegetable oil

FRYING

8 cups peanut oil

2 cups lard *(see page 136)*

Hot sauce, for serving

SERVES 4

FRIED CHICKEN LIVER PÂTÉ SALAD

Mike Lata, chef and owner of FIG in Charleston, holds a high honor. He makes a chicken liver pâté that everyone I know (chef, restaurateur, food writer, food lover) says the same thing about: "best chicken liver pâté I have ever tasted in my life, hands down." Mike is generous with sharing his technique and recipe, and though we have talked it through a half dozen times, I am now convinced that he made a Robert Johnsonesque deal at a crossroads in the Low Country.

This recipe is inspired by both my mother's (who also makes an unbelievable pâté) and Mike's. We take our version to a little spicier place and then after slicing, we put a quick fry on it and serve it on a salad with a sweet herb vinaigrette and pickled vegetables. Admittedly, frying is to cover the fact the Mike's version still wins. . . .

ingredients

"New Slang" —The Shins

PÂTÉ

1 pound chicken livers, rinsed and trimmed of veins

¼ cup bacon fat, melted

½ cup clarified unsalted butter *(see page xxiii)*

2 large eggs

¼ cup heavy cream

1 teaspoon salt

1 teaspoon freshly ground white pepper

¾ teaspoon cayenne

1 pinch of ground cloves

2 tablespoons brandy

1 pound bacon, thinly sliced

FRYING

3 cups lard *(see page 136)* or peanut oil

3 cups Seasoned Flour *(page xxvi)*

3 cups Egg Wash *(page xxvii)*

SALAD

4 large handfuls frisée or other bitter lettuce

3 tablespoons minced shallots

2 hard-boiled eggs, minced

6 tablespoons Fresh Herb Vinaigrette *(page xxvii)*

½ cup sliced Spicy Pickled Okra *(see page 61)*

½ cup pecan pieces, toasted

Salt and freshly ground black pepper

Grainy Mustard *(page 94)*, for serving

SERVES 8

Preheat the oven to 275°F. Place the chicken livers in a food processor and puree until smooth. With the processor running, slowly drizzle in the bacon fat and butter until emulsified.

In a separate bowl, whisk the eggs until frothy, and then whisk in the heavy cream. Blend the liver mixture into the cream, and then stir in the salt, white pepper, cayenne, cloves, and brandy.

To bake the pâté: Line a pâté mold with plastic wrap and the thinly sliced bacon, with enough bacon hanging over the edges to cover the pâté. Pour the pâté mixture into the prepared mold. Cover with bacon and wrap plastic over the top to seal. Set the mold in a water bath, so that the water comes three-quarters of the way up the side of the mold. Bake for 1 hour, or until set. Remove from the oven, cool, and chill until completely set. Once completely chilled, it can be easily unwrapped and sliced.

To fry the pâté: Slice the pâté ½ inch thick, then cut each slice into quarters. In a large cast-iron skillet, heat the lard to 375°F. Dust the pâté nuggets in the seasoned flour and knock off any excess. Dip the pieces in the egg wash and then coat again with the seasoned flour. Carefully drop the pieces, in batches, into the lard and brown lightly, 3 to 4 minutes, turning occasionally. Transfer to a plate lined with paper towels to drain.

To make the salad: Toss the frisée with the shallots, eggs, vinaigrette, okra, and pecans in a stainless-steel bowl. Season to taste with salt and pepper. Divide among serving plates and top each with a slice of the fried pâté and a drizzle of mustard.

CORNMEAL-FRIED OYSTERS WITH BLACK PEPPER BUTTERMILK RANCH

Little in this world comes as close to perfection as a deftly fried oyster. The perfectly browned, crunchy, and slightly sweet outside against the tender and briny inside is a heavenly chorus of outstandingness. I know that the cavalry of naysayers is gathering to say that nothing matches the purity of freshly sliced toro or the subtlety of a citrus-brightened scallop *crudo*. But I'll take good fried oysters any day of the week.

Oysters will pair with a tremendous number of things from a simple cocktail sauce to a velvety béarnaise or paired with New Orleans–Style Rémoulade (page 106) will carry you to your favorite Mardi Gras moment you have ever had . . . or wanted to have. Here we add a tangy Black Pepper Buttermilk Ranch as a simple yet delicious exclamation point.

"Being Around" —The Lemonheads

In a large cast-iron skillet, heat the peanut oil to 375°F. Blend together the cornmeal, salt, and cayenne in a bowl.

Drain the oysters and dredge them in the seasoned flour, knocking off any excess. Dip the oysters in the egg wash, and then coat them with the seasoned cornmeal.

Working in batches, fry the oysters in the hot oil until golden brown, 3 to 4 minutes. These should fry very quickly. You do not want to compromise the texture of the oyster. Ideally, you'd like to create a crispy shell filled with an oyster that has just barely warmed.

Remove the oysters with a slotted spoon and drain them on a plate lined with paper towels. Sprinkle the chives on top and serve with the ranch dressing.

ingredients

10 cups peanut oil
3 cups yellow cornmeal
2 teaspoons salt
½ teaspoon cayenne
20 freshly shucked oysters
(Gulf of Mexico oysters are the best)
6 cups Seasoned Flour *(page xxvi)*
6 cups Egg Wash *(page xxvii)*
¼ cup minced fresh chives
2 cups Black Pepper Buttermilk Ranch
(recipe follows)

SERVES 4

BLACK PEPPER BUTTERMILK RANCH

1½ cups Homemade "Duke's" Mayonnaise *(page 93)*
1 cup buttermilk
¼ cup chopped fresh flat-leaf parsley
¼ cup chopped celery leaves
3 tablespoons chopped fresh chives
1 tablespoon freshly squeezed lemon juice
5 teaspoons Dijon mustard
2 teaspoons onion powder
2 teaspoons garlic powder
1½ teaspoons salt
1 tablespoon black pepper

MAKES ABOUT 3 CUPS

Whisk together the mayonnaise, buttermilk, parsley, celery leaves, chives, lemon juice, mustard, onion and garlic powders, and salt and pepper to taste in a stainless-steel bowl and let stand at room temperature for 30 minutes. Taste and adjust the seasoning as needed. Store chilled in a glass jar or plastic container for up to 2 weeks.

CHICKEN-FRIED DUCK
WITH CARAMELIZED ONION GRAVY

Chicken-fried steak is not something you see on menus in New Orleans very often, and it doesn't pop up much in Mississippi either. As much as it pains me to credit our neighbors to the west, food historians have located its roots in Texas. With some similarity to wiener schnitzel, it is an excellent way to make use of inexpensive cuts of beef, veal, or pork. Whatever the case may be, it hit me like a lightning bolt the first time I ever had it, so we play with a number of versions, including this one with duck breast and caramelized onion gravy.

ingredients

"If You Want Me to Stay" —Sly and the Family Stone

4 whole duck breasts, skin removed and reserved *(about 5 ounces each)*

1 medium yellow onion, very thinly sliced from root to tip

1 teaspoon sugar

¼ teaspoon salt

2 teaspoons fresh thyme leaves

Freshly ground black pepper

6 cups Seasoned Flour *(page xxvi)*

6 cups Egg Wash *(page xxvii)*

4 cups panko bread crumbs

6 tablespoons peanut oil

2 tablespoons lard *(see page 136)*

¼ cup all-purpose flour

½ cup Dark Chicken Stock *(page 31)*

¾ cup whole milk

SERVES 4

Slice the reserved duck skin into thin strips and pat dry with a paper towel. In a 10-inch sauté pan over medium heat, cook the strips of duck skin until golden brown and crispy, stirring constantly. Remove the duck cracklings from the pan and drain on paper towels. Pour off the duck fat into a glass measuring cup; return 3 tablespoons of the fat to the sauté pan.

Add the onion, sugar, salt, and thyme to the pan and cook, stirring, over medium heat until the onion turns transparent and wilts, 5 to 7 minutes. Decrease the heat to low and continue cooking for 20 minutes, stirring constantly, until the onion has caramelized and turned a light brown. Remove from the heat and set aside.

Cut an incision horizontally into the thickest part of each duck breast, so that when opened up like a book, it will lay flat on the table and have a uniform thickness. Place the breasts between two pieces of plastic wrap and, using a meat-tenderizing hammer, gently pound the breasts to ¼ inch thick. Peel the plastic back and lightly season both sides of each pounded breast with salt and pepper.

Dredge the duck breasts in the seasoned flour, knocking off any excess. Dip them in the egg wash and then roll in the bread crumbs. Place the prepared duck breasts on a plate.

In the cast-iron skillet, heat 1 tablespoon more of the reserved duck fat, 2 tablespoons of the peanut oil, and 1 tablespoon of the lard over medium heat until you see very light wisps of smoke begin to rise from the pan. Put two of the prepared breasts into the hot oil and brown for about 1½ minutes. Flip and brown on the second side for 1 minute or until golden brown. Transfer to a plate lined with paper towels to drain. Add another 2 tablespoons of the peanut oil and the remaining 1 tablespoon lard to the skillet and heat. Cook the remaining two breasts and transfer to the plate to drain. Hold the cooked breasts warm in a very low oven.

Add the remaining 2 tablespoons peanut oil and 2 more tablespoons of the reserved duck fat to the skillet. Whisk in the all-purpose flour until smooth. Continue to whisk for 2 more minutes, just until the flour begins to take on a "nutty" aroma and a very light brown color. Whisk in the stock and milk and bring to a simmer. Stir in ½ cup of the caramelized onions and season the gravy with salt and black pepper to taste. Spoon the gravy over the fried duck, or serve on the side from a gravy boat, if you prefer.

PAN-FRIED DUCK RILLETTES

These are not the truest rillettes in the world. The predecessor of American potted meat or deviled ham, rillettes are stewed, shredded pork, traditionally stored in earthenware jugs and capped with fat to keep preserved in a larder all the way through winter. They are typically scooped out and spread on warm, crusty bread as a snack. This recipe is mostly traditional, though we finish the Rillettes a little differently. These are crispy and salty and are great with a spot of Tomato Jam (page 105), Spicy Pepper Jelly (page 86), or Pickled Peach Relish (page 118).

"The Only Living Boy in New York" —Simon and Garfunkel

Cut the pork jowl into 1-inch cubes and combine with the duck legs, bacon, stock, onions, thyme, rosemary, garlic, bay leaves, red pepper flakes, and brandy in a large saucepan and bring slowly up to a simmer over medium-low heat.

Let simmer for about 3 hours, or until the pork pulls apart easily with a fork. Strain the liquid and reserve. Discard the bay leaves and place the meat and vegetables in a food processor.

Skim ¾ cup of fat from the top of the reserved liquid and add it to the meat in the processor. Pulse until the meat is roughly chopped and then transfer to a large bowl. Stir in the bread crumbs and combine well. Cover a baking sheet with plastic wrap and spread the rillettes evenly across the sheet. Cover with plastic wrap and place a second baking sheet on top, pressing to evenly disperse the rillettes in an even layer across the pan. Place in the refrigerator, set two gallons of milk (or other comparable weight) on top of the baking sheet, and let sit overnight.

Remove the rillettes from the refrigerator and remove the top baking sheet and plastic wrap. Grasping the edges of the bottom layer of plastic, flip the rillettes over onto a cutting board, peel off and discard the plastic, and cut the rillettes into 1-inch squares. Dust the squares with seasoned flour, knocking off any excess.

Heat ½ inch peanut or olive oil in a cast-iron skillet over medium heat until almost smoking. Working in batches, brown the rillettes on both sides. Serve on lightly toasted bread dotted with peach relish.

ingredients

½ pound pork jowl or fatback
4 duck leg quarters *(do not trim fat)*
2½ cups chopped bacon
2 cups Dark Chicken Stock *(page 31)*
1½ cups roughly chopped yellow onions
2 teaspoons fresh thyme leaves
2 teaspoons chopped fresh rosemary
3 cloves garlic, thinly sliced
2 dried bay leaves
1½ teaspoons red pepper flakes
¼ cup brandy
1½ cups panko bread crumbs
3 cups Seasoned Flour *(page xxvi)*
Peanut oil, for frying
Lightly toasted bread, for serving
Pickled Peach Relish *(page 118)*, for serving

MAKES ENOUGH FOR 30 BITE-SIZE PORTIONS

OKRA AND GREEN ONION HUSH PUPPIES

I wrote this recipe for a meal honoring Bill Neal at the James Beard House in 2002. Hush puppies were a menu staple at Crook's Corner, and Bill was entirely responsible for guiding me along the path that brought me to my love for okra.

I had tucked it away after that meal and almost forgotten about it until my dear friend Jenny Dirksen invited me to come cook at the Big Apple BBQ Block Party in New York City. I had no idea what I was getting myself into, and even when I was ordering cornmeal by the ton and eggs by the hundreds of dozens, I still failed to realize how bad it was going to be.

Our general manager/wartime *consigliere*, Jim Weems, stood over those fucking fryers with me on the edge of Madison Square Park during the hottest weekend New York has seen since the last Ice Age. And best as we can estimate, we fried somewhere in the vicinity of 35,000 hush puppies between the two of us. We were as beat after those two days as I have ever been, and I swore I'd never cook another goddamned hush puppy as long as I lived. That lasted all of about six months; the damn things are just too good. These are great with a tangy barbecue sauce.

"Jesus Built My Hotrod" —Ministry

ingredients

Preheat the oven to 350°F.

Toss the okra together with the olive oil, 1 teaspoon of the salt, and 2 teaspoons of the black pepper in a stainless or glass bowl. Spread the okra in a single layer on a baking sheet and bake for 15 to 20 minutes, until tender. At the same time, put the whole, unshucked corn in the oven and roast for 30 minutes.

Remove the okra, cool, and chop finely by hand or in a food processor. Remove the corn, cool, shuck, and carefully remove the kernels from the cobs. Discard the cobs.

Blend together the cornmeal, the remaining 1 tablespoon salt, the remaining 5 teaspoons black pepper, the cayenne, sugar, baking powder, and baking soda in a stainless-steel bowl.

In another large bowl, whisk together the eggs, milk, buttermilk, and bacon fat. Blend the dry mixture into the wet ingredients, and then stir in the okra, corn, and green onions.

Let stand for 20 minutes at room temperature for the cornmeal to hydrate and the batter to thicken. If you have the luxury of time, refrigerate the batter for up to 24 hours before frying. It will tighten even further and fry up a little better.

Heat a cast-iron skillet filled with 2 inches of peanut oil to 350°F. Scoop out 1-ounce portions (about the size of a small ice cream scoop) of the hush puppy mix and drop them carefully into the hot oil. Fry until they float and are golden brown on both sides, 3 to 4 minutes.

Serve these hot with the sauces of your choice.

- ½ pound fresh okra
- 2 tablespoons pure olive oil
- 1 tablespoon plus 1 teaspoon salt
- 7 teaspoons freshly ground black pepper
- 3 medium ears sweet corn in the husks
- 6 cups yellow cornmeal
- 1 teaspoon cayenne
- 1 tablespoon sugar
- 1 tablespoon baking powder
- 1 tablespoon baking soda
- 6 large eggs
- 2 cups whole milk
- 2 cups buttermilk
- ¼ cup bacon fat
- ¾ cup chopped green onions
- Peanut oil (*or half vegetable oil and half lard; see page 140*), for frying
- Fresh Herb Tartar Sauce (*page 107*), Rémoulade (*page 106*), ketchup, or your favorite barbecue sauce, for serving

SERVES 8 TO 10

PAN-FRIED CATFISH WITH ROASTED JALAPEÑO TARTAR SAUCE

I would be entirely remiss—nay, derelict—in my recording if I passed over one of Mississippi's greatest contributions to the culinary world: farm-raised, freshwater catfish. Catfish has always suffered from the perception of being a third-class seafood, lingering in the same breath with the likes of tilapia and cod, a half step up the ladder from buffalo fish and others used primarily for cat food and lamp oil.

The frostbitten and fishy product that gave catfish this bad reputation, due to outdated and low-quality freezing technique and equipment, is now a thing of the past. Individual Quick Freezing (IQF), which involves blast-freezing individual fillets in a matter of moments and encasing each in a thin protective frozen shell, all but eliminates the threat of freezer burn. So slowly thawed fillets are almost indiscernible from fresh.

Catfish is sweet and flaky when handled and cooked properly, and it is a forgiving product to work with. When it's cooked fresh, I enjoy it as much as almost any small-flake white fish. To boot, it is high in both omega-3 and omega-6 fatty acids, each of which fights LDL ("bad") cholesterol.

ingredients

"Harlem River Blues" —Justin Townes Earle

3 cups yellow cornmeal

3½ teaspoons salt

¾ teaspoon cayenne

2 teaspoons freshly ground black pepper

1½ teaspoons ground cumin

1 teaspoon ground coriander

Finely grated zest of 2 limes

4 (5- to 7-ounce) freshwater catfish fillets

Peanut oil, for frying

6 cups Seasoned Flour *(page xxvi)*

6 cups Egg Wash *(page xxvii)*

Roasted Jalapeño Tartar Sauce *(see Note)*

SERVES 4

Combine the cornmeal, 2 teaspoons of the salt, and ½ teaspoon of the cayenne in a stainless-steel bowl and set aside.

Combine the remaining 1½ teaspoons salt, the remaining ¼ teaspoon cayenne, the black pepper, cumin, coriander, and lime zest in a stainless-steel bowl. Then sprinkle about half of this mixture over the fillets. Flip them over and season the other side with the remaining mixture.

In a large cast-iron skillet, heat about 1 inch of peanut oil to 375°F. Dredge the fillets in the seasoned flour, shaking off any excess. Dip in the egg wash, and then dredge them in the seasoned cornmeal. Gently place two of the fillets in the oil and cook until golden brown, 7 to 8 minutes. Transfer to a plate lined with paper towels to drain. Repeat with the remaining fillets. Serve warm with the tartar sauce on the side.

Note:

For the Roasted Jalapeño Tartar Sauce, follow the directions for the Fresh Herb Tartar Sauce on page 107, substituting lime juice and zest for the lemon juice and zest. Also add 1 minced, roasted jalapeño and 1 teaspoon ground cumin.

GARLIC-FRIED FROG'S LEGS
SAUCE PIQUANT

Spahr's Seafood, which sits on the south side of Highway 90 on the way to where we used to duck hunt in Theriot, Louisiana, is the first place I remember eating sauce piquant. (It is no longer in its original location, as that space burned years ago, but they are still there, just down the road a bit.) It was an alligator sauce piquant, and while the alligator was entirely unremarkable, the intention was unarguably divine. My brother Richard and I devoured multiple plates one Sunday night after a Saints game, on our way to an annual goose hunt in Gueydan, Louisiana.

In the time since, I have had masterful sauce piquants made with everything from squirrel and rabbit to seafood. It truly is one of the great "clearinghouse" dishes that you can use almost anything in, and, if your base is solid, the final product is exceptional. This one is particularly good for young and tender frog's legs.

"Without You" —Junip

ingredients

Season the frog's legs with the salt, black pepper, and cayenne. In a medium cast-iron Dutch oven, heat the garlic olive oil over medium heat until the surface begins to shimmer. Dredge the frog's legs in the seasoned flour, knocking off any excess. In batches, brown the legs in the oil until golden brown all over, 3 to 5 minutes. Transfer to a plate lined with paper towels to drain.

In the same pan, melt the butter, whisk in the all-purpose flour, and cook to make a light brown roux (see page 43). Stir in the onions, bell peppers, celery, and garlic and cook for about 3 minutes, or until the vegetables are tender. Stir in the tomatoes, parsley, thyme, tarragon, and bay leaves and combine well.

In a small saucepan, warm the stock and stir in the tomato paste, blending until smooth. Add to the roux-vegetable mixture and combine well. Return the frog's legs to the Dutch oven and simmer over low heat for 35 to 40 minutes. Check every 15 minutes and add more stock if it appears the sauce is beginning to get dry. Add the Tabasco and season to taste with salt and black pepper.

Note:
Sauce piquant, like most things in south Louisiana, is typically served over warm white rice.

- 3½ pounds large frog's legs, patted dry
- 2½ teaspoons salt
- 1 tablespoon freshly ground black pepper
- 1½ teaspoons cayenne
- 3 tablespoons Garlic Olive Oil *(page xxvii)*
- 3 cups Seasoned Flour *(page xxvi)*
- ½ cup unsalted butter
- ½ cup all-purpose flour
- 1½ cups small-dice yellow onions
- 1 cup small-dice green bell peppers
- ¾ cup small-dice celery
- 10 cloves garlic, thinly sliced
- 4 cups chopped tomatoes
- 3 tablespoons chopped fresh flat-leaf parsley
- 2 tablespoons fresh thyme leaves
- 2 tablespoons chopped fresh tarragon
- 2 bay leaves
- 3 cups Dark Chicken Stock *(page 31)*
- ½ cup tomato paste
- 1½ teaspoons Tabasco hot sauce

SERVES 8

DEEP SOUTH "RAMEN" WITH FRIED POACHED EGGS

I was 47 years old before I ever let instant ramen noodles pass my lips. Out of childish curiosity, I finally gave them a try one Sunday afternoon. As is frequently the case, I was at the grocery store famished and, as a result, uninhibited. I should never be let loose in this condition. I always make catastrophic purchases. On this particular trip, packaged ramen noodles caught my eye. I saw, I purchased, I rushed home, I "cooked." They were disgusting.

Immediately following this unfortunate event, I was on an extended trip to Los Angeles and found myself unintentionally touring what I was told were the best ramen shops in LA. Whether that was actually the case or not, I immediately fell in love with "authentic" ramen. I had it with fish, shrimp, lobster, pork, chicken, and beef. This got the wheels turning; I returned home and started to work on a recipe that incorporated all the sensibilities of authentic ramen (flavorful broth, hearty noodles, a touch of protein, crispy vegetables, and, usually, an egg of some variety), but I made it my own.

Dashi is a very clean, flavorful stock that is the base for ramen. It is often little more than water flavored with kelp (seaweed) and dried bonito flakes (salted dried fish). It is a marvel of simplicity and incredibly good for you. Ours is a total bastardization of the traditional, which we fortify with pork to put the Deep South in it.

ingredients

"He Needs Me" —Jon Brion

5 cups Ham Stock *(page 33)*
2 teaspoons Bluegrass Soy Sauce *(see Notes)*
2 teaspoons fish sauce
2 teaspoons bonito flakes
(available at Asian specialty stores)
3 drops of liquid smoke
½ teaspoon salt
¼ teaspoon red pepper flakes

SERVES 4

To make the dashi: Combine the stock, soy sauce, fish sauce, bonito flakes, Liquid Smoke, salt, and red pepper flakes in a large saucepan and bring to a simmer over medium heat. Decrease the heat to low and simmer for 5 minutes. Immediately remove from the heat, strain the dashi, discarding any solids, and set aside.

Notes:

Bluegrass Soy Sauce is made by Bourbon Barrel Foods out of Louisville, Kentucky. It marries organic American soybeans and repurposed bourbon barrels with Asian tradition. It's great stuff and easily available online, but if you must, you can substitute a high-quality import just as well.

FRIED POACHED EGGS

2 tablespoons plus 2 teaspoons champagne vinegar
2½ teaspoons salt
4 large eggs
2 tablespoons extra-virgin olive oil
1 teaspoon freshly ground black pepper

Bring 8 cups water, the vinegar, and 2 teaspoons of the salt to a simmer in a medium saucepan over medium heat. Decrease the heat to low. Crack the eggs carefully into 4 separate cups. Slowly tip each of the cups into the simmering water, gently adding the egg. With a slotted spoon, carefully keep the eggs separated. The whites will start to color almost immediately. As soon as they turn completely opaque, remove the eggs with the slotted spoon and drain on a plate lined with paper towels.

Meanwhile, heat the olive oil in a nonstick skillet over medium heat. Sprinkle the remaining ½ teaspoon salt and the pepper over the eggs and immediately place the eggs in the skillet to cook for 3 minutes, or until both sides are crisp.

ASSEMBLY

2 cups cooked buckwheat noodles
2 cups shredded pork shoulder barbecue *(with no sauce)*
2 tablespoons sesame seeds, toasted
1 cup whole celery leaves
½ cup thinly sliced Spicy Pickled Okra *(page 61)*
4 dashes of black vinegar *(see Note)*

Cook the buckwheat noodles according to the package instructions. Divide the warm noodles among warm serving bowls. Divide the pork among the bowls as well. Pour 1 cup hot dashi over the pork and noodles in each bowl (you will have 1 cup left over; reserve for another purpose). Place 1 egg in each bowl and sprinkle with the sesame seeds. Garnish with the celery leaves and pickled okra, and sprinkle with black vinegar.

Note:

Black vinegar is available at Asian specialty stores and online, of course. It's a touch sweet and molassesy.

CORN DOG BATTER

2 cups yellow cornmeal
2 cups all-purpose flour
1 teaspoon baking soda
¾ teaspoon salt
3 tablespoons sugar
1 teaspoon onion powder
½ teaspoon cayenne
3 cups buttermilk
½ cup whole milk
3 tablespoons unsalted butter, melted
2 large eggs

Blend together the cornmeal, flour, baking soda, salt, sugar, onion powder, and cayenne in a stainless-steel bowl.

In a separate bowl, whisk together the buttermilk, milk, butter, and eggs. Whisk the wet ingredients into the dry ingredients until evenly blended and smooth. Let stand at room temperature for 20 minutes.

FRYING AND SERVING

4 cups peanut oil
2 cups lard *(see page 136)*
2 cups Seasoned Flour *(page xxvi)*
Ketchup and/or mustard, for serving

Heat the oil and lard together in a medium Dutch oven to 375°F. Dredge the dogs in the seasoned flour and knock off any excess. Dip them in the batter and allow the excess to drip off briefly. Gently place the dogs in the hot oil and cook until golden brown, about 5 minutes. Remove and drain them briefly on a plate lined with paper towels. Serve with ketchup or mustard.

SHRIMP AND LOBSTER CORN DOGS

One of my wife's favorite things about our experiments at the restaurants is that my fascination with carnival food and re-creating iconic American packaged foods never dies. We have made Foie Gras Funnel Cakes, Elephant Ears with Pork and Caramelized Onion Ragout, and Wild Mushroom Pop Tarts. We have made riffs on Reese's Peanut Butter Cups, Snickers, and Twinkies. This was one of the first items we rolled out, and it was a huge hit, with both my bride and the general public. It's relatively painless to make and a great party offering. These are great with our Roasted Tomato Ketchup (see below) and Yellow Mustard (page 93).

"We Had to Tear This Muthafucka Up" —Ice Cube

ingredients

To make the corn dogs: Combine the lobster, shrimp, shallots, garlic puree, chives, bread crumbs, mustard, cream, eggs, lemon zest and juice, cayenne, and salt and white pepper in a food processor. Pulse quickly just to combine. You do not want to puree this mix or add any air to the eggs, or else they will rise when they cook. They are meant as a binder only.

Spoon the seafood mix into a ziplock bag and seal. Cut a corner off the bag and pipe a fat line of the mixture onto 8 (12-inch-long) pieces of plastic wrap. You want the seafood lines to be about as long as a typical hot dog, but they should be a little fatter. Fold the plastic over the mixture and roll the "sausages" up tightly. Grabbing the ends of the plastic, roll the sausage across the counter so that it tightens while you hold the ends. Fold the ends in toward the center and then roll the sausages in aluminum foil to secure them. If you are not proceeding immediately, refrigerate the uncooked sausages.

Fill a medium soup pot with 4 quarts water and bring to a boil over high heat. Lower the heat to medium and drop the sausages into the boiling water. Poach for 12 minutes. Remove them from the water and let them cool in their wrappers. Refrigerate for 2 hours or as long as overnight.

Remove the sausages from the refrigerator and peel off the aluminum foil and plastic wrap. Insert a bamboo skewer into one end of each of these "dogs" and push until the skewer goes about three-quarters of the way through the dog.

1 pound cooked lobster claw and tail meat, chopped

½ pound shelled, fresh shrimp, chopped *(26 to 30 count)*

2 medium shallots, minced

1 teaspoon finely minced garlic

2 tablespoons chopped fresh chives

½ cup toasted bread crumbs

2 tablespoons Grainy Mustard *(page 94)*

6 tablespoons heavy cream

2 large eggs, whisked until broken up

Finely grated zest and juice of 1 lemon

½ teaspoon cayenne

Salt and freshly ground white pepper

SERVES 8

ROASTED TOMATO KETCHUP

8 medium tomatoes, cored, halved, and deseeded	1 tablespoons peanut oil	1½ teaspoons garlic powder
4 tablespoons olive oil	½ cup minced yellow onion	¼ teaspoon allspice
2 teaspoons salt	2 teaspoons minced garlic	¼ teaspoon ground clove
2 teaspoons freshly ground black pepper	4 tablespoons dark brown sugar	½ teaspoon cayenne pepper
1 tablespoon fresh thyme leaves	½ teaspoon smoked paprika	⅓ cup white wine vinegar
	1½ teaspoons onion powder	2 tablespoons tomato paste

Preheat the oven to 325°F. Place the tomato halves, cut side up, on a parchment-lined cookie sheet. Drizzle with the olive oil and sprinkle with the salt, pepper, and thyme leaves. Bake for 2 hours, or until the tomatoes begin to dry out. Remove and let cool.

Place the tomatoes and the remaining ingredients in a Vita Mix and blend on high until smooth. Add water, if needed, to achieve your desired ketchup consistency.

CRISPY PIG'S EAR "FRITES" WITH COMEBACK SAUCE

My good friend and culinary superhero Sean Brock made some fried pig's ears with some of the best barbecue sauce I have ever tasted and served them in a lettuce wrap for a Southern Foodways Alliance event we both worked in New York City several years ago. We have all played with ears for years, but the cut struck me as perfect to do a knockoff on French fries. Here we use our pickled pig's ears and thinly slice them, dust them very lightly with flour, and give them a quick fry to crisp them up. Comeback Sauce is a one of the great Mississippi contributions to the culinary cannon. On first blush, it doesn't seem all that special, but once you've tasted it, you'll put it on everything from French fries to green salad.

"Lookin' for Love" —Johnny Lee

Heat the lard in a medium Dutch oven to 375°F. Dredge the pig's ears strips in the flour, knocking off any excess. Drop these carefully into the pot and fry until the edges begin to crisp, 2 to 3 minutes. Transfer with a slotted spoon to a plate lined with paper towels to drain. Serve immediately with the aioli.

ingredients

6 cups lard *(see page 136)*
4 whole Pickled Pig's Ears *(page 68)*, **sliced into thin strips**
3 cups Seasoned Flour *(page xxvi)*
Comeback Sauce *(recipe follows)*

SERVES 8

COMEBACK SAUCE

2 cups Homemade "Duke's" Mayonnaise *(page 93)*
4 teaspoons finely minced garlic
3 tablespoons finely minced yellow onions
4 tablespoons ketchup
½ cup chili sauce
4 teaspoons pure olive oil
2½ teaspoons smoked paprika
1 teaspoon black pepper
4 teaspoons Worcestershire sauce *(page 97)* or store bought
2 tablespoons lemon juice
1½ teaspoons mustard powder
2½ teaspoons Crystal Hot Sauce
½ teaspoon salt

MAKES ABOUT 2 CUPS

Combine all of the ingredients in a food processor and blend until smooth. Store in glass or plastic covered containers. The Comeback will keep refrigerated for 7 to 10 days.

PIMENTO CHEESE FRITTERS

The Southern Foodways Alliance, though fronted by John T. Edge, is actually run by the great and powerful Oz. The person behind the curtain is the beautiful and disturbingly organized Mary Beth Lasseter. Mary Beth is one of the wonderful souls on this planet for whom I would do anything. So when she came up to me at an SFA event where I was trying to feed 300 starving intoxicants and shoved a Tupperware container full of the "best pimento cheese in the world" under my nose and simply said, "make this fried," I did. And they were so good that we started serving them at City Grocery immediately.

While you will have to wait for John Fleer and Ashley Christensen to publish their books, which will most certainly contain recipes for the most transcendent pimento cheese you will ever eat, here is ours. It is muscular, with a touch of heat on the back end but a little sweetness from the pickles.

"Rocket Man" —Elton John

To make the pimento cheese: Combine the cheddar, Havarti, cream cheese, pickles and juice, Tabasco, pimentos, and mayonnaise in a stand mixer fitted with the paddle attachment, and blend well. Season with the salt, black pepper, and cayenne. Cover and refrigerate to set up for 45 minutes. (Leftover pimento cheese will keep, stored in a covered container, for up to 10 days in the refrigerator.)

Form the cheese filling into ¾-ounce balls, place on a parchment-lined baking sheet, and return to the refrigerator to set up again.

Heat a cast-iron skillet filled with 2 inches of peanut oil (lard if you want really good hush puppies, though half oil and half lard will do) to 350°F on a candy or frying thermometer.

Remove the pimento cheese balls from the refrigerator and dip them in the seasoned flour, then the egg wash, and then the panko. After coating the fritters, you can hold them for several hours before you fry them and they will be fine, kept covered and refrigerated.

Fry the fritters in the hot oil until golden brown, 3 to 5 minutes. Transfer to a plate lined with paper towels to drain.

Wait several minutes before eating, or you *will* end up at the hospital needing a skin graft in your mouth. And we all know where they take that skin for grafting from.

Note:

Seasoned cornmeal will give your fritters a more hush puppyesque finish. To season cornmeal, in a small stainless-steel mixing bowl, combine 2 cups yellow cornmeal, 1 teaspoon salt, 2 teaspoons freshly ground black pepper, 1½ teaspoons onion powder, and ½ teaspoon cayenne and blend well together.

ingredients

PIMENTO CHEESE

2 cups coarsely shredded extra-sharp cheddar cheese

1 cup coarsely shredded Havarti cheese

1 cup cream cheese

¾ cup chopped bread-and-butter pickles

6 tablespoons pickle juice

2 teaspoons Tabasco hot sauce

½ cup chopped canned pimentos

½ cup Homemade "Duke's" Mayonnaise *(page 93)*

1½ teaspoons salt

2½ teaspoons freshly cracked black pepper

½ teaspoon cayenne

MAKES ABOUT 4½ CUPS

FRYING

Peanut oil or lard *(see page 136)*

3 cups Seasoned Flour *(page xxvi)*

3 cups Egg Wash *(page xxvii)*

Panko bread crumbs or seasoned cornmeal, for rolling *(see Note)*

SERVES 8 TO 10

Chapter 7

SAUTÉING & SEARING

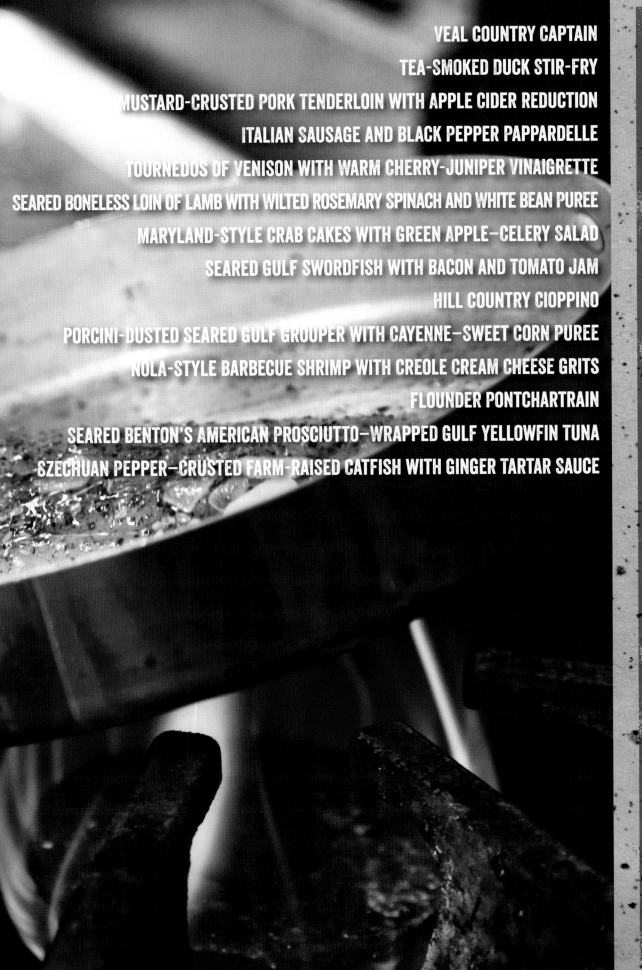

VEAL COUNTRY CAPTAIN — 157

TEA-SMOKED DUCK STIR-FRY — 158

MUSTARD-CRUSTED PORK TENDERLOIN WITH APPLE CIDER REDUCTION — 159

ITALIAN SAUSAGE AND BLACK PEPPER PAPPARDELLE — 160

TOURNEDOS OF VENISON WITH WARM CHERRY-JUNIPER VINAIGRETTE — 162

SEARED BONELESS LOIN OF LAMB WITH WILTED ROSEMARY SPINACH AND WHITE BEAN PUREE — 163

MARYLAND-STYLE CRAB CAKES WITH GREEN APPLE–CELERY SALAD — 165

SEARED GULF SWORDFISH WITH BACON AND TOMATO JAM — 166

HILL COUNTRY CIOPPINO — 167

PORCINI-DUSTED SEARED GULF GROUPER WITH CAYENNE–SWEET CORN PUREE — 169

NOLA-STYLE BARBECUE SHRIMP WITH CREOLE CREAM CHEESE GRITS — 170

FLOUNDER PONTCHARTRAIN — 172

SEARED BENTON'S AMERICAN PROSCIUTTO-WRAPPED GULF YELLOWFIN TUNA — 173

SZECHUAN PEPPER–CRUSTED FARM-RAISED CATFISH WITH GINGER TARTAR SAUCE — 174

Chapter 7

SAUTÉING & SEARING

SAUTÉING & SEARING

The sauté station in a professional kitchen is the ultimate prize every aspiring young cook has his or her eyes on. Dishes off this station are all cooked *à la minute* (to order, for immediate service). They are unforgiving and require a higher degree of skill, ostensibly, than most stations in the kitchen. The action is fast and furious on a busy sauté station. On one particularly brutal Valentine's night at an Italian restaurant where I once worked, I cooked 170 Veal Scallopini Milanese, and there were seven other dishes on that sauté station that had to be cooked as well. No smoke breaks that night.

For a dinner party, these dishes have some pluses and some minuses. Because of their nature, they will require you to be squarely in front of the stove immediately before serving dinner. If you are serving multiple courses for a dinner, you will have to leave the table to make the final preparations. On the other hand, if your friends like being in the kitchen, you can show off your mad skills, and your finished product will be as fresh as it can be.

VEAL COUNTRY CAPTAIN

Vishwesh Bhatt, our *chef de cuisine* at Snackbar, has perhaps the deftest hand with blending spices into beautiful rubs for meats and for additions to sauces that I have ever seen. It is inspiring to watch him, effortlessly and without deliberation, throw together a garam masala blend delicious enough to inspire Johnny Apple to pen a few lines about him in the *New York Times* (which he did in the winter of 2002).

I can't say how much I have loved working alongside Vish for almost 20 years or how much I have gleaned from him and his family. (His dear sweet mother was one of the finest cooks I have ever known.)

This dish (with chicken instead of veal) was one of Bill Neal's favorites. It is a wonderful expression of history through food. It clearly illustrates the importance that the Indian spice trade played in the Low Country of South Carolina and northern coastal Georgia that Bill loved. Traditional recipes call for generic, store-bought curry powder, but taking the time to blend your own garam masala really elevates this dish. Thanks, Vish . . . Bill would be very proud, I think.

"I Wanna Be Your Dog" —The Stooges

ingredients

Slice the veal into 1½-ounce medallions. Place the medallions between sheets of plastic wrap and pound with a meat tenderizer until ⅛ inch thick. Season the medallions on both sides with the salt, black pepper, and garam masala.

In a medium saucepan over medium heat, melt the butter and 1 tablespoon of the bacon fat, and sauté the onions and garlic until transparent but not browned. Add the green and yellow bell peppers and sauté until tender. Stir in the chopped tomatoes, thyme, curry powder, and red pepper flakes and bring to a simmer. Stir in the stock, crushed tomatoes, and currants and bring to a boil. Simmer for 35 minutes over medium-low heat, stirring occasionally.

Heat two large ovenproof sauté pans until hot. Divide the remaining 1 tablespoon bacon fat and the olive oil equally between each pan and swirl to coat the bottom of the pans. Carefully lay in the veal medallions. Brown them on one side, and then turn over and brown slightly on the second side, about 1 minute per side. Remove from the pan and reserve.

Add 3 tablespoons wine to each pan and swirl briefly to deglaze. Pour half of the tomato sauce into each sauté pan. Return the medallions to the pans and spoon the sauce over the top. Place the pans in the oven for 10 minutes.

Remove the pans from the oven, transfer the medallions to individual serving plates, whisk 4 tablespoons of the cold butter into the sauce in each pan, and season to taste with salt and black pepper. Divide the sauce over the medallions and serve.

1 pound veal top round, trimmed
1½ teaspoons salt
5 teaspoons freshly ground black pepper
1 tablespoon Garam Masala *(recipe follows)*
2 tablespoons unsalted butter
2 tablespoons bacon fat
1 cup sliced yellow onions *(cut root to tip)*
1 tablespoon minced garlic
½ cup julienned green bell peppers
¾ cup julienned yellow bell peppers
2 cups chopped tomatoes
2 teaspoons fresh thyme leaves
2 teaspoons Madras curry powder
¼ teaspoon red pepper flakes
1 cup Veal Stock *(page 30)* or unsalted beef broth
1 cup crushed tomatoes, with their juices
½ cup dried currants
2 tablespoons pure olive oil
6 tablespoons dry red wine, preferably Burgundy
½ cup cold unsalted butter, cubed

SERVES 4

GARAM MASALA

MAKES ¼ CUP

1 tablespoon cumin seeds
1½ teaspoons coriander seeds
1½ teaspoons cardamom pods
1½ teaspoons black peppercorns
1 teaspoon ground cinnamon
1 teaspoon ground ginger
½ teaspoon whole cloves
½ teaspoon ground nutmeg
½ teaspoon crushed dried bay leaves

Preheat the oven to 350°F. Place the cumin, coriander seeds, cardamom, peppercorns, cinnamon, ginger, cloves, nutmeg, and bay leaves in a small ovenproof sauté pan or on a very small baking sheet. Bake for 5 to 7 minutes, until you can smell the fragrances of those spices coming off the pan. Allow the spices to cool briefly and then grind in a spice grinder to a fine powder. Extra garam masala can be stored in sealed glass or plastic containers for about 6 months.

TEA-SMOKED DUCK STIR-FRY

This recipe takes a bit of commitment, but I have removed several of the traditional steps to make it less daunting than it would be otherwise. I've always been a huge fan of fried rice. It's such a quick fill up that doesn't weigh you down, and you can load it with as many vegetables as you want. The smoky-sweet fatty unctuousness of the duck is a refreshing departure from the traditional pork, chicken, or shrimp.

ingredients

"Last Time" —Ike Reilly

JASMINE RICE

2 tablespoons unsalted butter

¼ cup small-dice yellow onions

2 tablespoons minced garlic

2 tablespoons peeled and minced fresh ginger

2 cups jasmine rice

3 tablespoons mirin

2 tablespoons rice wine vinegar

3 cups Dark Chicken Stock *(page 31)*, warmed to a simmer

SMOKED DUCK

6 tablespoons soy sauce

2 green onions, chopped

2 tablespoons peeled and minced fresh ginger

2 teaspoons red pepper flakes

2 whole (5- to 7-ounce) duck breasts, fat scored into a diamond pattern

2 cups soaked hickory chips *(see Note, page 203)*

STIR-FRYING

1 tablespoon toasted sesame oil

2 tablespoons pure olive oil

½ teaspoon red pepper flakes

Smoked duck breasts

½ cup thinly sliced yellow onions

½ cup small julienned carrots

½ cup small julienned celery

½ cup snow peas, thinly sliced lengthwise

2 tablespoons plus 1 teaspoon peeled and minced fresh ginger

3 cups cooked jasmine rice

2 tablespoons soy sauce

3 tablespoons chopped fresh cilantro

2 tablespoons chopped fresh flat-leaf parsley

½ cup sliced green onions

SERVES 4

To make the rice: In a medium saucepan, melt the butter over medium heat. Stir in the onions and garlic and sauté until transparent. Stir in the ginger and sauté again briefly, stirring constantly.

Stir in the rice until coated completely with the onion mixture. Add the mirin and rice wine vinegar and combine well. Add the stock, cover, decrease the heat to low, and simmer slowly for 15 to 17 minutes, just until the rice has absorbed all of the liquid.

Remove the saucepan from the heat, dump the rice onto a baking sheet, spread it out into an even layer, and refrigerate to cool immediately.

To smoke the duck: Combine 3 cups water, the soy sauce, green onions, ginger, and red pepper flakes in a medium saucepan and bring to a boil over high heat. Remove immediately from the heat and cool to room temperature. Pour the liquid over the duck breasts in a shallow, glass dish. Cover and refrigerate for at least 2 hours, or if possible, overnight.

Prepare a stovetop smoker with the soaked chips and place it over medium heat. Remove the breasts from the marinade and arrange them on the rack as soon as the smoke begins to rise from the chips. Cover the smoker and allow the breasts to smoke for 8 to 10 minutes. Immediately remove the breasts from the smoker and set aside to cool. Once cooled, slice the breasts across the grain into thin slivers; cut the medallions into ¼-inch-thick strips and set aside.

To assemble the stir-fry: Heat the sesame and olive oils and red pepper flakes in a wok over high heat. When the oils begin to shimmer, toss in the prepared duck. Sauté over high heat until the duck begins to crisp up, then remove from the pan.

Add the onions, carrots, and celery to the wok and sauté, stirring constantly, until tender. Add the snow peas and ginger and sauté briefly. Stir in the 3 cups of rice and soy sauce and combine well. Stir-fry for 5 to 6 minutes, until the rice begins to brown slightly. Return the duck to the wok and combine. Add the cilantro and parsley. Spoon into bowls, top with the green onions, and serve.

MUSTARD-CRUSTED PORK TENDERLOIN WITH APPLE CIDER REDUCTION

I'll put a well-cooked heritage breed pork tenderloin up next to just about anything. With the fresh herbs and Dijon on this one, you really don't need much of anything else. A drizzle of a nicely infused olive oil and a sprinkle of finishing salt never hurts, but the cider reduction works spectacularly. I love to serve this with Salt-Roasted Turnip Puree (recipe follows).

"Boom Boom Boom" —The Iguanas

Sprinkle each of the pork tenderloins with about 2 teaspoons each of salt and black pepper. Place, covered, in the refrigerator until ready to cook.

In a medium bowl, blend together both mustards, the honey, 2 tablespoons of the fresh rosemary, 2 tablespoons of the shallots, and the garlic until well combined. Rub the mustard mixture evenly all over the tenderloins, and then dredge them lightly in the bread crumbs, knocking off as much excess as you can.

In a large, ovenproof sauté pan, briefly heat 3 tablespoons of the clarified butter over medium heat, about 45 seconds. Gently place the tenderloins in the pan and brown them on all sides. Place the pan in the oven for 7 to 8 minutes, until the tenderloins reach an internal temperature of about 135°F. Remove the tenderloins from the pan and set aside on a cutting board to rest for 3 to 5 minutes. This will keep them from releasing their juices when they are sliced for serving.

Return the sauté pan to the stovetop over medium heat. Add the remaining 2 tablespoons clarified butter and the remaining 2 tablespoons shallots and sauté until the shallots are transparent. Add the stock, cider, sugar, and remaining 2 teaspoons rosemary and bring to a simmer. Reduce the liquid by just over half. Turn off the heat and let cool for about 10 seconds. Then vigorously whisk in the cold cubed butter.

Slice the tenders crosswise into ½-inch-thick medallions, drizzle each portion with the cider reduction, and serve immediately.

ingredients

2 pork tenderloins *(about 1 pound each)*
Salt and freshly ground black pepper
¾ cup Dijon mustard
½ cup Grainy Mustard *(page 94)*
3 tablespoons honey
2 tablespoons plus 2 teaspoons chopped fresh rosemary
¼ cup grated shallots
2 teaspoons minced garlic
4 cups panko bread crumbs
5 tablespoons clarified unsalted butter *(see page xxiii)*
3 tablespoons Dark Chicken Stock *(page 31)*
¼ cup fresh apple cider
1½ teaspoons sugar
3 tablespoons cold unsalted butter, cubed

SERVES 4

SALT-ROASTED TURNIP PUREE

1 large russet baking potato, peeled
1 medium yellow onion, peeled
3 medium fresh turnips, peeled
1 (3-pound) box Morton's kosher salt
4 tablespoons cold unsalted butter, cubed
3 tablespoons sour cream
3 tablespoons heavy cream
1 tablespoon fresh thyme leaves
2 teaspoons freshly ground white pepper
1½ teaspoons finely minced garlic

SERVES 4

Preheat the oven to 400°F. In a medium saucepan, cover the potato and onion with cold water. Place the pan on the stovetop over high heat and bring to a boil. Decrease the heat to medium and simmer until the potato is done enough to easily push a knife through it, about 25 minutes. Drain the potato and onion, and push the potato and onion through a food mill. Alternatively, you can puree them in a food processor.

Place the peeled turnips in a small baking dish and cover completely with salt. Cover with aluminum foil and roast for 25 minutes, until a knife can be pushed through with little resistance. Once the turnips are knife-tender, immediately remove them from the salt (it will be caked a little hard and the turnips will have to be broken out). Immediately force the hot turnips through a food mill, or puree in a food processor. Combine with the potato and onion. Blend in the butter, sour cream, heavy cream, thyme, white pepper, and garlic and blend until fully combined.

ITALIAN SAUSAGE AND BLACK PEPPER PAPPARDELLE

I have done two turns through Italian kitchens and eaten enough of the Americanized versions of Italian "classics" to kill Clemenza four or five times over, if we are to be honest about the authenticity of this dish. In Italy I am yet to stumble upon what we call "Italian sausage," but the pasta itself in this dish is very much Italian. I love making pasta by hand. Nothing comes close to it for flavor and texture, and it takes just a moment to cook. As a time-saver, basic dough for pasta can be made in a food processor, and even if the processor technique is not remotely traditional, it is a great convenience for the home cook who wants to make pasta from scratch.

So while this dish doesn't pretend to be authentic, it is exceptional and full of delicious flavors. It is partly borrowed from my dear friend Gwen Higgins, and it takes me right back to the kitchen at Aurora in Chapel Hill every time I taste it.

"If Drinkin' Don't Kill Me (Her Memory Will)" —George Jones

ingredients

BLACK PEPPER PAPPARDELLE

3 cups all-purpose flour, plus more for dusting the work surface

1½ teaspoons salt

4 teaspoons finely ground black pepper

3 large eggs, lightly beaten

4 teaspoons extra-virgin olive oil

Note: This will make more pasta than you will need to feed 4 people, but the cut pasta can be dried or frozen and used later.

SAUCE

2 tablespoons pure olive oil

2 teaspoons minced garlic

½ cup thinly sliced red onions

½ cup thinly sliced sweet red bell peppers

1½ teaspoons red pepper flakes

1½ cups ½-inch-thick sliced hot Italian sausage

½ cup brandy

½ cup Ham Stock *(page 33)*

24 strips Black Pepper Pappardelle

3 tablespoons cubed unsalted butter, cubed

¼ cup plus 2 tablespoons freshly grated Parmesan cheese

3 tablespoons chopped fresh flat-leaf parsley

SERVES 4

To make the pasta: Place the flour, salt, and black pepper in a food processor and pulse to combine. With the processor running, add the eggs and olive oil. The mixture should immediately resemble a coarse meal. Stop the processor and remove the top. The mixture should hold together when you pinch it. Remove the blade and press the dough into a ball that holds together. Place the dough on a floured cutting board and knead for 3 to 4 minutes, adding flour as needed, until the dough has a smooth consistency.

Cut the dough into quarters. Run each piece sequentially through the widest setting of a pasta machine, folding the dough in half or thirds after each pass, until the dough looks homogenous and smooth. Dial the roller down two notches and run the dough through again. Roll the pasta to just under the thickness of an LP. (Yes, I know I am dating myself; use a CD for reference if you prefer.) If the dough gets too thin the pepper will cause tears, in which case fold it in half, return to the next thickest setting, and roll again.

Lay the pasta on a cutting board and cut it into 4-inch lengths. Cut these lengthwise into 1-inch widths. Sprinkle the pasta with flour, cover with a moist kitchen towel, and refrigerate until needed.

To cook the pasta: Fill a medium soup pot with water salted to the salinity of seawater, and bring to a boil over high heat.

To make the sauce: In a large sauté pan over medium heat, warm the olive oil until the surface begins to shimmer but not smoke. Stir in the garlic, onions, and peppers and sauté just until the vegetables begin to wilt. Add the red pepper flakes and Italian sausage and sauté until the sausage begins to brown very lightly.

Carefully stir in the brandy. *The pan will likely flame from the alcohol.* Don't panic. Gently cover the pan with a lid or a pan of equal size and the fire will die immediately. Remove the lid and add the stock. Allow the liquid to reduce by three-quarters over medium heat.

Meanwhile, drop the pasta into a strainer or colander and lower into the boiling water. Cook for 1½ to 2 minutes or until the pasta floats. Drain briefly and dump into the sauté pan with the sauce. Stir in the cold butter and Parmesan cheese and continue stirring until fully combined. Divide evenly among serving bowls and sprinkle each with a little parsley.

MY EXPERIENCE WITH REAL PASTA

The New Orleans I grew up in during the 1960s and '70s was a town dotted with a plethora of mom-and-pop Italian restaurants. The "Creole Italian" that evolved through the middle part of the twentieth century there made for a menu of extremely rich and garlic-heavy items. Those menu items frequently utilized local seafood, but the sauces were mostly heavy with cream, slow-cooked "red gravy," and/or Parmesan cheese. There was lots and lots of pasta, but it wasn't until I went off to college that I first had the pleasure of handmade pasta. My first taste was astounding. I remember the mouthful as though it happened yesterday. I was on a weekend trip with a friend's family to their cabin in West Virginia. The cabin had no running water or power. It was the dead of winter and we literally had to get up in the middle of the night, bundle up, and walk 30 or 40 yards through the snow to use the outhouse, when we had to "go." They loved and embraced everything about the primitive conditions, and we spent a long weekend making, proofing, and baking bread, along with cooking different meats over an open hearth. And ultimately, one afternoon, we were mixing, kneading, rolling, and cutting fresh pasta.

Pasta making started to make its appearance in the early 1980s in the American cooking magazines, and Atlas pasta machines began to pop up in specialty stores. Pasta making was the "it" thing for home cooks, right after Chicken à la King and right before sun-dried tomatoes.

As I got into cooking professionally, several years down the road, the seed of interest planted that weekend in West Virginia immediately began to grow and has been flourishing ever since. It may have fallen out of vogue over the years, but it's never out of fashion.

TOURNEDOS OF VENISON
WITH WARM CHERRY-JUNIPER VINAIGRETTE

There is enough wild white-tailed deer taken each year around Oxford during hunting season that our local slaughterhouse does zero killing of hogs and cattle from early November until early February because they are so busy processing all the animals brought to them. There's lots of deer meat to go around.

The problem here is that when deer are in season, cherries are not (and vice versa). The sweetness of the cherries and the floral, earthy, eucalyptus flavors of the juniper go too well together with the venison to not make this dish, though. Fortunately, farm-raised venison is available year-round. If you want to do this with wild venison during deer season, you can substitute frozen cherries or reconstituted dried ones for an equally good result.

 ingredients

"Hate to Say I Told You So" —The Hives

VENISON

3 whole venison tenderloins
(8 to 9 ounces each)
3 tablespoons Garlic Olive Oil *(page xxvi)*
2 teaspoons salt
2 teaspoons freshly ground black pepper

VINAIGRETTE

3 tablespoons extra-virgin olive oil
6 tablespoons pure olive oil
1 tablespoon minced shallots
1 teaspoon minced garlic
5 teaspoons Dijon mustard
¼ cup red wine or apple cider vinegar
½ cup chopped fresh cherries
2 teaspoons honey
1½ teaspoons ground juniper berries
2 teaspoons fresh thyme leaves
¾ teaspoon salt
1¼ teaspoons freshly ground black pepper
1 tablespoon bacon fat

SERVES 4

To prepare the venison: Rub the tenderloins with 2 tablespoons of the garlic oil and the salt and pepper and set aside.

To make the vinaigrette: Combine the olive oils, shallots, garlic, mustard, vinegar, cherries, honey, juniper berries, thyme, salt, and pepper in a blender and puree until smooth. Set aside.

To finish cooking the venison: In a medium, ovenproof sauté pan, warm the remaining 1 tablespoon garlic oil and the bacon fat over medium heat until the fat begins to shimmer on the top. Gently place the tenderloins in the pan and brown on all sides, and then place the pan in the oven for 4 minutes, until the venison has reached an internal temperature of about 125°F.

Transfer the tenderloins to a cutting board to rest for 3 minutes. Slice into ½-inch-thick medallions and drizzle with the vinaigrette.

HILL COUNTRY CIOPPINO

Seafood, as a general rule, needs little more than a quick cook, citrus, and a sprinkling of salt and pepper to achieve its full potential. Overthinking typically leads to its ruination. This is a north Mississippi version of an Italian classic. It was the Friday night weekly special at Snackbar and, it seemed, no matter how much we made of it, we just couldn't make enough. It has to be made *à la minute* for it to be at its best. The seafood should just finish cooking in the broth as it is served alongside grilled, crusty sourdough with a healthy application of butter.

"Love on a Farmboy's Wages" —XTC

ingredients

In a large sauté pan over medium heat, sauté the onions, garlic, fennel, and celery in the bacon fat and butter, stirring constantly until they begin to wilt, about 6 minutes. Stir in the tomatoes, salt, and pepper and combine well. Continue to sauté another 4 to 5 minutes. Add the shrimp, white fish, crawfish tails, clams, and crab. Turn the heat to high and stir until the shrimp just begin to turn pink all over. Add the herbs, red pepper flakes, bay leaves, tomato paste, lemon juice, and white wine and bring to a simmer. Stir in the stock and bring to a boil. Lower the heat to medium and simmer for 3 minutes. Remove from the heat, distribute the seafood evenly among 4 bowls. Swirl the butter into the remaining broth until full incorporated and pour over the seafood. Serve immediately with grilled bread.

½ cup small dice yellow onions

2 teaspoons finely minced garlic

¼ cup small dice fennel bulb

¼ cup small dice celery

1 tablespoon bacon fat

1 tablespoon butter

1½ cups seeded and chopped tomatoes

1½ teaspoons salt

2½ teaspoons freshly ground black pepper

8 medium shrimp *(16 to 20 count)*

8 ounces white fish of your choice, such as catfish or grouper drum, cut into ½-ounce pieces

6 ounces crawfish tails

8 clams, washed *(make sure they are tightly closed)*

4 ounces of jumbo lump blue crabmeat *(or about 10 claws)*

3 tablespoons mixed chopped basil, thyme, rosemary, and parsley

1½ teaspoons red pepper flakes

2 bay leaves

1 tablespoon tomato paste

1 tablespoon freshly squeezed lemon juice

½ cup white wine

4 cups Shrimp Stock *(page 34)*

3 tablespoons cold butter, cubed

Grilled bread, for serving

SERVES 4

PORCINI-DUSTED SEARED GULF GROUPER WITH CAYENNE–SWEET CORN PUREE

Grouper is prolific on the Gulf Coast. Still somewhat exotic 25 years ago, it was relegated to fine dining restaurants and was a little more obscure in its usage. Today this beast is the toast of the town everywhere. Gulf Coast seafood shacks all sport a fried, grilled, or broiled grouper sandwich. That said, it is still an outstanding choice whenever you find it. Its thick fillets flake into giant, sweet, thumb-size chunks as delicious as any cold-water white fish I have ever had. The porcini dust adds a perfume that fills the room, and the spicy-sweet corn puree provides a creamy, balanced base. This goes very nicely with a simple salad of bitter greens.

"Novocaine Rhapsody" —Dean Gray

ingredients

To cook the grouper: Drizzle the fish with the olive oil to coat thoroughly and sprinkle evenly with the salt, pepper, and porcini powder.

Heat the butter in a medium skillet. Gently place the grouper in the hot pan and brown lightly on the first side. Flip the fillets over and tilt the pan slightly so the butter accumulates on the side closest to you. Using a large spoon, baste the fish with the hot butter as the second side browns. Spoon 6 or 8 spoonfuls of the hot butter over each of the pieces, and then flip them again, spooning the butter over the other side.

Spoon the sweet corn puree (recipe follows) onto serving plates and top with the grouper fillets. Sprinkle with chopped fresh herbs.

4 (6-ounce) fillets fresh grouper
3 tablespoons pure olive oil
2 teaspoons salt
3 teaspoons freshly ground black pepper
5 teaspoons porcini powder
(available at specialty food stores)
½ cup clarified unsalted butter *(see page xxiii)*
1 tablespoon chopped fresh herbs

SERVES 4

CAYENNE–SWEET CORN PUREE

2 tablespoons clarified unsalted butter *(see page xxiii)*
2 tablespoons minced shallots
2 teaspoons minced garlic
3 cups roasted sweet corn kernels
½ teaspoon cayenne
2 tablespoons heavy cream
3 saffron threads *(a small pinch)*
1 teaspoon salt
2 teaspoons freshly ground black pepper
3 tablespoons cream cheese

In a small sauté pan, heat the butter over medium heat and sauté the shallots and garlic until transparent. Add the corn kernels, cayenne, and cream and bring just to a simmer. Transfer this mixture to a blender and puree. Blend in the saffron, salt, pepper, and cream cheese. Set aside.

NOLA-STYLE BARBECUED SHRIMP WITH CREOLE CREAM CHEESE GRITS

There are two popular versions of barbecued shrimp in New Orleans and, oddly, neither is what most people might think. New Orleans barbecued shrimp never see open fire, charcoal, or smoke. The most common version you see today was pioneered by Gerard Maras at Mr. B's Bistro in the French Quarter and is a stovetop sauté heavy on Worcestershire and garlic and finished with a healthy dose of cold butter, which gives it a spicy and creamy texture. The other was born on Napoleon Avenue at Pascal's Manale and is a butter-baked version heavy on black pepper, rosemary, and garlic. Both versions are perfect for sopping up with cloud-light Leidenheimer's French bread, but the former lends itself to much greater interpretation when it comes to sides to serve it with.

I worked the station at Mr. B's that turned out this dish as well as an outstanding pasta jambalaya. It was insanely busy. Prep for my station on a regular weekend night included cubing up two cases (72 pounds) of butter to finish these two dishes. It was a monster, but if you could work that station, you could work just about any one, anywhere.

You will not need 72 pounds of butter for this, but trust me, use exactly what I tell you; though fatty, this is a perfectly acceptable occasional treat, especially if you get your hands on some good fresh shrimp. As much as I love a contrasting texture in my dishes, the creamy grits here are a great counterpunch to the boldness of the Worcestershire. The Creole Cream Cheese (a south Louisiana primitive farmer's cheese) paired with a hint of raw garlic stand up to the bold flavor of the shrimp.

"I Don't Wanna Know" —Lil' Band O' Gold

ingredients

20 head-on, unpeeled shrimp *(26 to 30 count)*

1½ teaspoons salt

2 teaspoons freshly ground black pepper

2 tablespoons pure olive oil

1 tablespoon bacon fat

2 shallots, sliced

4 cloves garlic, thinly sliced

2 teaspoons black peppercorns

1 lemon, sliced
(rind included, but stem and blossom ends discarded)

2 cups Worcestershire Sauce *(page 97)*
or store bought

1 tablespoon chopped fresh rosemary

2 teaspoons fresh thyme leaves

2 teaspoons red pepper flakes

2 dried bay leaves

½ cup dry white wine

¾ cup Veal Stock *(page 30)*

3 tablespoons clarified unsalted butter
(see page xxiii)

3 tablespoons heavy cream

½ cup cold unsalted butter, cubed

3 tablespoons chopped fresh flat-leaf parsley

½ cup thinly sliced green onions

SERVES 4

To cook the shrimp: Remove the shrimp heads and peel the shrimp, leaving the tails attached. Reserve the shells. Cut a groove down the spine of each shrimp (this will cause them to "butterfly" when they cook and increase the delicious surface area). Sprinkle the shrimp with the salt and pepper and set aside.

Heat the olive oil and bacon fat in a medium saucepan over medium heat. Add the shrimp shells and heads and stir until they all have turned pink. Add the shallots and garlic and sauté until they turn transparent. Stir in the black peppercorns, lemon slices, Worcestershire, rosemary, thyme, red pepper flakes, bay leaves, wine, and stock. Bring to a boil, lower the heat, and reduce by half, 12 to 15 minutes. Strain the reduced shrimp stock and reserve.

In a large sauté pan over medium heat, heat the clarified butter until it begins to shimmer. Add the shrimp and cook, turning once as the shrimp begin to turn pink. Add the reserved shrimp stock to the pan. Bring to a simmer and reduce the sauce until it is thick and syrupy. Swirl in the cream and combine completely. Whisk in the cold butter until completely combined, and then blend in the parsley.

Serve the shrimp and accompanying sauce over the grits and scatter with the green onions.

GRITS

2 cups Dark Chicken Stock *(page 31)*

2 cups whole milk

1 cup stone-ground grits *(not instant or quick)*

4 tablespoons unsalted butter

2 teaspoons minced garlic

2 teaspoons salt

1 tablespoon freshly ground black pepper

¾ cup Creole cream cheese *(page 170)*, substitute commercial cream cheese, if need be

In a medium saucepan, bring the stock and milk to a boil over medium heat. (Be careful as this approaches a boil, since it will foam up in a hurry and spill over.) Whisk in the grits and lower the heat slightly. Continue whisking for about 10 minutes. Taste to make sure the grits are cooked through and tender. Stir in the butter, garlic, salt, pepper, and cream cheese and set aside, keeping warm.

FLOUNDER PONTCHARTRAIN

"Pontchartrain" describes a preparation that is, at times, disturbingly ubiquitous. It is little more than sautéed blue crab over a piece of lightly sautéed white fish. I had to lay down the law several years ago with a fistful of crab-happy cooks who put crabmeat on almost everything (fried green tomatoes, veal, beef fillet, Caesar salad, and so on), not because it wasn't delicious, but because the prolific use looked one-dimensional. That being said, it is still an excellent preparation and one that's very easy to pull off. Leftover sautéed crabmeat makes a killer omelet, by the way.

Lake Pontchartrain, the gigantic puddle that borders the north side of New Orleans (I call it a puddle because its deepest natural point is only about 12 feet), was a natural home to a huge population of Gulf blue crabs, because of its protected surroundings and plentiful food. Commercial crabbing in the lake is but a shadow of what it once was, but the dish remains in memoriam.

"Well Well Well" —The Woodentops

ingredients

4 (5-ounce) flounder fillets

4 teaspoons bay oil *(see below)*

3½ teaspoons salt

5 teaspoons freshly ground black pepper

4 teaspoons finely grated lemon zest

5 tablespoons clarified unsalted butter *(see page xxiii)*

2 cups Seasoned Flour *(page xxvi)*

2 tablespoons minced shallots

1 teaspoon minced fresh garlic

1 cup fresh lump blue crabmeat

2 teaspoons freshly squeezed lemon juice

2 teaspoons dry white wine

1 tablespoon chopped fresh flat-leaf parsley

SERVES 4

Preheat the oven to 450°F. Rub both sides of the flounder fillets with bay oil and sprinkle with 2 teaspoons of the salt, 3 teaspoons of the black pepper, and the lemon zest.

Heat a large, ovenproof sauté pan with 3 tablespoons of the clarified butter over medium heat. Dredge the flounder in the seasoned flour and knock off any excess. Place the fillets gently in the warmed butter and brown them until golden on one side. Flip carefully onto the second side and place the pan in the oven for 5 to 6 minutes to finish cooking through.

In a medium sauté pan over high heat, warm the remaining 2 tablespoons clarified butter. Stir in the shallots and garlic and sauté until transparent. Add the crabmeat and season with the remaining 1½ teaspoons salt and 2 teaspoons pepper, stirring gently so as to not break up the lumps of crabmeat. Add the lemon juice and white wine and reduce by half. Stir in the parsley.

Place the flounder fillets in the center of the serving plates and spoon the hot crabmeat over the top. Try not to start eating before you get to the table.

FLAVORED OILS

This recipe calls specifically for bay oil, but this technique works with just about any dried herb or spice to achieve the same effect with different flavor. This technique was first proffered by Jean-Georges Vongerichten more than 25 years ago and continues to be an essential tool in our flavoring profiles.

Place dried bay leaves in a spice grinder and grind to a fine powder. In a small, sealable container, mix 1 tablespoon of the ground bay leaves with enough boiling water to make a thick paste (a tiny bit thinner than that of wasabi). Stir the mixture to fully combine, and let steep for 5 minutes. Add ¾ cup of a neutral-flavored oil like peanut, seal the container, and shake vigorously until blended and cloudy. Let settle for several hours and then shake again. Continue this process for 24 hours. Let settle, and decant the flavored oil off into another container. Discard the solids. This will keep for about 1 month.

SEARED BENTON'S AMERICAN PROSCIUTTO–WRAPPED GULF YELLOWFIN TUNA

People wax romantically about Allan Benton for his ability with ham and bacon. I am reluctant to do so because I feel like another chef on the bandwagon. The bottom line is: 1) Allan is one of the finest hard-working, humble, honest, uncompromising, and enjoyable people you will ever have the pleasure of meeting; and 2) he makes, simply, the best country ham there is. I could not be more fortunate than I am to call him friend. Allan is the calm in the middle of my storm, the man I love to call when the chips are down, because his voice and kindliness can always cheer me up. He is one of the finest people I have ever been blessed to know.

Tuna and salty ham are as natural a pairing as peanut butter and jelly. The addition of Old Bay is just a kiss on the cheek from God. This is great cooked on the grill as well, with a drizzle of chimichurri (see page 98) and a baked summer squash casserole.

"Jell" —Let's Active

Rub the tuna blocks with the olive oil and sprinkle with the pepper and Old Bay. Lay the prosciutto slices out flat and sprinkle them evenly with the meat glue. Roll the tuna up inside the ham, wrap tightly with plastic wrap, and refrigerate for about 2 hours.

Heat the clarified butter in a medium sauté pan over medium heat until the butter shimmers. Unwrap the tuna pieces from the plastic wrap and place them gently into the pan (prosciutto seam side down) to sear. Brown the fish on all sides, basting constantly with the butter, for 3 to 4 minutes.

Remove, slice into ½-inch-thick medallions (this should still be rare in the middle), and serve immediately.

Note:

Transglutimanase is a naturally occurring enzyme that causes bonding between protein substances. It is known as "meat glue" because it quite literally can be used to fuse two pieces of protein together. The enzyme that causes the bonding is the same one that causes blood to coagulate. It is produced commercially through animal blood extraction and/or fermentation. It has gotten some negative press due to unethical use by some chefs who are "gluing" together scraps of beef to pass off as high-end fillet. Used responsibly it has no unethical or unhealthy implications. It adds no flavor and only enhances the appearance of the final product. Transglutimanase is available through the Modernist Pantry online. It is a living enzyme that is packaged in vacuum-sealed pouches and is stable at room temperature. After breaking the seal, freezing is recommended in order to extend the product's life. You can prepare this dish by "toothpicking" or tying the ham securely and achieve a nice result.

ingredients

4 (6-ounce) pieces fresh tuna
(if you can get your fishmonger to cut these into rectangular blocks, rather than steaks, you will increase the rare center portion when sliced)

2 tablespoons olive oil

1 tablespoon freshly ground black pepper

2½ teaspoons Old Bay Seasoning

4 paper-thin slices Benton's Smokehouse American Prosciutto

4 teaspoons transglutimanase
("meat glue"; see Note)

5 tablespoons clarified unsalted butter
(see page xxiii)

SERVES 4

SZECHUAN PEPPER—CRUSTED FARM-RAISED CATFISH WITH GINGER TARTAR SAUCE

Catfish is definitely considered one of the redheaded stepchildren of the food world—decidedly an unwarranted reputation. While it will never have the robust flavor of swordfish or the toothy texture of tuna, well-raised fresh catfish can stand shoulder to shoulder with a tremendous number of the world's flaky white fish. There is absolutely nothing second-rate about fresh, quality, pond-raised catfish. And the best of those, hands-down, came from Mississippi, I am proud to say.

The zesty shot in the arm from the Szechuan peppercorns here is a nod to the Asian population in the Mississippi Delta, who have adopted our ingredients and folded them into their foodways. If you look hard enough in the Delta, you can still find the odd spot serving interesting twists on traditional dishes. One of my favorites was a grocery store on Highway 61 just south of the "crossroads" in Clarksdale, where they served sweet and sour frog's legs and stir-fried pig's tails. It was one of my favorite stops on the way to duck camp. This dish goes great with Okra and Green Onion Hush Puppies (page 143).

ingredients

"Chelsea Hotel No. 2" —Leonard Cohen

2 (7- to 9-ounce) fresh catfish fillets

4 teaspoons salt

5 teaspoons ground Szechuan peppercorns

1 cup cornmeal

1 cup all-purpose flour

½ teaspoon baking soda

1 teaspoon ground ginger

½ teaspoon cayenne

½ cup clarified unsalted butter *(see page xxiii)*

2 teaspoons toasted sesame oil *(optional)*

2 cups Egg Wash *(page xxvii)*

Ginger Tartar Sauce *(see Note)*

SERVES 2

Carefully slice each catfish fillet horizontally into two thin slabs (you will end up with pieces roughly the same size as the original fillets, just thinner). Season the pieces with 2 teaspoons of the salt and the Szechuan peppercorns.

In a shallow baking dish, combine the cornmeal, flour, baking soda, the remaining 2 teaspoons salt, the ginger, and cayenne. Blend together well.

Heat the butter and sesame oil in a large skillet over medium heat until the butter shimmers. Working with one piece at a time, dredge the catfish in the cornmeal, dip in the egg wash, and then dredge in the cornmeal again. Place the fillets carefully into the hot butter. Brown on the first side, and then flip to cook on the other side, about 2 minutes per side.

Remove the fillets from the pan, drain briefly on a plate lined with paper towels, and serve with the tartar sauce.

Note:

For the Ginger Tartar Sauce, prepare the Fresh Herb Tartar Sauce on page 107, adding 3 tablespoons peeled and grated fresh ginger and substituting rice wine vinegar for the vinegar reduction.

Chapter 8

ROASTING & BRAISING

STEEN'S SYRUP-BRAISED PORK BELLY 180

SATSUMA AND CLOVE-BRAISED LAMB SHANKS 182

HERB AND GARLIC ROASTED POULET ROUGE 183

PAN-ROASTED DUCK BREAST "FRISÉE" AUX LARDONS 185

BOURBON-BRAISED PORK CHEEKS 186

TOMATO-BRAISED GROUPER 187

OSSO BUCO WITH ROSEMARY AND ENGLISH PEA RISOTTO 189

ROASTED QUAIL STUFFED WITH TRUFFLE BREAD PUDDING 190

PAN-ROASTED SOFT SHELLS WITH ROASTED TOMATO-VERMOUTH PAN BUTTER 191

RABBIT CACCIATORE 193

ROASTED AND STUFFED SPECKLED TROUT 194

Chapter 8

ROASTING & BRAISING

ROASTING & BRAISING

Welcome to the chapter where we address the Barry White of cooking techniques. There is little as romantic and seductive as a roast, osso buco, pork belly, or what-have-you slowly cooking and filling your house with its smell. It is intoxicating and entrancing, like the strains of Barry in low light with a glass of red wine. It's a beautiful romance.

Roasting and braising are the processes that require the most patience, sometimes the most preparation, and, certainly, the most time. If you are prepared to dedicate the time and love to these dishes, the results are decidedly more soulful than most anything else you can cook.

Every year for Christmas lunch, my mom used to cook a magnificent pork crown roast. Everyone helped prepare that meal and set the table. It was always, with the exception of the occasional obligatory bickering, a joyful affair.

As I went about my duties on those Christmas mornings, I could not help but watch, with transfixed fascination, as that roast turned from an anemic raw blob of meat and bone into this marvelous Escoffian masterpiece. My mother was the mistress of the transformation, and it took hours of her constantly opening the oven door, spooning pan liquid and drippings over the meat and bones to achieve the desired result. At the end, she would fill the center with a wild rice stuffing and always drizzled something sweet around the outside. My dad would let me help him in the feverish process of turning the pan drippings into gravy (I freaking love gravy), but little mattered to me at that point except for seeing the flash of the steel carving knife and fork to get all of it on our plates.

Roasting and braising have decidedly cold-weather implications and traditionally require a significant amount of time fussing, but an overnight slow cooker brisket or pressure-cooked pork pot roast are convenient time-savers any time of year. And they can be accomplished without leaving the oven running for hours at a time in the heat of summer.

STEEN'S SYRUP-BRAISED PORK BELLY

Pork belly is a magical thing when handled the right way. Because of the fat content and resulting forgivingness, almost anyone can look like a seasoned pro bringing slabs of belly to the table. To make it a little more palatable to the general public (some people, like my wife, immediately condemn it to the too fatty, unhealthy category), we trim a significant amount of the surface fat away, leaving more pure protein in the finished product.

The Steen's Syrup Mill in Vermilion Parish, in south Louisiana, has been producing an outstanding, subtle, and smooth cane syrup for just over 100 years. To my mind, it is one of the most seminal artisanal food products from the state. It is simple, honest, and delicious. It works perfectly with pork because it is flavorful but not cloyingly sweet. It brings an earthiness to this dish that is truly unique. A good-quality, unsulfured molasses or fresh honey will do the trick as well, but if you can get your hands on Steen's, buy several cans.

ingredients

"Basket Case" —Green Day

3 tablespoons salt
3 tablespoons dark brown sugar
1 tablespoon freshly ground black pepper
2 teaspoons red pepper flakes
1 (5-pound) slab pork belly
3 tablespoons pure olive oil
1½ cups thinly sliced yellow onions
2 tablespoons minced garlic
1 cup peeled, small-dice carrots
1 cup small-dice celery
2 tablespoons fresh thyme leaves
10 cups Ham Stock *(page 33)*
2½ cups Steen's cane syrup

SERVES 6

The night before you want to serve this dish, combine the salt, sugar, black pepper, and red pepper flakes in a small bowl. Trim the pork belly into a tidy rectangle and remove any surface fat that is obviously gratuitous. Rub the spice blend evenly into the pork belly. Cover with plastic wrap, place on a large baking sheet, and refrigerate overnight.

When ready to cook, prepare a hot charcoal fire. Unwrap the pork belly, pat it dry, and rub off any excess spice mix. Place the pork belly on the hot grill and cook briefly, just until both sides are well marked. If you do not want to grill the meat, you can still make this dish: Alternatively, coat the pork belly all over with a little olive oil and place it in a large braising pan over high heat. Sear the meat quickly, just until brown on both sides, and remove from the heat.

Preheat the oven to 325°F. In a large braising pan over medium heat, heat the olive oil until it shimmers. Sauté the onions and garlic until they begin to wilt. Stir in the carrots and celery and sauté again until they begin to soften. Blend in the thyme and heat through. Push the vegetables to one side and lay the pork belly in the pan with the vegetables. Add the stock and Steen's, cover with aluminum foil, and braise in the oven for 3 hours, or until very tender.

Remove the pan from the oven and let cool briefly. Carefully remove the belly from the pan and let rest at room temperature while you finish the sauce.

Strain the braising liquid into a medium saucepan, discard the vegetable solids, and bring to a simmer over medium heat. Lower the heat to maintain a simmer and skim off any fat that floats to the top. Once most of the fat has been removed, turn the heat back up, and reduce the sauce until it thickens. Season to taste with a touch more Steen's, or salt and pepper.

Cut the belly into equal portions and arrange on serving plates. Pour the thickened sauce over the top of each piece and serve.

SATSUMA AND CLOVE-BRAISED LAMB SHANKS

I have always been fond of the flavor of lamb. Good lamb is distinctly gamey for a farm-raised protein, and the flavor holds up through slow cooking even better than pork, beef, or duck. Because of its robust flavor, it pairs well with super-sweet south Louisiana Satsumas (a thin-skinned, seedless, sweet cousin of the tangerine) and a hint of clove. Once it begins cooking, it could not smell any more like Christmas. These go perfectly with Rosemary-Stewed Flageolet (use the White Bean recipe on page 163 and substitute flageolet beans, if you can get them; otherwise, just serve with the Stewed White Beans) and wilted spinach or kale.

ingredients

"Delta Lady" —Leon Russell

2 teaspoons salt

2 teaspoons freshly ground black pepper

¼ teaspoon ground cloves

1 tablespoon roughly chopped fresh rosemary

1 teaspoon garlic powder

1 teaspoon onion powder

6 whole lamb shanks *(10 to 12 ounces each)*

7 tablespoons pure olive oil

1 cup minced yellow onions

2 tablespoons minced garlic

⅓ cup peeled, small-dice carrots

⅓ cup small-dice celery

1½ cups tawny Port

10 Satsumas, zested, peeled, and segments separated

4 cups Veal Stock *(page 30)*

6 cups Dark Chicken Stock *(page 31)*

SERVES 6

Prepare a hot charcoal fire. Preheat the oven to 300°F. Blend together the salt, pepper, cloves, rosemary, and garlic and onion powders in a small bowl. Rub the shanks with 3 tablespoons of the oil, sprinkle them with the spice blend, and rub it in thoroughly.

Place the shanks on the charcoal grill and brown completely on all sides until well marked. Immediately remove from the heat and set aside.

In a large braising pan over high heat, warm the remaining 4 tablespoons oil and sauté with the onions and garlic until translucent. Stir in the carrots and celery and continue to cook for 6 to 8 minutes, or until they just begin to soften.

Add the shanks to the pan and deglaze the pan with the Port, stirring and scraping the bottom of the pan to loosen any caramelized vegetables sticking to the bottom. Add the Satsuma segments and both stocks and bring to a boil.

Cover the pan tightly with aluminum foil and place in the oven for 5 hours, or until the meat is tender and begins to fall off around the bone.

Remove the pan from the oven and gently transfer the shanks to warm serving plates. Strain the cooking liquid into a glass container and discard the vegetable solids. Place 2 cups of the cooking liquid in a small saucepan over medium heat to simmer briefly. Skim any fat from the top as the sauce simmers. Season to taste with salt and pepper and serve over the top of the shanks. Sprinkle lightly with Satsuma zest.

HERB AND GARLIC ROASTED POULET ROUGE

My dear friend Randy Yates, who was our first bar manager at City Grocery, confided in me years after we opened that the first night I cooked for him in my first apartment in Oxford, on a 1940s electric stove, and completely charred a store-bought chicken, almost made him quit before we opened, thinking I was a total clown.

My intention and what I lectured our staff on in those early days of the restaurant was that we were making simple but perfectly executed food from ingredients of unyielding quality. All we needed to do was gain the trust of our guests, and the curve of ambition would follow that seduction.

Chicken was the thing I went on about the most. "Anybody can look like a rock star with a lamb rack and some sweet shit. But if you can blow their socks off with chicken, *then* you've done something." I repeated it time and again. So when I pulled the blackened bird from my Flintstones oven, Randy's misgivings were completely understandable.

Fortunately, our technique fares much better with care, a reliable heat source, and significantly less red wine. For this recipe I use a poulet rouge, a French heritage breed chicken. (Ashley Farms in North Carolina does a wonderful job of raising these delicious birds.) You can use any 3- to 4-pound free-range chicken. I strongly recommend avoiding factory-farmed chickens, because of their disease, awful living conditions, and utterly anemic flavor profile. You can skip the brining step, if you must, but it definitely helps with the moisture content and final flavor of the meat. Timing and temperature control are critical in the process. This is a little tricky, and the odds are that you will botch this a time or two before you perfect the technique, but it is well worth the effort. Go on, be the real David Lee Roth of flightless yard birds. I'm about to tell you how.

"Do Whatcha Wanna" —Rebirth Brass Band

ingredients

The night before you want to serve this dish, submerge the birds in the poultry brine and refrigerate overnight. If you want to brine and cook the same day, keep the chickens in the brine for at least 3 hours.

When ready to cook, preheat the oven to 425°F. Remove the birds from the brine and pat dry. With you fingers, gently work the skin away from the breasts of the chickens, being careful not to tear the skin.

Mix the butter with 1 teaspoon of the salt, 2 teaspoons of the black pepper, the minced garlic, and the mixed fresh herbs until evenly combined. Set 3 tablespoons of the flavored butter aside. Divide the remaining butter and rub an equal amount under the skin of each of the chickens.

Toss the onion, celery, sliced garlic, thyme, the remaining 1½ teaspoons salt, and the remaining 2 teaspoons pepper with the olive oil in a bowl. Stuff each of the cavities of the chickens with the vegetable mixture. Rub the outside of the chickens with the reserved 3 tablespoons flavored butter and place the birds in a large baking dish.

Bake for 20 minutes, or until the skin begins to change color. Lower the heat to 375°F and continue to cook for 20 additional minutes. As soon as the thigh reaches an internal temperature of 160°F, briefly turn on the broiler function of the oven and watch closely until the chickens brown completely. This will take only a couple of minutes.

Transfer the chickens from the oven to a platter or cutting board and let rest for 5 minutes before carving. Pour the cooking juices into a small saucepan, and add any that gather around the resting chickens. Place the pan over medium heat and slowly whisk in the flour. Simmer gently until the gravy thickens. Taste before serving. If it seems a little salty for your liking, add a splash of chicken broth or water to dilute the salt. Simmer and thicken again. Serve over the roasted chicken.

2 (3- to 4-pound) whole chickens

4 quarts Poultry Brine *(page 200)*

¾ cup unsalted butter

2½ teaspoons salt

4 teaspoons freshly ground black pepper

2 teaspoons minced garlic

2 tablespoons minced mixed fresh herbs *(see Note)*

1 large yellow onion, quartered

2 celery stalks, chopped

6 cloves garlic, sliced

2 teaspoons fresh thyme leaves

3 tablespoons pure olive oil

2 tablespoons all-purpose flour

SERVES 4 TO 6

Note:

Use whatever herbs you have on hand. Thyme, rosemary, sage, parsley, and tarragon are among my favorites. Summer savory, basil, chervil, and chives are nice additions as well. The makeup of the blend is not as important as just having the bright flavors of fresh green herbs.

LARDONS

5 teaspoons lard *(see page 136)*
½ pound slab bacon, cut into ½-inch cubes

Warm the lard in a medium cast-iron skillet over medium heat and add the bacon cubes. Cook, stirring constantly, until the bacon crisps slightly. Transfer from the pan to a plate lined with paper towels to drain. Leave the bacon fat in the pan. You will use it to make the vinaigrette and cook the duck breast.

VINAIGRETTE

4 teaspoons reserved bacon fat, warmed until liquid
3 tablespoons extra-virgin olive oil
3 tablespoons red wine vinegar
1 tablespoon Dijon mustard
2 tablespoons minced shallots
¼ teaspoon salt
½ teaspoon freshly ground black pepper

Whisk together the bacon fat, olive oil, vinegar, mustard, shallots, salt, and pepper in a small bowl, and set aside.

SALAD

4 medium handfuls Scarlet Frills mustard greens
1 medium shallot, sliced into thin rings
1 tablespoon fresh thyme leaves
1 teaspoon salt
2 teaspoons freshly ground black pepper

Place the mustard greens, reserved lardons, shallot, thyme, salt, and pepper in a stainless-steel bowl and toss briefly.

PAN-ROASTED DUCK BREAST "FRISÉE" AUX LARDONS

This book is dreadfully devoid of salad offerings, not because I have anything against them but because there wasn't a natural place for them. I wasn't going to include a chapter on "tossing" and open myself to endless amounts of ridicule from friends and detractors. "Squirting" will bring all the derision I need. As a result, salads dot the landscape, but they have no country of their own here.

I remember my first *salade frisée aux lardons* on a driving trip around the French countryside in my twenties. On one of those completely carefree afternoons, we were bouncing from wine tasting to wine tasting, and the last thing anyone needed was a long and heavy meal to spoil the rhythm, so we dropped into a little mom-and-pop bistro on the side of the road. The *salade lardons* that arrived under my nose that day was stunning in its complexities, especially considering how simple a salad it is. The brightness of the vinegar played against the sweet saltiness of the bacon. The bitterness of the lettuce paired magnificently with the earthiness of the poached egg. It was as close to a perfect dish (particularly with some crusty bread to get every drop of the egg yolk) as you can get.

For ours I use a variety of mustard green called Scarlet Frills. It is not as bitter as frisée, but it has a wonderfully peppery bite. Lots of farmers' markets are carrying it these days. If you can't find it, frisée or even arugula will do. Actually, you can use almost any salad green, but without the odd structure and bitter quality of the ones I have listed, the salad doesn't stick the same landing.

"Clash of Cultures" —Bobby Charles

ingredients

To cook the duck breasts: Preheat the oven to 425°F. Sprinkle both sides of the duck breasts with the salt and pepper.

Heat the cast-iron skillet with the remaining bacon fat in it over medium heat. Place the breasts gently in the pan and brown on both sides. Decrease the heat to low and continue to turn, spooning hot fat over the breasts, until they brown lightly on both sides. Transfer the pan to the oven and cook for 6 to 8 minutes, until the breasts reach an internal temperature of 125°F. Remove from the oven and transfer the breasts to a cutting board to rest. Pour any excess fat into a heatproof container to save for a later use, and set the skillet aside.

Pour the vinaigrette into the skillet used to cook the duck and swirl for a moment until warm and liquid. Pour it over the greens and toss the salad thoroughly. Divide it among large serving plates. Slice the duck breasts into thin slices and lay a few slices neatly on top of each portion.

To poach the eggs: Bring a large saucepan with 4 quarts water and the white vinegar to a boil over medium heat. Decrease the heat to low and keep at a low simmer.

Place the lip of each ramekin as close to the surface of the simmering water as possible and quickly tip the eggs into the water. The eggs will separate naturally as they cook, but you can gently nudge them apart with a slotted spoon as the whites begin to cook, if it makes you feel better. After they cook through and become opaque, but before the yolks become solid, about 2½ minutes, use a slotted spoon to gently scoop the eggs out of the water. Drain briefly on paper towels, and place one on top of each salad. Sprinkle the eggs with salt, pepper, and the fresh parsley and serve.

DUCK BREASTS

2 (6- to 7-ounce) duck breasts, skin scored in a diamond pattern through the fat but not into the flesh

1 teaspoon salt

1½ teaspoons freshly ground black pepper

POACHED EGGS

6 tablespoons white vinegar

4 large eggs, each cracked gently into a ramekin

Salt and freshly ground black pepper

2 tablespoons chopped fresh flat-leaf parsley

SERVES 4

BOURBON-BRAISED PORK CHEEKS

Some folks are convinced that cheeks are just a cute name for some random cut, but the cheek is actually the cheek muscle. In beef, pork, and lamb, this bite is one of the most prized items to come from a braise. They literally fall apart once they are fully cooked because they are so tender. Anything more than the gentlest of simmers will cause them to turn into shredded nothingness.

Cheeks are not the easiest cuts of meat to find, but they are entirely worth the effort. I recommend finding a friendly butcher shop and getting cozy with the guys working there. They may look burly and act brusque, but most of these guys have a genuine interest in their work and love the challenge of sourcing or harvesting an unusual cut. You'll be one of the cool kids, asking for cheeks. I know . . . thank me later. If anyone ends up getting married as a result of this union, I get to perform the wedding service, okay? No bullshit—I am an ordained minister in the Universal Life Church and I work *very* cheap. These go nicely over Creamy Garlic-Parmesan Grits (recipe follows) and any kind of braised greens.

ingredients

"City of New Orleans" —Willie Nelson

12 pieces pork cheeks *(about 2 pounds total)*
1 tablespoon salt
4 teaspoons freshly ground black pepper
2 cups Seasoned Flour *(page xxvi)*
2 tablespoons bacon fat
2 tablespoons Garlic Olive Oil *(page xxvi)*
1 tablespoon minced garlic
¾ cup sliced yellow onions
½ cup peeled, small-dice carrots
1 cup chopped fresh tomatoes
1½ cups plus 2 tablespoons bourbon
2 sprigs fresh rosemary
1 teaspoon red pepper flakes
3 cups Veal Stock *(page 30)*
3 cups Ham Stock *(page 33)*
2 dried bay leaves
1 tablespoon dark brown sugar

SERVES 4

Preheat the oven to 325°F. Trim the pork cheeks of any obvious gristle, fat, and sinew. Sprinkle with the salt and pepper and dredge in the seasoned flour, knocking off any excess.

In a medium braising pan over medium heat, warm the bacon fat until it begins to shimmer. Gently place the cheeks in the pan, brown each side, and transfer to a plate.

Add the garlic oil to the pan and heat till it shimmers. Stir in the garlic, onions, carrots, and tomatoes and sauté until the carrots begin to soften. Return the cheeks to the pan and carefully pour in the 1½ cups bourbon. There is a very good chance that your bourbon will flame up now. Simply place a lid over the pan and the flames will extinguish immediately. Remove the lid and add the rosemary, red pepper flakes, both stocks, and bay leaves and bring back to a simmer.

Cover the pan and braise in the oven for 2 hours, or until the cheeks are tender. Spoon the cheeks out and keep warm while you finish the sauce. Strain the braising liquid into a small saucepan, discard the vegetable solids, place over medium heat, and bring to a simmer. Lower the heat to maintain a simmer and skim off any fat that floats to the top. Once all the fat has been removed, turn the heat back up and reduce the sauce until it begins to thicken. Whisk in the sugar and the remaining 2 tablespoons bourbon. Serve over the cheeks on top of the grits.

CREAMY GARLIC-PARMESAN GRITS

2 cups whole milk
2 cups Dark Chicken Stock *(page 31)*
4 teaspoons finely minced garlic
1 cup stone-ground grits *(see Note)*
6 tablespoons cold unsalted butter, cubed
3 tablespoons heavy cream
¾ cup freshly grated Parmesan cheese
1¼ teaspoons salt
1½ teaspoons freshly ground black pepper

SERVES 4

In a medium saucepan over medium heat, bring the milk, stock, and 2 teaspoons of the garlic to a simmer. As soon as the liquid begins to simmer, whisk in the grits. (Be careful, because if this gets to a boil unwatched, the milk will bubble up furiously and boil over, making a bad mess on your stovetop.) Decrease the heat to medium-low and whisk the grits for 7 to 9 minutes, until they are fully cooked. (When cooked, the grits should have a little firmness to them when bitten.)

Whisk in the cold butter, the remaining 2 teaspoons garlic, the cream, Parmesan, salt, and pepper and combine well. Serve immediately. If the grits end up sitting for a bit, they will thicken up. If this happens, add a touch of warm chicken stock and stir the grits, loosening them to a consistency that you like.

Note:
There are few things that I will tell you there are absolutely no substitutes for, but stone-ground grits is one of them. There is absolutely zero comparison between stone-ground and quick or instant grits. The gold standard of grits is Anson Mills. Glenn Roberts, owner of the company, is perhaps the most fascinating man in our industry. His knowledge of the history of food of the South Carolina Low Country and the provenance of hundreds of different species of edible plants and fruits is patently unparalleled. His product line at Anson Mills reflects perfectly his dedication to this understanding and his desire to preserve the integrity of foods otherwise relegated to memory and legend. That being said, any stone-ground product you can put your hands on will be a huge step up from other varieties.

TOMATO-BRAISED GROUPER

Fish is rarely ever braised because the traditional "braise" is usually reserved for tougher cuts of meat, to tenderize them and coax subtle flavors from their flesh and bone. Fish simply doesn't need this treatment—and if it does, it likely shouldn't be eaten. In this case, however, a whole fillet, braised quickly with a load of fresh green herbs, tomatoes, and lemon, produces an incredibly bright and tender result. The flavor of the grouper is still able to shine through.

This is particularly good for a dinner party because you can brown the fish in advance (an hour or so) and hold it until you are ready to finish the dish by popping it into the oven for 10 to 12 minutes.

ingredients

"eBay" —Weird Al Yankovic

5 tablespoons extra-virgin olive oil
2 tablespoons minced garlic
1 cup thinly sliced red onions
¾ cup small-dice fennel bulb
6 cups chopped fresh tomatoes
2 tablespoons chopped fresh basil
1 tablespoon chopped fresh tarragon
2 tablespoons chopped fresh flat-leaf parsley
1 tablespoon chopped fresh oregano
1 tablespoon chopped fresh rosemary
Finely grated zest and juice of 2 lemons
½ cup dry white wine
4 (5- to 7-ounce) grouper fillets
1½ teaspoons salt
2 teaspoons freshly ground black pepper
4 tablespoons cold unsalted butter, cubed

SERVES 4

Preheat the oven to 450°F. In a medium saucepan, heat 3 tablespoons of the oil over medium heat until the surface of the oil begins to shimmer. Sauté the garlic, onions, and fennel until the onions are translucent. Stir in the tomatoes, basil, tarragon, parsley, oregano, rosemary, lemon zest and juice, and white wine and combine well. Lower the heat to maintain a simmer, stirring constantly, for 12 to 15 minutes.

Sprinkle the grouper fillets with the salt and black pepper.

In a large, ovenproof sauté pan, heat the remaining 2 tablespoons oil over medium heat until it shimmers. Gently place the fish in the hot oil, allow it to brown nicely, and flip the pieces over. Cook for 2 minutes more, and then ladle the tomato mixture over the fish. Place the pan in the oven, uncovered, to cook for 5 minutes. Transfer the fish carefully to serving plates and return the pan to medium heat. Whisk in the cold butter, turn the heat off, and whisk until the butter is fully incorporated. Be careful that the butter just blends into the sauce but does not fully melt or it will separate. (The butter can be omitted, but it serves to keep the sauce a little tighter.) Spoon the sauce over the fish and serve immediately.

ROSEMARY AND ENGLISH PEA RISOTTO

2 tablespoons pure olive oil

2 tablespoons minced shallots

2 teaspoons minced garlic

1 cup fresh English peas

1 tablespoon chopped fresh rosemary

2½ cups Arborio rice

½ cup dry white wine

8 cups hot Dark Chicken Stock *(page 31)*, plus more if needed

1 teaspoon salt

2 teaspoons freshly ground black pepper

2 tablespoons cold unsalted butter, cubed

3 tablespoons freshly grated Parmesan cheese

SERVES 4

Warm the oil briefly in a medium saucepan over medium heat. Stir in the shallot and garlic and cook until they are transparent. Add the English peas and rosemary and warm through. Using a wooden spoon, stir in the rice and coat completely with the oil, stirring constantly. Stir in the white wine, lower the heat slightly, and stir until the wine is completely absorbed. Immediately add ½ cup of the stock, continuing to stir until it is absorbed. Then add another ½ cup stock, and continue in this way until all of the stock has been added and absorbed. Taste the rice to see if it is cooked all the way through. There should be only the tiniest resistance when you bite through a grain. If the rice is satisfactory, stir in the salt, black pepper, and butter and combine completely. Blend in the Parmesan and keep warm until ready to serve.

OSSO BUCO WITH ROSEMARY AND ENGLISH PEA RISOTTO

Seeing Sinatra in the early 1990s, as his career and life were coming to a close, was certainly nothing like I imagine it would have been seeing him at the Sands with Count Basie in the early 1960s. However, the experience of sitting in Piero's, just off the Strip in Las Vegas, swilling red wine and eating their famous osso buco with a pack of friends, doesn't seem to have changed over that same time. I'm absolutely certain that it was everything in 1994 that it was in 1964.

In the early '90s, Vegas was going the way of Disney World. Show girls gave way to circus clowns. Seedy became sterile, but Piero's was one of the few old-school holdouts. Once you crossed the threshold, you might as well have hurtled back 40 years. It is leathery, and the dark corners hold a certain gravity and possessed a density all their own. The smell of 50 years of cigar and cigarette smoke pervades everything yet never approaches offensiveness. The journey from the hostess stand to the table always feels like a gauntlet of wiseguy scrutiny, but once you reach your seat, you are definitely one of the gang.

Their osso buco was always exceptional and inspired me to duplicate it immediately. If those tender, red wine–braised shanks aren't good enough on their own, they are traditionally served with Parmesan risotto, simple but as rich and decadent as they come. The risotto version we do is studded with rosemary and English peas.

"I Can't Explain" —The Who

ingredients

Preheat the oven to 325°F. Sprinkle the veal pieces with salt and black pepper.

Heat the oil in a medium Dutch oven over medium heat until the surface begins to shimmer. Dredge the meat in the flour, knocking off any excess, and place in the Dutch oven. Lightly brown on both sides, then transfer to a plate.

Add the garlic, onions, carrots, and celery to the pot and sauté until the vegetables are tender and begin to brown slightly, 7 to 8 minutes. Return the shanks to the pot and stir in the red wine. Stir, scraping the bottom of the pan to loosen any of the bits clinging to the pan. Add the rosemary and stock and bring to a simmer. Place the lid on the Dutch oven and cook in the oven for 3 hours. The meat is done when it easily separates from the bone. Remove the pot from the oven.

When ready to serve, scoop some risotto into each warmed, rimmed serving plate. Gently transfer 1 piece of the veal from the pot to each plate.

Skim off any fat from the top of the remaining sauce and discard. Puree the remaining sauce and vegetable solids with an immersion blender (or you can do it in an upright blender) until smooth. Season to taste with salt and black pepper, and whisk in the cold butter cubes until smooth. Ladle the sauce equally over each shank.

4 (3- to 4-inch-thick) slices veal shank
Salt and freshly ground black pepper
6 tablespoons Garlic Olive Oil *(page xxvi)*
2 cups Seasoned Flour *(page xxvi)*
2 tablespoons minced garlic
¾ cup chopped yellow onions
½ cup peeled and chopped carrots
½ cup chopped celery
1 cup dry red wine
3 sprigs fresh rosemary
6 cups Veal Stock *(page 30)*
Rosemary and English Pea Risotto *(left)*
3 tablespoons cold unsalted butter, cubed

SERVES 4

ROASTED QUAIL STUFFED WITH TRUFFLE BREAD PUDDING

We started playing with savory bread puddings in the early 1990s. I wanted to create something that mimicked turkey dressing but was slightly more sophisticated with a sexier texture. A rosemary bread pudding was the first thing to come of this experiment, and it met with a remarkable response. We tweaked it a number of times before we finally arrived at the truffle, which sits at the corner of Decadence and Hedonism. I mean, when there is enough truffle hanging around that you are adding it to bread pudding, something is going either incredibly right or incredibly wrong. In our case, I like to think it was the former.

This is a great cool spring evening dish. Serve the quail with Spicy Summer Pea Soup (page 47) and drizzled with a touch of unsulfured molasses. Shiitake mushrooms make an excellent substitution for the truffles if they are unavailable.

 ingredients

"Heavy Metal Drummer" —Wilco

3 large eggs
1 cup half-and-half
½ cup peeled roasted garlic cloves
1½ teaspoons salt
4 cups day-old bread, torn into small pieces
1 tablespoon chopped fresh rosemary
1 tablespoon chopped fresh sage
¼ cup black truffle shavings
(fresh truffle shredded with a Microplane grater)
1 tablespoon truffle oil
2 tablespoons unsalted butter, melted
2 teaspoons freshly ground white pepper

SERVES 4

To make the bread pudding: In a stainless-steel bowl, whisk together the eggs and half-and-half until thoroughly combined.

Place the roasted garlic on a wooden cutting board and sprinkle lightly with a pinch of salt. Using the blade of a chef's knife, mash the roasted garlic into a smooth paste, working the blade back and forth over the garlic. Whisk this paste into the egg mixture.

Add the torn bread to the bowl and use your hands to blend the mix well. Stir in the rosemary, sage, truffle shavings, truffle oil, and butter and season with the 1½ teaspoons salt and the white pepper.

QUAIL

4 (2- to 3-ounce) whole semi-boneless quail
1½ teaspoons salt
2 teaspoons freshly ground black pepper
2 tablespoons extra-virgin olive oil

Preheat the oven to 450°F. Sprinkle the inside and outside of each quail evenly with the salt and pepper. Stuff the cavities of each quail with equal amounts of the bread pudding and secure the legs across the abdominal opening with butcher's string.

In a large, ovenproof sauté pan, heat the olive oil over medium heat until it begins to shimmer. Gently place the quail, breast side down, in the oil and brown for 2 to 2½ minutes. Turn over onto their backs, place the pan in the oven, and roast for 8 minutes. The internal temperature of the stuffing should register 120°F. Serve immediately.

PAN-ROASTED SOFT SHELLS WITH ROASTED TOMATO-VERMOUTH PAN BUTTER

I love soft-shell blue crab as much as any foodstuff on the entire planet. My sweet friend Alex Guarnaschelli cooks them every year at a lunch for Southerners attending the James Beard Awards. Hers are so good that I hold out having my first of the year until that Monday lunch. She never disappoints.

Early in my career at City Grocery, I got a call from a wonderfully nice gentleman named John Shoup, who had produced the Great Chefs series for PBS for years. He wanted to come to Oxford and feature the restaurant and three dishes that felt we could really stand by. This is one of the recipes I decided to do. It is an amazing dish that, no matter how hard you try, just looks terrible on the plate. We tried unsuccessfully for hours to give it a pretty presentation, but fortunately the flavors are incredible and made up for its lack of visual cooperation. After what seemed like an eternity, John finally piped up after tasting it and said, "Who gives a damn what it looks like? This is amazing! Plate it and shoot it!"

In the early summer, we are into local greenhouse tomatoes because we just have a hard time waiting for summer slicers. While hothouse tomatoes usually aren't a suitable slicing tomato, they work very nicely roasted, as their natural sugars concentrate and really blossom when treated this way. This is a very quick dish that will need to be assembled right before you serve it. Serve over a simple rice pilaf and prepare to be the hit of the dinner-party circuit.

"Low Rider" —War

ingredients

Preheat the oven to 275°F. On a baking sheet lined with parchment paper, place the tomatoes, cut side up, and sprinkle with the salt and pepper. Drizzle with the olive oil and distribute the garlic and thyme evenly over the top of each tomato half. Bake for 4 hours. Check regularly after the second hour, as you want these tomatoes to cook but not dry out. Remove from the oven and let cool. When they have cooled, chop roughly and reserve.

Increase the oven temperature to 450°F. In a large, ovenproof sauté pan, heat 2 tablespoons of the garlic oil over medium heat until it begins to shimmer. Dust the soft-shell crabs lightly in the seasoned flour, knocking off any excess. Gently place them in the hot oil and brown on both sides. Place the pan in the oven and roast for 6 minutes. Remove and carefully place on serving plates.

Add the remaining 1 tablespoon garlic oil to the pan over medium heat and sauté the red onions until transparent. Stir in the chopped roasted tomatoes and warm through. Add the vermouth and lemon zest and juice, combine well, and bring to a simmer. Whisk in the cold butter, immediately turn off the heat, and whisk until the butter is completely incorporated. Season to taste with salt and pepper. Spoon the sauce over the crabs and serve immediately.

4 whole large tomatoes, cored, halved, and deseeded

1 teaspoon salt

1 teaspoon freshly ground black pepper

4 teaspoons extra-virgin olive oil

4 cloves garlic, thinly sliced

2½ teaspoons fresh thyme leaves

3 tablespoons Garlic Olive Oil *(page xxvi)*

4 large fresh soft-shell crabs

1½ cups Seasoned Flour *(page xxvi)*

½ cup thinly sliced red onions

2 tablespoons dry vermouth

Finely grated zest and juice of 1 lemon

3 tablespoons cold unsalted butter, cubed

SERVES 4

RABBIT CACCIATORE

I spent some of my formative culinary years working in a "classical country Italian" restaurant helmed by a young Italian chef from Reggio Emilia, in the Emilia-Romagna region of northern Italy. I was first exposed to traditional cacciatore made from that region by my chef, Fernando. It was the exact kind of dish that resonated with every part of me. Fernando's cacciatore was usually made with chicken, and his sauce was lighter than most I had had before. It completely moved me. Years later, I was on a driving trip with my parents in Tuscany in early spring. Asparagus was just beginning to come into season, and it seemed like every little trattoria we stopped at had its own version of wild boar cacciatore. I couldn't get enough.

Oddly for the South, for years we didn't sell very much rabbit. Folks just didn't get after it like everything else we'd put in front of them. But every year at Easter just for laughs, we would put rabbit on the menu as a special, and the board would light up with orders for it. It was crazy, so much so that we started garnishing the plates with halved Brach's jelly beans, just to illustrate how twisted people were. They ate, thankfully, in spite of our vitriolic garnish. This dish was the result of one of those Easters and my wonderful Italian experiences.

Take the time to make some homemade fettuccine (use the pappardelle recipe on page 160, omitting the black pepper) to serve this over, and you will likely be as happy as you have ever been.

"Girl, You Have No Faith in Medicine" —The White Stripes

ingredients

- 8 (4- to 6-ounce) rabbit hindquarters
- 4 teaspoons salt
- 4 teaspoons freshly ground black pepper
- ¼ cup roughly chopped fresh oregano
- Garlic Olive Oil *(page xxvi)*
- 2 cups Seasoned Flour *(page xxvi)*
- 5 tablespoons pure olive oil
- 1 cup small-dice yellow onions
- ¾ cup small-dice green bell peppers
- 3 tablespoons thinly sliced garlic
- 4 cups sliced cremini mushrooms
- 2½ cups chopped fresh tomatoes *(substitute canned San Marzano plum tomatoes if tomatoes are not in season)*
- 2 tablespoons fresh thyme leaves
- 1 tablespoon chopped fresh rosemary
- 3 cups crushed tomatoes, with their juices
- 1½ cups Dark Chicken Stock *(page 31)*, plus more if needed
- ½ cup dry Marsala
- Freshly grated Parmesan cheese, for serving
- Roughly chopped fresh flat-leaf parsley, for serving

SERVES 8

Season the rabbit with salt and pepper, 3 tablespoons of the oregano, and some garlic oil. Lightly dust each quarter with the seasoned flour, shaking off any excess.

In a large braising or roasting pan or Dutch oven, heat the olive oil over medium heat until the surface begins to shimmer. Brown the rabbit legs, two or three at a time, and reserve. Add the onions, bell peppers, and garlic to the pan and sauté until they begin to sweat. Add the mushrooms and chopped fresh tomatoes and sauté for an additional 5 to 7 minutes. Stir in the remaining 1 tablespoon oregano, the thyme, and rosemary and combine well.

Return the rabbit legs to the pan, add the crushed tomatoes, stock, and Marsala, and bring to a low simmer. Lower the heat to maintain a simmer, covered, for 45 minutes. Remove the lid and check every 15 minutes or so; if the sauce appears to be drying out, add more stock, a cup at a time as needed. If you need to add additional stock, be careful: The rabbit gets very tender as it cooks and may fall apart if you stir too vigorously. Uncover, season with salt and pepper, and simmer for an additional 15 minutes, being very careful not to burn the tomatoes.

Serve immediately, garnished with a sprinkling of Parmesan and parsley.

ROASTED AND STUFFED SPECKLED TROUT

My dad is a total hard-ass when it comes to fishing. We call him "Fish Nazi." He's funnier than shit, but still *way* too serious when it comes to putting fish into the boat. We fish for speckled trout about an hour and a half south of New Orleans (we do it whenever I can find the time to sneak away; fortunately, you can literally fish year-round in south Louisiana). Adolph Currence knows, down to the precise minute, when we need to leave the house on any given day to be on the water in Bastian Bay the second the fish start biting. Negotiations the night before we leave over wake-up time are always a source of laughter. The conversation is invariably the same, with the same result.

Dad: Son, what time do you want to get up in the morning?

Me: What time do you want to leave?

Dad: 4:45.

Me: Why don't you shake me at 4:20, then?

Dad: Are you planning to have coffee before we leave?

Me: Of course.

Dad: Well, then I'll just get you up at 4.

Me: It doesn't take me 20 minutes to microwave a cup of coffee, Dad.

Dad: Well, we need to pull out at exactly 4:45. I'll just get you up at 4. Make sure you put your coffee in Styrofoam . . . and save the cup.

Me: Why do we even have this fucking conversation?

Dad: What do you want to have for lunch tomorrow?

Me: Why don't you just tell me what I am going to eat and let's just save the aggravation.

As entertaining as it is, it is rare when we don't come back with 60 to 70 pounds of trout. They are thin, sweet fillets that broil, pan-fry, or deep-fry very nicely. They need little more than lemon, salt, and pepper for any of these preparations to be astounding. For this dish, I use butterflied, skin-on whole fish. Crisped up, the skin is delicious, and the stuffing of lemon and fresh herbs adds a sweet and slightly tart finish to the dish. This needs nothing but a little green salad to ride alongside it.

ingredients

"New Year's Day" —U2

4 (10- to 12-ounce) whole, scaled, and butterflied speckled trout *(or substitute rainbow trout)*

1½ teaspoons salt

2 teaspoons freshly ground black pepper

1 lemon, thinly sliced, including the rind

12 sprigs fresh thyme

8 sprigs fresh flat-leaf parsley

4 sprigs fresh rosemary

4 sprigs fresh sage

12 fresh basil leaves, torn

1 tablespoon bacon fat

2 tablespoons Garlic Olive Oil *(page xxvi)*

SERVES 4

Preheat the oven to 425°F. Lay the trout open, flesh side up, on a cutting board. Sprinkle with the salt and pepper and distribute the lemon slices, thyme, parsley, rosemary, sage, and basil evenly among the 4 trout. Close the trout around the stuffing, and pat dry with paper towels.

In a large, nonstick, ovenproof sauté pan, heat the bacon fat and garlic oil over medium heat until the oil just begins to show wisps of smoke. Place the fish carefully in the pan and allow to fully brown. Flip over and immediately place the pan in the oven to roast for 6 minutes. Flip the fish back to the first side and roast for an additional 4 minutes. Serve immediately.

chapter 9
BRINING & SMOKING

NO-FAIL THANKSGIVING TURKEY — 200

SMOKED SCALLOP "CRUDO" — 203

SMOKED CHICKEN SALAD — 204

HICKORY-SMOKED SALMON CAKES WITH MARINATED LENTILS AND DILL AIOLI — 205

SMOKED CENTER-CUT PORK CHOPS WITH ROASTED CLOVE APPLESAUCE — 206

SMOKED WHOLE BEEF TENDERLOIN — 209

PECAN-SMOKED DUCK WITH MOLASSES LACQUER — 210

SMOKED BEETS WITH CHARRED PECANS AND BUTTERMILK–GOAT CHEESE CREMA — 211

SMOKED GLAZED BABY CARROTS — 212

SMOKED ENDIVE — 215

SMOKED MUSHROOM TAMALES — 216

Chapter 9

BRINING & SMOKING

BRINING & SMOKING

Most of you who spend every big holiday worrying over the bird are about two paragraphs and a few cupfuls of salt away from dazzling your family with the finest turkey they have ever eaten. Birds, you see, because of the whole flying thing, are remarkably lean and free of intramuscular fat (that is, with the obvious exception of farm-raised duck, which is fatty like an Ossabaw hog). It is precisely that fat content that gives pork, beef, and lamb their flavor and tenderness, and its absence is precisely why birds, in general, are very prone to drying out when cooked. Load that dry turkey sandwich with enough mayonnaise (fat and eggs) and, all of a sudden, you have deliciousness.

Well, brothers and sisters, I am here to help. Follow my instructions and you can become the maestro of the anemic holiday protein. What's more, apply those principles to chicken, duck, quail, squab, emu, or whatever and you will come out with a much superior product. It's as simple as placing the bird in a saltwater-based brine for 8 to 12 hours before you cook or smoke it. The brine can be flavored with almost anything you like; heck, we brine our fried chicken in salted Coca-Cola at Big Bad Breakfast and in buttermilk and hot sauce at City Grocery. Our turkey brine is flavored heavily with Worcestershire, and I love molasses with quail or guinea hen. I provide you with several basic brines, but encourage you to experiment and develop your own.

You may wonder why I have lumped brining and smoking together in the same chapter. That's because we also brine a lot of our proteins, other than birds, before we smoke them. Smoking is such a low and arid process that it can frequently lead to a dried-out finished product no matter how fatty. A little extra hydration can really make a difference with that.

Finally, I'll touch on some stovetop smoking techniques in this chapter. As difficult as it may seem, you can actually smoke small portions of different items in a stovetop setup without the threat of an apartment full of uninvited firemen. I do recommend a good hood system if you are going to try this, but if you don't mind a little smoky smell and can crack the windows, then go nuts. Smoking is simple, it's sexy, and it's fun. Again, this is a simple technique that will make you the envy of your friends. And let's face it—that is what it's all about.

NO-FAIL THANKSGIVING TURKEY

When I worked for the Brennans family in New Orleans at Mr. B's Bistro, they would distribute turkeys to the staff at the holidays. Chef Gerard Maras took this duty very seriously. Not content with giving out thoughtlessly roasted, half-assed turkeys, he took his turkey preparation the extra mile and actually smoked the turkeys for the staff before they were handed out. There were probably 80 to 90 employees at Mr. B's then, so there were a lot of turkeys to handle. One of the cooks' instructions was to prepare a simple saltwater bath to dunk the turkeys in overnight before we smoked them. The hot smoke on those birds produced some of the finest turkey I had ever had. My immediate thought was that if saltwater could produce that good a result, additional flavoring could only be better.

The first Thanksgiving after opening City Grocery, we decided to make a holiday meal for the needy. It put my theory to work, and we cooked about 20 of the most delicious turkeys I had ever dreamed of. It turns out there weren't as many needy folks in Oxford as we had thought, so there was lots of leftover bird, and not a bite of it went uneaten. This is how I cook turkey to this day. Although I will add a little injection solution (see Note) with some extra butter and garlic, which does *exactly* what you think it does . . . *boom*, right in the mouth.

ingredients

"More Than I Can Do" —Steve Earle

POULTRY BRINE

10 quarts very warm water

3½ cups salt

4 cups Worcestershire Sauce *(page 97)* **or store bought**

20 fresh sprigs thyme

10 dried bay leaves

½ cup chopped fresh sage

1 cup Crystal Hot Sauce

½ cup black peppercorns, toasted and roughly crushed

TURKEY

1 (12- to 14-pound) turkey
(if you can buy free-range, they are excellent)

Extra-virgin olive oil, for rubbing the turkey

Salt and freshly ground black pepper

Super-Bonus Gravy *(recipe follows)*

SERVES 8
(PLUS LEFTOVERS FOR SANDWICHES FOR DURING THE FOOTBALL GAME)

To make the brine: In a 5-gallon, food-grade bucket, combine the warm water and salt. Stir until it has completely dissolved. Stir in the Worcestershire, thyme, bay leaves, sage, hot sauce, and peppercorns and combine well.

Remove the giblets from the turkey and reserve. Rinse the bird inside and out. Place it in the brine, making sure it is submerged. If needed, add more water until it is completely covered. You may need to weight the turkey down with a plate. Cover and refrigerate overnight.

Preheat the oven to 350°F. Remove the turkey from the brine and pat dry with paper towels. Place the bird in a large roasting dish and spread the giblets around it to roast for your gravy. If you choose to inject the turkey (see Note), this is the ideal time to do it. (I use equal parts olive oil and melted butter with a little hot sauce and black pepper.) Rub the outside of the turkey with the oil and sprinkle generously with salt and pepper. Cover the turkey with aluminum foil and place the pan in the oven.

Roast the turkey for 2½ hours. Remove the foil and sink a meat thermometer into the thickest part of the breast and then the leg. The internal temperature should read about 165°F. Return the turkey to the oven, uncovered, to brown for an additional 20 minutes. With a sturdy pastry brush, baste the bird with its own juices every 5 minutes until golden brown. Make the gravy with the pan drippings and serve immediately.

Note:
Among the many gifts of culinary ingenuity that south Louisiana Cajuns have gifted the rest of the world is the turkey marinade injector. This came along with the early 1980s movement of frying turkeys. The injection gives the turkey an extra blast of flavor and moisture. Kits with a typically fat-heavy, spicy liquid for this are widely available at most grocery stores and include a pint jar of marinade and a large hypodermic syringe. Fill the syringe with liquid and inject it throughout the muscles of the turkey before cooking, and you simply get a better bird. These days, I usually make my own injection. Olive oil, Tabasco, Pickapeppa sauce, molasses, and butter are all regular ingredients in my improvised marinades.

SUPER-BONUS GRAVY

4 tablespoons unsalted butter, melted
¼ cup turkey fat, from the top of
the turkey drippings
½ cup all-purpose flour
Remaining turkey drippings
3 cups Dark Chicken Stock *(page 31)*
½ cup dry sherry
¼ teaspoon Accent
1 teaspoon Kitchen Bouquet
Roasted giblets from the turkey pan, chopped

MAKES ABOUT 5 CUPS

In a small saucepan over medium heat, whisk together the butter, turkey fat, and flour until well combined and the roux begins to bubble. Whisk in the remaining drippings from the roasting pan, the stock, sherry, Accent, and Kitchen Bouquet and blend together well. Add the giblets, decrease the heat to low, and let simmer, stirring constantly, until thickened.

Serve over the aforementioned turkey, if you can get it to the table without drinking it . . . or maybe that is just my problem.

CARVING A TURKEY

Carving the turkey gets way more of a bad rap than it deserves. Cutting up a bird is neither hard to understand nor hard to execute. I think it suffers a dark reputation due to the fact that most folks only face the chore once or twice a year. Given the understanding of a couple of basic things, carving up a bird could not, actually, be a much simpler task. The nice thing about this lesson is that, once you understand these basic tenets, you will be able to carve everything from squab and grouse to turkey and emu, as their basic skeletal structure is the same. So here are the two basic things you need to know: 1) you always want to cut major muscle groups away from the bird, off the bone, working on a level board to cut; and 2) all birds have a vertical breastbone that separates the two breast halves and provides a guide for their easy and efficient removal.

So let's imagine you have removed the bird from the oven. It's on your great-grandmother's Wedgwood serving platter and everyone has had a chance to admire your handiwork. Set a small cutting board next to the turkey and proceed like this:

+ Remove the bird to the cutting board.

+ Orient the turkey so the "butt end" is facing you. Grasp the thigh quarter on whichever side you are most comfortable with and slowly pull it down toward the table. Pierce the skin in the area between the thigh and the body and make small slices to help pull the thigh away from the bird until the joint attaching the thigh to the carcass is exposed. Gently slice through this joint, cut the skin along the back of the bird, and transfer the thigh to the cutting board.

+ Using your finger, locate the thin flexible bone down the center of the breast and run the knife along it on the same side as the thigh you just removed. Place the tongs in the incision and gently pull the breast away from the carcass, slicing slowly at the underside of the breast, tracing the tip of the knife along the rib cage around the side of the bird. Follow the cut up around the neck portion of the bird and separate the breast from the carcass, so all that remains is the joint connection between the wing and the carcass. Gently slice through this joint and transfer the breast to the cutting board.

+ Repeat with the thigh and breast on the opposite side.

+ Separate the legs and thighs at the knuckle that joins them. Slice the meat away from the bone in chunks.

+ Remove the wings from the upper portion of the breasts and slice the breasts into medallions across the grain of the meat, which runs head to toe.

+ The real prize on the bird, however, still remains on the carcass. Flip the bird on its side, and where the thighbone connects to the carcass, along the back will be a large thumb-size piece of dark meat tucked away in its own little compartment. This is called the "oyster." There is one on the opposite side as well, and these are the two most delicious bites of your bird.

+ All that's left to do is to throw the carcass in a pot with some vegetables and make turkey gumbo.

+ Feel free to thank me later for making you look like a stud. Make checks payable to the "Buy John Currence's Daughter a Pony Fund."

SMOKED SCALLOP "CRUDO"

I have thought that April Bloomfield is an absolute genius from the very first meal I had at the Spotted Pig, but she rocketed past my ability to describe her talents when I ate at the original John Dory in the Meatpacking District in the spring of 2009. She coaxed sublime flavors from fish with the help of little more than salt, butter, olive oil, and citrus, which I found remarkable.

I hit on this dish after a remarkable meal with Traci Des Jardins, Mary Sue Milliken, April, and Gabrielle Hamilton at the new Dory after the James Beard Awards in 2011. I had a remarkable scallop *crudo* at that dinner and immediately thought about adding a hint of smoke to it. Bacon and scallops are lovely together, but bacon chunks would be too heavy for a crudo, so the idea of a quick stovetop smoke came to mind. The result is outstanding and a great first course with a really crisp white wine.

"Gathering Flowers for the Master's Bouquet" —Stanley Brothers

ingredients

Remove the side muscle from each of the scallops and coat with the pure olive oil. Sprinkle evenly with ½ teaspoon of the salt and the white pepper. Set aside.

Prepare a stovetop smoker with the soaked wood chips and place it over high heat for 2 to 3 minutes, until the chips begin smoking heavily. Place the scallops on the perforated rack in the smoker, close the lid, and immediately turn off the heat. Allow the scallops to smoke for about 3 minutes. Remove them from the smoker and refrigerate immediately.

When ready to serve, slice each scallop horizontally into 3 medallions and arrange them on serving plates. Drizzle with the extra-virgin olive oil, lemon juice, and lemon zest. Sprinkle with the black pepper, fennel pollen, and the remaining ½ teaspoon salt. Garnish with the serrano pepper, celery leaves, and chives.

Notes:

Camerons are extremely simple to use and they are a simple to clean stovetop smoker. In a time when absolutely everything seems to be over-thought and over-built, the Camerons smoker is a refreshing breath of minimalism. It is little more than a lightweight stainless-steel box with a tight-fitting lid and raised screen for placing your meat over wood chips, which merely sit on the bottom of the smoker and are heated by the stove heat source. It is magnificently simple. Cameronsproducts.com offers a number of smokers and accessories, including a number of different wood chips. Play with the different smokes and see which you like the smell and flavor of best. We use primarily oak, pecan, hickory, and cherry because those are the most common hardwoods available to us. They all lend a sweet, smoky flavor, but oak smells the strongest and it also burns the hottest.

Fennel pollen is available at specialty food stores and widely online. It is the actual pollen from the flower of the fennel plant. It is slightly sweet and definitely carries a note of licorice. It is a nice addition to salads and to finished fish dishes, and it's particularly good with raw oysters. It is, admittedly, an extravagant flourish, but one that sets dishes apart when employed.

8 large diver scallops
(little bay scallops will not work for this dish)

2 tablespoons pure olive oil

1 teaspoon salt

1 teaspoon finely ground white pepper

¾ cup soaked wood chips *(see Notes)*

3 tablespoons extra-virgin olive oil

2 teaspoons freshly squeezed lemon juice

Finely grated zest of 1 lemon

1 teaspoon freshly ground black pepper

¼ teaspoon fennel pollen *(see Notes)*

1 serrano pepper, deseeded and thinly sliced

2 teaspoons roughly chopped celery leaves

1½ teaspoons thinly sliced fresh chives

SERVES 4

SMOKED CHICKEN SALAD

One of my favorite childhood memories was going downtown to Canal Street in New Orleans with my grandmother Lucy when she wanted to go shopping. I don't remember anything about the shopping itself, but I knew it meant that we got to get dressed up like we were going to church and to ride the streetcar all the way down St. Charles Avenue, through the oaks and past the matronly architectural masterpieces that dot that trail. Those trips ultimately included a stop at one of the downtown lunch counters. Those counters, catalysts for the advancement of civil rights in the early 1960s, were always bustling and charged with energy. It amazed me, even then, to see the throngs of people who would wait for the simplest white bread sandwiches, egg plates, griddled skinny burgers, and milk shakes. More often than not, I settled on a chicken salad sandwich. The construction of toasted white bread; cooked chicken with mayonnaise, celery, and basic seasoning; and a crispy leaf of iceberg lettuce was a monument to minimalism. And as much as anything else, I loved watching my grandmother, very deliberately, take off her gloves to eat when it arrived.

In this version, the traditional recipe is dressed up a little by smoking the chicken lightly. And in a nod toward the Southern tradition of adding something sweet, I use muscadine grapes when they are in season. There really is little more Southern than muscadines, and they add a unique flavor to the finished product.

ingredients

"Born with a Tail" —The Supersuckers

BRINING AND SMOKING

1 (3- to 4-pound) whole frying chicken
6 quarts Poultry Brine *(page 200)*
1¼ cups soaked wood chips *(see Note, page 203)*

SALAD

½ cup plus 2 tablespoons Homemade "Duke's" Mayonnaise *(page 93)*
2 tablespoons Grainy Mustard *(page 94)*
2 teaspoons fresh thyme leaves
2 teaspoons chopped fresh rosemary
1 tablespoon chopped fresh flat-leaf parsley
½ cup chopped roasted peanuts
2 tablespoons minced shallots
¼ cup minced celery and celery leaves
2 teaspoons salt
2 teaspoons freshly ground black pepper
1½ cups quartered, seeded muscadine grapes *(see Notes)*

MAKES ENOUGH FOR 8 TO 10 SANDWICHES

To brine the chicken: Submerge the chicken in the cooled brine and let sit for at least 2½ hours, or overnight in the refrigerator if possible.

To smoke the chicken: Remove the chicken from the brine and let drain. Using a large kitchen knife, split the chicken down the breast and cut through the backbone, so that it will lay flat in the stovetop smoker. (If you are using a larger outdoor smoker, you can alternatively leave the chicken whole.) Prepare the smoker with the soaked wood chips and place on the stove over high heat. As soon as the chips begin to smoke, place the chicken on the rack and close the smoker tightly. Lower the heat to medium and cook the chicken to an internal temperature of 160°F, about 35 minutes.

Remove the chicken from the smoker, cool, and dice into ½-inch cubes. You should have 5 to 6 cups of diced chicken meat. Set aside, covered and refrigerated, until you are ready to make the salad.

To make the salad: Combine the mayonnaise, mustard, thyme, rosemary, parsley, peanuts, shallots, celery and celery leaves, salt, and pepper in a large bowl and blend together well. Stir in the chicken and grapes and toss to fully coat. Cover and refrigerate for 2 hours before serving.

Notes:
There is a reason you so frequently see chicken salad served on toasted white bread or in a lettuce cup. That is because good chicken salad is so flavorful that it needs little more than that. As much as I love this chicken salad on plain white toast, I will freely admit that it is even more exceptional on a croissant.

Muscadine or scuppernong grapes are quintessentially Southern. Though rarely seen highlighted on menus, they certainly have a place in new Southern cooking. Muscadines have a unique flavor that I can only compare to what I smell in marigolds. It is a very "green" flavor, off-putting to some. When ripe, muscadines can be cloyingly sweet, but they make a nice accent to lightly cooked sauces and a bright sweet bite as an addition to chicken salad.

HICKORY-SMOKED SALMON CAKES WITH MARINATED LENTILS AND DILL AIOLI

Knowing I am about to invite a pile of e-mails and death threats from every salmon-fishing advocacy group on the planet, I am going to say it anyway. I really don't like salmon most of the time. It is, more often than not, a nasty, anemic, farm-raised, smelly mess. That being said, I have had both farm-raised and wild salmon that were absolutely crushing, they were so good. Problem is: 1) there's lots of shitty salmon out there; and 2) most chefs take for granted that it is a fatty fish and easy to cook. And for that reason, they frequently screw it up. Handled well and respectfully selected, it can be more than formidable. In this dish, we barely finish the pieces in hot smoke to the point where the flake is still moist and then form them into cakes that we pan-fry and serve on top of a light salad and some marinated lentils. It's a great lunch or brunch item.

"Androgynous" —The Replacements

ingredients

Brush the salmon with the oil and sprinkle with the salt and pepper. Prepare a stovetop smoker with the soaked wood chips and place it on the stove over high heat. As soon as the chips begin to smoke, place the salmon on the rack in the smoker and close the lid tightly. Lower the heat to medium and smoke for 7 minutes. Remove the lid and check the center for doneness. The flesh should have just turned milky in the center. Remove the fish from the smoker and let cool.

Place the egg, cream, mustard, mayonnaise, shallots, jalapeño, celery, lemon zest, and thyme in a medium bowl and blend together well. Flake the cooled salmon into the egg mixture. Mix to combine well, but try not to break up the salmon flakes any more than necessary.

Form into 4 equal-size cakes (or 8 if you prefer to serve 2 smaller cakes). Dredge in the seasoned flour, shake off any excess, dip in the egg wash, and then roll in the bread crumbs until evenly coated. Cook immediately, or cover and refrigerate for up to 2 days.

Heat the clarified butter in a medium skillet over medium heat until it begins to shimmer. Carefully place the cakes in the hot pan. Brown them on one side, flip them over, and brown on the second side.

Make a bed of the greens and marinated lentils on each plate. Arrange the salmon cakes on top and add a small dollop of the dill aioli.

2 (6-ounce) salmon fillets *(try to get them the same shape and size so they smoke evenly)*

2 teaspoons pure olive oil

1 teaspoon salt

1 teaspoon freshly ground black pepper

¾ cup soaked hickory chips *(see Note, page 203)*

1 large egg

2 tablespoons heavy cream

5 teaspoons Grainy Mustard *(page 94)*

1 tablespoon Homemade "Duke's" Mayonnaise *(page 93)*

1 tablespoon minced shallots

2 teaspoons deseeded and minced jalapeño pepper

1 tablespoon minced celery

Finely grated zest of 1 lemon

2 teaspoons fresh thyme leaves

3 cups Seasoned Flour *(page xxvi)*

3 cups Egg Wash *(page xxvii)*

1½ cups panko bread crumbs

4 tablespoons clarified unsalted butter *(see page xxiii)*

4 handfuls mixed baby greens

Marinated Lentils *(recipe follows)*

Dill Aioli *(recipe follows)*

SERVES 4

MARINATED LENTILS

1½ cups green lentils
2 teaspoons finely minced garlic
4 tablespoons small yellow onions
2 tablespoons finely diced carrots
1 fresh bay leaf
6 thyme sprigs
1 teaspoon salt
1½ teaspoons ground black pepper
2½ cups Dark Chicken Stock
3 tablespoons Fresh Herb Vinaigrette *(page xxvii)*
2 tablespoons minced shallots
2 tablespoons chopped fresh flat-leaf parsley
2 teaspoons minced capers

Combine the lentils, garlic, onions, carrots, bay leaf, thyme, salt, pepper, and chicken stock in a small saucepan and bring to a boil over medium heat. Decrease the heat to low and simmer until tender. Add a touch of stock if needed. Drain the lentils and chill in the refrigerator. Blend the lentils, vinaigrette, shallots, parsley, and capers together in a medium bowl. Cover and refrigerate until needed.

DILL AIOLI

½ cup Homemade "Duke's" Mayonnaise *(page 93)*
1½ teaspoons minced garlic
2 teaspoons chopped fresh dill
Finely grated zest and juice of 1 lemon
¼ teaspoon salt
¾ teaspoon freshly ground black pepper

Blend together the mayonnaise, garlic, dill, lemon zest and juice, salt, and pepper in a small bowl. Cover and set aside in the refrigerator to rest for 1 hour.

SMOKED CENTER-CUT PORK CHOPS WITH ROASTED CLOVE APPLESAUCE

Though I admit that a good piece of smoked brisket is exceptional, there is no equivocation in my mind about why God put pigs on this planet. They are simply the perfect animal for barbecue. Shoulders, hams, ribs, belly, you name it—it is easily smoked and turned into something killer. Sorry, all you good folks out there flailing your arms about beef ribs, brisket, and whatnot, the pig wins hands down. You goofballs in western Kentucky trying to sell people on old-ass barbecue mutton, well, I can only assume you know how fruitless arguing superiority would be.

As good as pork smoked to confit texture is, a light smoking and an oven finish on a more naturally tender cut like the loin or tenderloin is subtle beauty. Cooked to a mid-rare to medium temperature (see the very important Note), these cuts are exceptionally tender and flavorful. A light smoke adds fruity notes to the finished product while allowing the true flavor of the meat to shine through.

Apples pair naturally with pork, and fall sweet apples work exceptionally well for this dish. The Lardo-Sautéed Green Beans go very well with the chops, too.

ingredients

"More Today Than Yesterday" —Spiral Staircase

BRINING AND SMOKING

4 cups very warm water

3 tablespoons salt

1 cup Crystal Hot Sauce

3 tablespoons unsulfured molasses

3 tablespoons Worcestershire Sauce *(page 97)* or store bought

2 tablespoons soy sauce

1 tablespoon crushed black peppercorns

2 teaspoons red pepper flakes

Leaves from 3 sprigs fresh rosemary

4 (10- to 12-ounce) double-cut pork chops

FINISHING AND SERVING

1½ cups soaked wood chips *(see Note)*

2 tablespoons Garlic Olive Oil *(page xxvi)*

2 teaspoons bacon fat

2 teaspoons salt

2 teaspoons freshly ground black pepper

Roasted Clove Applesauce and/or Lardo-Sautéed Green Beans *(recipes follow)*

SERVES 4

To brine the chops: Combine the water and salt in a large bowl and stir until the salt has dissolved. Stir in the hot sauce, molasses, Worcestershire, soy sauce, peppercorns, red pepper flakes, and rosemary. Add the chops and submerge them in the brine. Cover and refrigerate for at least 2 hours, or overnight if possible.

To smoke the chops: Prepare a stovetop smoker with the soaked wood chips and place it over medium heat until the smoke begins to rise from the chips. Place the pork chops on the rack, close the smoker, and decrease the heat to medium-low. You want to apply a little heat, but you do not want an extremely hot smoking chamber. Smoke the chops for 7 minutes, and remove them from the smoker.

To finish cooking the pork chops: Preheat the oven to 400°F. Heat the garlic oil and bacon fat in a large ovenproof skillet until the surface begins to shimmer. Sprinkle the chops with the salt and pepper and carefully place them in the hot pan. Brown them for 2 minutes on each side and place the pan in the oven for 4 minutes, or until the chops reach an internal temperature of 135° to 140°F. Serve immediately with the roasted applesauce.

Very Important Note:

You can *absolutely* eat rare or medium-rare pork without a threat to your health. The threat of eating undercooked pork comes from a variety of roundworm causing an abdominal condition known as trichinosis. Trichinosis in pigs has historically been caused by pigs being fed meat or carcasses of uncooked meat. Trichinosis is more frequently prevalent in wild game than in other animals, and a majority of the dozen or so cases reported each year are attributed to undercooked game, particularly bear (who frequently kill and eat other animals).

Note:

Soaking wood chips slows their burn and makes them last longer, ostensibly. In reality this is really only slightly true, but I do it anyway. My feeling is that every bit of flavor helps in the final product. I like soaking wood chips in different liquids because when the liquid does cook off, it will impart flavor to whatever you are smoking. I use wine, beer, whiskey, and, sometimes, soda for soaking chips. Using straight water will add a tiny bit of humidity to your smoking chamber, but it only slightly prolongs the burn of the chips.

ROASTED CLOVE APPLESAUCE

4 Red Delicious apples, peeled and cored

2 tablespoons unsalted butter, melted

8 whole cloves

2 tablespoons granulated sugar

½ cup bourbon

2 tablespoons apple cider vinegar

2 tablespoons dark brown sugar

1 tablespoon chopped fresh rosemary

1 tablespoon freshly squeezed lemon juice

1 small pinch of ground cloves

SERVES 4

Preheat the oven to 350°F and butter a glass baking dish. Brush the apples all over with the butter and stick each with 2 cloves, each on opposite sides of the apple. Place the apples in the baking dish and sprinkle the granulated sugar over them. Place in the oven and roast for 20 minutes.

Remove the apples from the oven and discard the cloves. Chop the apples roughly and place in a medium saucepan with the bourbon, vinegar, brown sugar, rosemary, lemon juice, and ground cloves. Place the pan over medium heat and bring to a simmer. Decrease the heat to low and cook for 15 minutes, or until the apples are completely soft, stirring occasionally to prevent scorching. Add a couple of tablespoons of water, as needed, if the sauce begins to dry out.

Scrape the apples into a blender and puree briefly. Serve warm or at room temperature.

LARDO-SAUTÉED GREEN BEANS

¼ cup plus 1 teaspoon salt

1 pound green beans, ends snapped off and strings removed

3 tablespoons small-dice lardo (see Note)

1 tablespoon pure olive oil

2 tablespoons finely minced shallots

1½ teaspoons freshly ground black pepper

In a medium saucepan, combine 3 quarts water and ¼ cup of the salt and bring to a boil over medium heat. Prepare an ice bath. Add the green beans to the boiling water and simmer for 2 minutes after the water returns to a boil. Immediately remove and plunge the beans into the ice bath to stop the cooking process. Drain the beans.

In a medium sauté pan over medium heat, warm the *lardo* with the olive oil. Brown lightly, 3 to 4 minutes. Stir in the shallots and warm very briefly. Increase the heat to medium-high and add the green beans. Toss or stir the green beans in the pan until they begin to warm and sprinkle with the remaining 1 teaspoon salt and the black pepper. Toss again and serve immediately.

Note:

Lardo is one of the most sublimely delicious flavors there is. It is a total surprise the first time you taste it. It doesn't scream delicious on paper. *Lardo* is cured hog back fat that is hung and aged for several months before slicing and eating. It is one of my very favorite flavoring fats. I consider it the "cake icing" of pork fat. Use it sparingly, because its flavor is very forward and can easily overwhelm other items in its company. It is wonderful in this application, and I also like to render the fat from it for vinaigrettes. It will be a little tough to source (it's available, usually, at good Italian butcher shops or online, but is well worth the effort.

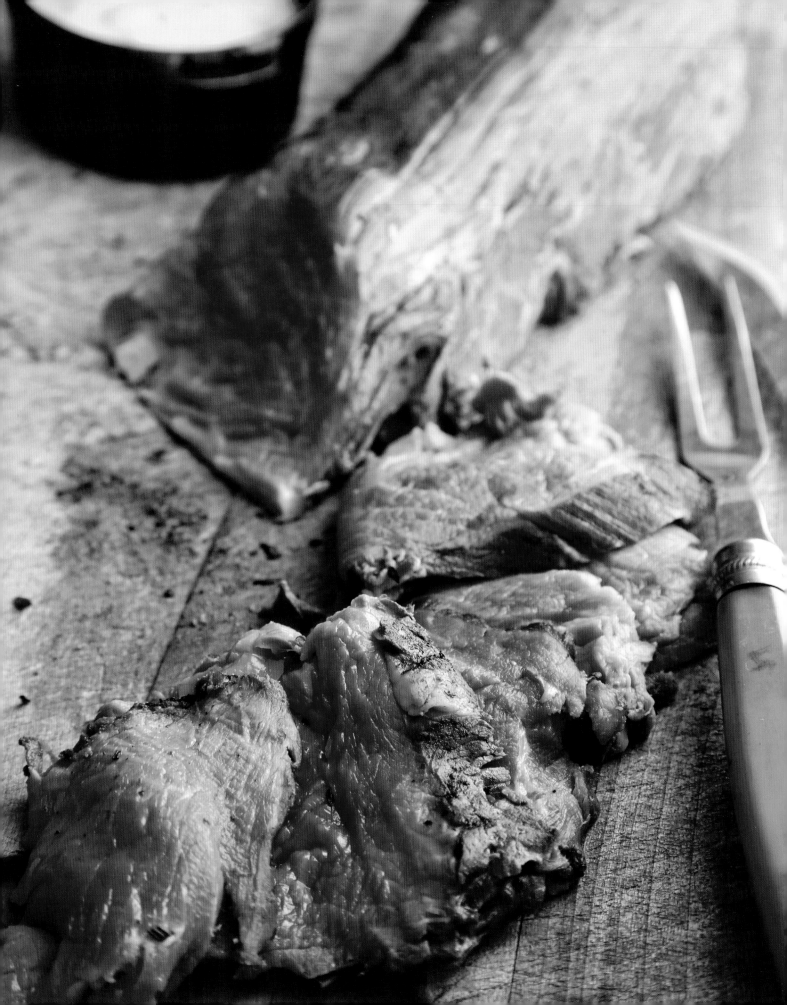

SMOKED WHOLE BEEF TENDERLOIN

There are few people in this world I enjoy cooking for at home more than my buddy Wright Thompson. Wright is larger than life and writes about people in a way that makes them all part of his bigger-than-life scale. I have known few people in my years who ever come close to equaling the joy that Wright takes in eating and drinking and being with others who do the same. The man is so happy at times that he comes apart at the seams. As a result, Wright invariably turns into an eight-year-old boy every time a giant portion of something edible crosses his peripheral plane. I have seen him nearly faint at the site of a 7-pound lobster in Maine, grin uncontrollably at giant bowls of pasta, and quiver at the sight of a steaming pizza pie. I swear he almost wet himself one night when we constructed this torpedo-size, bacon-wrapped, boiled-egg-and-cheese-stuffed pork thing at my house for a Super Bowl party. Really, I saw a drop of blood roll gently from the outside corner of his left eye the emotion wanted out so badly.

I decided I wanted to cook something for him after his return from a lengthy trip to Ghana to investigate the murder of an Olympic long-distance runner. During the trip, he had kept me abreast of his sojourns into the countryside for days at a time, where there simply wasn't any food at times for him to eat. Not that the food was weird or inedible—there was at times just nothing for him to eat for daylong stretches. It was a cold awakening for my beast of a friend. He talked about wanting a steak throughout the entire trip, so there was little doubt about what I needed to do for him.

Little evokes the response of a dinner-party crowd like a whole beef tenderloin, so that was what we cooked for my hungry buddy. I am not sure I have ever seen anyone quite so happy as Wright was when this came off the smoke.

"Uninspired" —The Connells

ingredients

To make the brine: Combine the water and salt in a large bowl and blend until the salt has completely dissolved. Stir in the Worcestershire, soy sauce, molasses, pepper, bay leaves, thyme, garlic, shallots, cardamom, and cinnamon.

To brine and smoke the beef: Preheat the oven to 450°F. Submerge the tenderloin in the brine, cover, and let sit for at least 2 hours, or overnight in the refrigerator if possible.

Prepare a large stovetop smoker with the soaked wood chips and place it over medium heat. Remove the tenderloin from the brine and pat dry. Place the tenderloin on the rack in the smoker. As soon as the chips begin to smoke heavily, close the top tightly and let smoke for 10 minutes.

In a large ovenproof skillet over medium heat, warm the oil until the surface begins to shimmer. Remove the tenderloin from the smoker and place it carefully in the hot pan. Brown it briefly on all sides and place in the oven for about 10 minutes. Check the temperature at the thickest point and remove from the oven as soon as it reaches 125°F (residual heat will continue cooking the tenderloin). Slice and serve with a simple green salad and Sweet Corn Pudding (page 224).

BEEF/PORK BRINE

12 cups very warm water

½ cup salt

1½ cups Worcestershire Sauce *(page 97)* or store bought

¾ cup soy sauce

¼ cup unsulfured molasses

3 tablespoons freshly ground black pepper

3 dried bay leaves

12 sprigs fresh thyme

12 cloves garlic, very thinly sliced

3 medium shallots, very thinly sliced

1 tablespoon crushed cardamom pods

½ teaspoon ground cinnamon

BRINING AND SMOKING

1 (5- to 6-pound) whole beef tenderloin, cleaned of all sinew and fat and the ends trimmed so that the tenderloin is relatively even in thickness

3 quarts Beef Brine *(see above)*

2 cups soaked wood chips *(see Note, page 203)*

2 tablespoons pure olive oil

SERVES 8 TO 10,
OR 2 MEDIUM WRIGHT THOMPSONS

PECAN-SMOKED DUCK WITH
MOLASSES LACQUER

The heavy fat of farm-raised duck cries out for vinegar, but the flavor profile almost demands something sweet. It is an easy go-to for chefs because people love the combination of sweet and salty. Farm-raised duck is a "safe" game choice for folks because there is absolutely nothing gamey about its flavor, and it cooks up extremely tender.

In the theme of using other people's garbage to make delicious food, in the fall, when the pecans begin to fall from the trees, they are gathered by the bagful and carried to the local feed stores and co-ops to be cracked. This leaves piles of pecan shells, dried and full of flavor. They are an excellent smoking fuel and a great recycled material to feel good about using, hippie.

ingredients

"Pulling Mussels (From the Shell)" —Squeeze

FOWL BRINE AND DUCK

6 cups very warm water

⅓ cup salt

1 cup apple cider vinegar

3 tablespoons unsulfured molasses

1 medium shallot, thinly sliced

1 tablespoon roughly crushed black peppercorns

6 sprigs fresh thyme

¼ cup rosemary leaves

2 dried bay leaves

2 teaspoons roughly crushed allspice berries

4 (5- to 7-ounce) whole boneless duck breasts
(wild birds are too tough for this dish)

MOLASSES LACQUER

5 tablespoons unsulfured molasses

¼ cup apple cider vinegar

1 clove garlic, very thinly sliced

1 tablespoon peeled and chopped fresh ginger

⅛ teaspoon cayenne

SMOKED DUCK

1 cup pecan shells

2 tablespoons Garlic Olive Oil *(page xxvi)*

2 teaspoons salt

2 teaspoons freshly ground black pepper

SERVES 4

To brine the duck: Combine the water and salt in a medium bowl and stir until the salt has dissolved. Add the vinegar, molasses, shallot, peppercorns, thyme, rosemary, bay leaves, and allspice and blend together well. Place the duck breasts in the brine, making sure they are submerged. Marinate in the refrigerator for at least 2 hours, or overnight if possible.

To make the molasses lacquer: Combine the molasses, vinegar, garlic, ginger, and cayenne in a small saucepan over medium heat and bring to a simmer. Decrease the heat to low and let reduce by half. Remove from the heat and set aside to cool briefly while you cook the duck breasts.

To smoke the duck breasts: Prepare a stovetop smoker with the pecan shells and place it on the stove over medium heat. Meanwhile, remove the breasts from the brine and pat dry. Score the duck breasts in a diamond pattern (through the skin but without cutting into the flesh to release as much of the fat as possible while cooking). Rub them all over with the garlic oil, salt, and pepper. Place the breasts in the smoker, flesh side down, and close the top. Decrease the heat to low and let the breasts smoke for 10 minutes. Remove and check the internal temperature with a meat thermometer. The meat should be 125° to 130°F at the thickest point.

To serve the duck, brush the breasts with the lacquer, slice across the grain of the meat (the grain runs on a duck breast), and serve. These go exceptionally well with Coal-Roasted Sweet Potatoes (recipe follows) and Collard "Choucroute Garnie" (page 121).

COAL-ROASTED SWEET POTATOES

4 medium sweet potatoes
Unsalted butter, for serving

SERVES 4

Build a large charcoal or wood fire. Prick the potatoes several times with the tines of a fork and wrap individually in aluminum foil. Once the fire has burned down to coals, bury the wrapped potatoes in the coals and let them cook undisturbed for 25 minutes. Carefully remove from the fire and pierce with a knife to see if they are done. Unwrap the potatoes, slice open, and slather with butter.

SMOKED BEETS WITH CHARRED PECANS AND BUTTERMILK–GOAT CHEESE CREMA

Beets, nuts, and creamy cheese (as vulgar as that may sound straight off the tongue) is a classic flavor combination. This dish has a particularly special place with me because it layers all the things I love to play against one another: earthy and refined, sweet and salty, hot and cold, and crunchy and smooth.

My sweet wife hates beets, but you can't fight the goodness in this dish, so just get over yourself and your dislike of beets (it's likely you only ever ate a canned beet anyway and don't know how good a freshly roasted one actually is if you say you don't like them). Go out and get this stuff and make a believer of yourself. That means you, Bess.

"I Want to Take You Home (To See Mama)" —Syl Johnson

To make the pecans: Preheat the oven to 350°F. Toss the pecans, butter, Worcestershire, and salt together in a bowl until well combined. Scatter the nuts in a single layer on a baking sheet. Toast the nuts for 5 minutes. Stir the nuts well with a spatula, return to the oven for another 3 minutes, and stir again. Continue this process until the pecans are dark brown and smell very nutty but are not burned. Remove from the oven, dump onto a cool plate, and let cool. Reserve until needed. The nuts can be made up to 3 days in advance.

To make the crema: Place the goat cheese in a medium bowl and work it with a whisk until it begins to soften and smooth out. Whisk in the buttermilk and lemon juice and whisk until smooth. Whisk in the thyme, salt, and pepper. Taste for seasoning and adjust as needed. Cover and refrigerate until needed. The crema may be prepared up to 2 days in advance.

To cook the beets: Preheat the oven to 350°F. Trim the beets, roots and tips, and wrap them individually in aluminum foil. Place them on a baking sheet and roast for 30 minutes. Using a small paring knife, pierce the largest of the beets. If the knife goes in easily, remove the beets from the oven and let cool. If the beets are still firm, roast for an additional 10 minutes, and then check again. When cool, remove the foil and, under cool running water, remove the skins. (This makes the process easier and keeps your hands from staining as badly. It has no effect on the flavor of the beets whatsoever.)

Slice the beets into 6 wedges each. Place the red beets in one bowl and the golden beets in another (red beets will stain the gold). Divide the olive oil, salt, and pepper among the bowls and toss each well.

Prepare a stovetop smoker with the soaked wood chips and place it on the stove over medium heat. As soon as the chips begin to smoke, place the red beets at one end of the smoker and the golden beets at the other. (They will likely touch in the center, which is fine.) Cover tightly with the lid and let smoke for 5 minutes. Turn off the heat and allow the beets to sit in the smoker for an additional 5 minutes. Transfer them to a plate.

To assemble: Equally divide the red and golden beets among serving bowls. Drizzle with the oil, vinegar, and crema. Sprinkle with the zest and horseradish. Scatter the pecans and herb flowers over the top. Dust with the finishing salt and black pepper.

Note:

Jean-Marc Montegoterro, master vinegar maker from Leon, France, produces the finest flavored vinegars I have ever had. Daniel Boulud explained to me that Jean-Marc was an old family friend and that years ago he had begun importing his friend's vinegars to use in his eponymous restaurant just east of Central Park. They are available through artisanflavor.com and well worth the effort and investment.

ingredients

PECANS

1 cup pecan halves

2 tablespoons unsalted butter, melted

1 tablespoon Worcestershire Sauce *(page 97)* or store bought

½ teaspoon salt

BUTTERMILK–GOAT CHEESE CREMA

½ cup crumbled goat cheese

½ cup buttermilk

1 tablespoon freshly squeezed lemon juice

1 teaspoon fresh thyme

½ teaspoon salt

¾ teaspoon freshly ground white pepper

BEETS

3 medium red beets *(4 to 5 ounces each)*

3 medium golden beets *(4 to 5 ounces each)*

2 tablespoons pure olive oil

2 teaspoons salt

Freshly ground black pepper

¾ cup soaked wood chips *(see Note, page 203)*

ASSEMBLY

¼ cup extra-virgin olive oil

2 tablespoons Huilerie Beaujolaise mango vinegar *(see Note)* or good-quality sherry vinegar

Zest of 1 lemon

2 tablespoons peeled and grated fresh horseradish

Mixed fresh herb flowers and sprouts *(or mixed chopped fresh herbs)*

Finishing salt *(see page xxi)*

Freshly ground black pepper

SERVES 4

SMOKED GLAZED BABY CARROTS

One of my greatest influences, Larkin Selman, who was the chef at Gautreau's in New Orleans, where I moved to work in the late 1980s, took our grandmother's glazed carrots to a different level with a brown sugar glaze spiked with just a hint of cinnamon. I used to love cooking them. Sticky and sweet, they were like chewable vitamins in that they tasted like candy but were actually somewhat good for you.

For my interpretation, we baptize the baby carrots in a salty, vermouth-tinged blanch before hot-smoking them. Then they hit the pan with a drizzle of Steen's cane syrup. Half of these suckers will not make it to the table—they are that good.

ingredients

"Floating Vibes" —Surfer Blood

SMOKED CARROTS

24 baby carrots with greens attached

6 tablespoons salt

1 cup dry vermouth

2 dried bay leaves

4 cloves garlic, sliced

1 medium shallot, sliced

1 tablespoon black peppercorns

¾ cup soaked wood chips
(see Note, page 203)

FINISHING AND ASSEMBLY

3 tablespoons cold unsalted butter

2 tablespoons minced shallots

3 tablespoons Veal Stock *(page 30)*

3 tablespoons Steen's cane syrup
(see page 180)

2 tablespoons dark brown sugar

½ teaspoon salt

1 teaspoon freshly ground black pepper

SERVES 4

To make the carrots: Trim the carrots, leaving 1 inch of the greens attached. Roughly chop the remaining greens and set aside.

Combine 3 quarts water, the salt, vermouth, bay leaves, garlic, shallot, and peppercorns in a large saucepan and bring to a simmer over medium heat. Boil for 3 minutes. Plunge the carrots into the liquid for 2 to 3 minutes after the water returns to a boil or until the carrots just begin to feel barely tender. Meanwhile, prepare an ice-water bath. Remove the carrots from the blanching liquid and plunge them immediately into the ice bath to cool and stop the cooking process.

Prepare a stovetop smoker with the soaked chips and place it over medium heat. As soon as the chips begin to smoke, place the carrots on the rack and cover tightly. Let smoke for 5 minutes, then remove the smoker from the heat (still covered) and let cool. Remove the carrots from the smoker.

To finish the carrots: Heat the butter in a medium sauté pan over medium heat until it begins to foam, being careful not to burn it. Stir in the shallots and sauté until transparent. Add the carrots and toss to fully coat with the butter. Blend in the stock, let it come to a boil, and reduce briefly. Stir in the Steen's syrup, brown sugar, salt, and black pepper until well blended with the carrots and simmer for 2 to 3 minutes, until the liquid becomes thick and syrupy. Sprinkle with the carrot greens and serve immediately.

SMOKED ENDIVE

Endive is truly one of the bitterest greens commonly consumed. I wasn't crazy about it early in my career . . . actually, I couldn't stand it. (I also didn't like cilantro, cauliflower, turnips, dill, Brussels sprouts, eggplant, or raisins. I have since corrected my ways.) It wasn't until I tasted some braised endive in Larkin Selman's kitchen that I realized how wrong I was about this magnificent green. I love its teeth-rattling bitterness, and I shave it into salads whenever I can get my hands on it. This preparation is great in the fall or winter. It goes spectacularly with the Bourbon-Braised Pork Cheeks (page 186).

"D-Nice" —Surgery

ingredients

Slice the endive in half lengthwise so that the root end continues to hold the head together. Drizzle with 1 tablespoon of the oil and sprinkle with the salt and pepper. Heat the remaining 2 tablespoons oil in a medium sauté pan over medium heat until it begins to shimmer. Carefully place the endive in the pan, flat side down, and brown lightly. Turn them over, add the stock, orange juice, and Grand Marnier, and bring to a simmer. Decrease the heat to low and simmer for 5 minutes, or until tender. Transfer the endive to a rack to drain.

Prepare a stovetop smoker with the soaked wood chips and place it over medium heat. As soon as the chips begin to smoke, place the endive on the rack and cover tightly. Lower the heat slightly and let smoke for 6 minutes. Turn the heat off and let sit for another 5 minutes. Remove the endive from the smoker and serve immediately, sprinkled with a touch of finishing salt.

6 large heads Belgian endive *(white or red)*

3 tablespoons pure olive oil

1½ teaspoons salt

1½ teaspoons freshly ground black pepper

2½ cups Veal Stock *(page 30)*

¼ cup freshly squeezed orange juice

2 tablespoons Grand Marnier

¾ cup soaked wood chips *(see Note, page 203)*

Finishing salt *(see page xxi)*

SERVES 4

SMOKED MUSHROOM TAMALES

North Mississippi has very little that is discernible in its foodways. I don't mean this in an ugly way. I have spent 20 years here, and studied the culinary landscape, and little can be cited when it comes to discussing what, of interest, patently has roots in the Mississippi kitchen. However, tamales are one of these things, and their existence is as much a study in history, class, and societal makeup as it is in culinary provenance. As best as we can tell, tamales came along with Latin migrant workers in the years after the Civil War, as the makeup of the agricultural workforce was changing. (That's my diplomatic way of explaining what the result of the "War of the Northern Aggression" was all about.)

Tamales were an enormously stable food item in the field. They could spend a hot summer morning in the shade on the side of a field without running the threat of making anyone sick. They are full of carbohydrates and are an excellent clearinghouse for whatever cooked protein you have laying around. All of the ingredients for making them are indigenous to the Mississippi Delta, so it is no surprise that locals picked up on them each year when the workers moved on. Tamales have, as a result, become positively Mississippi.

We have made dozens of versions of them with everything from meat and seafood fillings to chocolate and nuts. They require a little bit of labor but are the kind of thing that, when you set up to start making them, is as easy to make enough for 25 people as it is for 5. Even nicer, after they are steamed, they freeze beautifully.

ingredients   *"Drunken Angel"* —Lucinda Williams

MUSHROOM FILLING

1 cup medium button mushrooms, quartered
1 cup stemmed large shiitake mushrooms
1 cup medium cremini mushrooms
1 medium shallot, sliced
4 cloves garlic, sliced
½ cup sherry vinegar
¼ cup freshly squeezed lime juice
1 teaspoon ground cumin
1½ teaspoons salt
1 teaspoon freshly ground black pepper
1 cup soaked hickory wood chips

TAMALE DOUGH

½ cup roasted corn kernels *(see page 169)*
½ cup small-dice red onions
2 teaspoons minced garlic
¼ cup Dark Chicken Stock *(page 31)*
1 cup masa harina
1 teaspoon sugar
1 teaspoon salt
2 teaspoons crushed black peppercorns
1 teaspoon ground cumin
4 tablespoons cold unsalted butter
2 tablespoons lard *(see page 136)*
¼ cup fresh goat cheese

ASSEMBLY

Cornhusks, soaked for 30 minutes in warm water

SERVES 8

To make the mushroom filling: Combine all the mushrooms, the shallot, garlic, vinegar, 3 cups water, lime juice, cumin, salt, and pepper in a large saucepan and bring to a boil over medium heat. Let simmer for 4 minutes, then allow the mushrooms to cool in the liquid. Drain the mushrooms.

Prepare a stovetop smoker with the soaked wood chips and place on the stove over medium heat. As soon as the chips begin to smoke, place the mushroom mixture in the smoker and close the top tightly. Let them smoke for about 5 minutes. Turn off the heat and continue to smoke, covered, for an additional 5 minutes.

Transfer the mushrooms to a food processor and pulse until they are finely chopped but not pureed. Set aside while making the tamale dough.

To make the tamale dough: Puree the corn kernels, onions, garlic and stock in a food processor until smooth.

In a stainless-steel bowl, combine the masa harina, sugar, salt, crushed peppercorns, and cumin. Add the cold butter and lard and cut in until the dough resembles cornmeal. Cut in the goat cheese. Stir in the corn mixture until there are no lumps.

To assemble: Lay a large piece of soaked cornhusk (about 3 by 5 inches) on a flat surface. In the center, place 5 tablespoons of tamale dough and spread into a rectangle about 2 by 4 inches. Make a line of mushroom filling (2 to 3 tablespoons) lengthwise down the center of the tamale dough. Grasp the long edge of one of the tamales and roll the tamale into a tube, encasing the filling with the dough. Fold the ends over on the seam and rest the tamale on top of the folded ends so its weight holds the tamale together. Place the rolled tamale in the perforated pan of a steamer setup. Repeat this process with the rest of the tamales. Place the perforated pan over a pan of simmering water, cover, and steam for 45 minutes. Remove from the steamer and serve immediately. Alternatively, they can be refrigerated, covered with plastic wrap, for up to 48 hours and then rewarmed in a 350°F oven for 10 minutes.

Note:
Serve these with 3 cups of Roasted Cherry Tomato Marinara (page 85), adding the zest and juice of 2 limes and 2 teaspoons toasted and crushed cumin seeds.

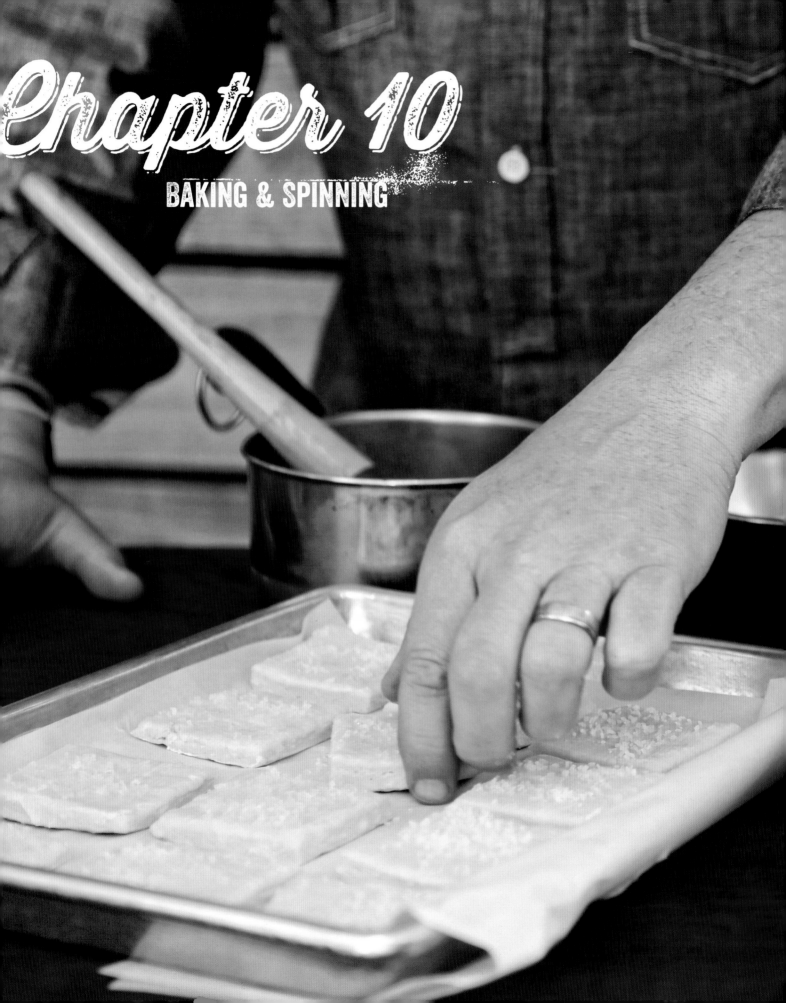

Chapter 10
BAKING & SPINNING

GRILLADES AND GRITS CASSEROLE	223
SWEET CORN PUDDING	224
CHICKEN SKIN CORNBREAD	225
CHOCOLATE CHESS PIE WITH WOODFORD RESERVE ICE CREAM	226
BANANAS FOSTER BREAD PUDDING WITH BROWN SUGAR–RUM SAUCE AND CANDIED PECAN "SOIL"	229
PEACH RICE PUDDING BRÛLÉE WITH BRANDY CHANTILLY CREAM	230
LOUISIANA STRAWBERRY AND MEYER LEMON CREPES	231
BANANA-WALNUT LAYER CAKE WITH VANILLA CREAM CHEESE ICING	232
BOURBON-PECAN PIE WITH TONKA BEAN ICE CREAM	234
PHYLLO-WRAPPED BOURBON-CLOVE POACHED PEARS À LA MODE	235
KITCHEN SINK COOKIE ICE-CREAM SANDWICHES	237
CHOCOLATE–PEANUT BUTTER CAKE	238
CAYENNE-PRALINE ICE CREAM	240
COMPRESSED SUMMER MELON WITH COUNTRY HAM POWDER	240
VANILLA BEAN–BUTTERMILK PANNA COTTA WITH BOURBON-MARINATED SUMMER CHERRIES	241
CHOCOLATE-ESPRESSO "JOLT" CAKE	243
SEZCHUAN PEPPER–BLUEBERRY COBBLER WITH FIVE-SPICE BUTTERMILK CREMA	244
PORK FAT BEIGNETS WITH BOURBON CARAMEL	247
LEMON-ROSEMARY SORBET WITH BENNE SEED SHORTBREAD	248

Chapter 10

BAKING & SPINNING

BAKING & SPINNING

I was fired from my first restaurant job for insulting a frat-boy customer who was berating his girlfriend for failing to express appropriate enthusiasm about his front-row tickets to Van Halen. Backstory: It was 1987 and "Van Halen" was touring for the first time with Sammy Hagar. I took this fact very personally, as I was a David Lee Roth man at the time. Sharing my opinion in a less than savory way with the young man did not sit well, and he reported me to the manager. I was ceremoniously dismissed for lacking the requisite social skills needed for front of the house employment, but apparently management thought my temperament was suited perfectly for kitchen work. The next morning I started as a dishwasher; I was, unknowingly, home.

During the course of my time in the kitchen, I was fortunate because both Bill Neal and his *chef de cuisine*, Fred Mueller, took a shine to me. I loved working in the kitchen and moved quickly from the dish pit to prep cook to line cook and ultimately to kitchen manager. At some point during this rapid ascent, the pastry chef decided to move on, and I was asked if I wanted to take on those duties as well. It was the first time in my career that I took a calculated risk and accepted a position I was entirely unqualified for, but I decided to tackle it anyway. Things would work out in my favor.

The pastry program was very straightforward, but demanding. Bill's tenet was simple. For a simple dish to take wings, the basic elements had to be executed precisely. So, if the piecrust for a pecan pie was not just perfectly flaky, or if the rest of the filling was so sweet it overran the flavor of the pecan, it then became just another forgettable pecan pie. And although I was, perhaps, the worst novice pastry chef ever to wield a bench scraper, the amount of time I spent one on one with Bill and Fred would serve me for the next 20 years.

The items in this chapter come from the pearls of wisdom I harvested during that time and applied to our pastry programs going forward. They are, for the most part, easy-to-execute recipes for dishes that most folks warm to easily. These are a sample of what our program was built on and what carried us through the first 15 or so years at City Grocery, before we were blessed with our superhuman pastry chef, Dwayne Ingraham.

We start here with a couple of baked savory items to round things out, but the rest are meant as meal finishers. These are the diabetic knockout punches of our repertoire.

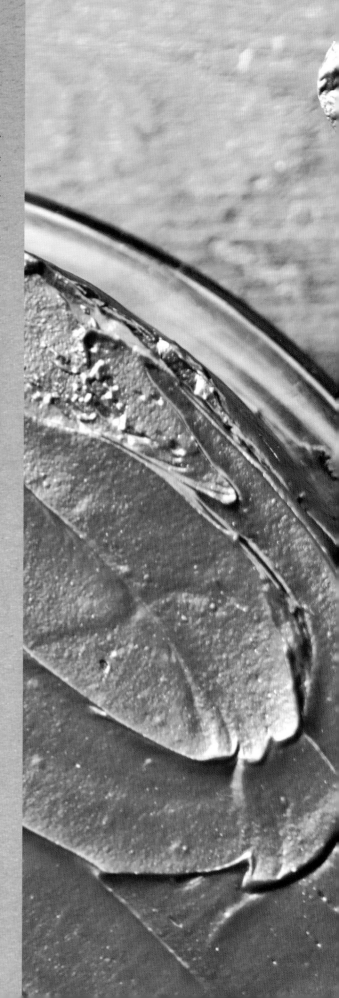

GRITS

4 cups whole milk
4 cups Dark Chicken Stock *(page 31)*
2 cups stone-ground grits
5 tablespoons butter, cubed
¾ cup cream cheese
¾ cup grated Parmesan cheese
2 tablespoons finely minced garlic
3 whole eggs, lightly beaten
2 teaspoons salt
1 tablespoon freshly ground black pepper

In a medium saucepan, over medium heat, bring the milk and stock to a simmer. As soon as the liquid begins to bubble around the edges of the pan, whisk in the grits. Continue whisking until the moment the grits begin to noticeably thicken, then switch to a wooden spoon and continue stirring. Decrease the heat to low and stir the grits for 12 to 15 minutes, or until, when tasted, the grits are cooked through. The minute the grits are done, remove from the heat. Stir in the butter, cream cheese, Parmesan, and garlic and combine thoroughly. Mix in the eggs and season with salt and pepper.

ASSEMBLE

2 teaspoons lard
½ cup Parmesan cheese

Preheat the oven to 350°F.

In a 12-inch cast-iron skillet, melt the lard over low heat to coat the bottom of the pan. Scoop half of the grits into the bottom of the pan and spread evenly across the pan. Layer in 1½ inches of grillades on top of the grits and then cover with the remaining grits evenly, and top with the remaining grillades. Sprinkle the Parmesan over the top and place on a baking sheet in the oven. Bake for 25 minutes, or until the cheese begins to brown lightly. Serve immediately.

Note:
This can be assembled and frozen in a casserole dish and it will keep for 2 months in the freezer. If you do this, remove from the freezer the night before to thaw in the refrigerator. Cook for a full 45 minutes if chilled. Insert a knife to test the warmth of the center.

GRILLADES AND GRITS CASSEROLE

I could not count the number of times that grillades saved me from the terminal effects of a hangover on a Sunday morning after a long weekend in New Orleans. So much so that I am not entirely convinced traditional recipes don't include a fistful of aspirin.

My mom made a particularly good version, gently pounding each cutlet of veal individually to achieve its perfect tenderness. Traditional recipes call for a tedious preparation that can take hours to just get in the pan. It was the method I ascribed to religiously until a nameless employee scorched an entire batch the morning before a huge wedding brunch we were hosting. We hurriedly hit the local grocery and cobbled together the recipe fast, gave it a nice simmer, and slid into the event right "under the wire." The grillades were excellent and no one knew the difference.

Here we make the grillades in advance, cook the grits, and assemble the dish so that all it needs is a few minutes in the oven. It is easily frozen and a marvel of simplicity to get together for a brunch.

Warning: Side effects of consumption can be prolonged naps, lethargy, procrastination, and/or periods of general unproductivity. Feelings of bliss and contentment are not uncommon. If sluggishness persists for more than a couple of days, see your doctor.

"Fight Test" —The Flaming Lips

ingredients

To make the grillades: Sprinkle the pork and beef cubes with salt and pepper and toss to distribute evenly. Dredge the cubes in 1 cup of the flour, knocking off any excess and set aside briefly. In a medium soup pot, heat the bacon fat over high heat until the surface begins to shimmer. Add the floured meat cubes and brown evenly on all sides. Remove from the pot and reserve. Lower the heat to medium.

Whisk in the remaining 4 tablespoons of flour, scraping any caramelized bits from the bottom of the pan. Whisk until the roux (paste) turns a light golden brown. Stir in the onions, garlic, celery, and peppers and sauté, stirring constantly, until the vegetables begin to wilt, 5 to 6 minutes. Add the tomatoes, tarragon, and thyme; combine and stir for an additional 3 minutes. Stir in the red wine and combine completely. Add the stock, bay leaves, Tabasco, and Worcestershire and bring to a boil. Lower the heat to low and simmer for 90 minutes, or until the meat is tender. Season to taste with salt and pepper. Stir in the green onions and set aside until ready to assemble, but do not chill, unless you will not be cooking until much later or the next day.

2 pounds mixed pork and beef stew meat, cut into ½- to ¾-inch cubes

2 teaspoons salt

2 teaspoons freshly ground black pepper

1 cup plus 4 tablespoons all-purpose flour

4 tablespoons bacon fat

½ cup small dice yellow onions

4 cloves garlic, finely minced

6 tablespoons small dice celery

½ cup small dice green bell peppers

½ cup small dice red bell peppers

3 medium tomatoes, seeded and small diced

2 tablespoons chopped tarragon

2 teaspoons fresh thyme leaves

½ cup red wine *(whatever kind you are sipping on while you are making this)*

3 cups Dark Chicken Stock *(page 31)*

2 fresh bay leaves

2 teaspoons Tabasco hot sauce

1 tablespoon Worcestershire Sauce *(page 97)* or store bought

1 cup thinly sliced green onions

SERVES 8 TO 10

SWEET CORN PUDDING

In the height of the summer there is, for a very brief window of time, an abundance of corn available locally. It is, without question, never better than straight off the stalk. Tomatoes can stand 24 hours at room temperature, sweet potatoes are arguably better after being given a week or so in the air, and squash can survive heinous abuses, but corn is brightest in the moments after it is picked. So when corn hits, we use it in everything that we can to try to deliver that experience.

This iteration combines the elements of south Louisiana maque choux and traditional corn pudding. It makes an outstanding accompaniment for the Roasted Poulet Rouge (page 183) or the Tomato-Braised Grouper (page 187).

ingredients

"Drown in My Own Tears" —Ray Charles

2 whole eggs, lightly beaten

¼ cup melted butter

¼ cup heavy cream

1½ teaspoons cornstarch

½ cup small dice yellow onions

2 teaspoons finely minced garlic

1 tablespoon minced jalapeño pepper

½ cup small dice red bell peppers

2 tablespoons bacon fat

½ cup seeded and diced tomatoes

2 tablespoons fresh thyme leaves

½ teaspoon salt

1½ teaspoons freshly ground black pepper

¼ cup chopped cooked bacon

2½ cup roasted corn kernels
(see page 169)

1 cup Panko bread crumbs

SERVES 4

Preheat the oven to 325°F.

Whisk together the eggs, butter, cream, and cornstarch in a small stainless-steel bowl and set aside.

In a medium sauté pan over medium heat, sauté the onions, garlic, jalapeño, and red bell peppers in the bacon fat until they begin to wilt, about 2 minutes. Turn the heat off and stir in the tomatoes, thyme, salt, and pepper and blend together briefly. Stir in the bacon and corn kernels and cool for 5 minutes. Add the egg mix, combine well, and stir in the bread crumbs and incorporate evenly.

Divide the mix evenly among 4 small (4-inch) cast-iron skillets brushed with a neutral flavored oil (alternately this can be done in a single batch in an 8-inch cast-iron pan). Bake for 25 minutes or until the center of the pudding is set when the pan is jiggled. Serve warm immediately.

CHICKEN SKIN CORNBREAD

This recipe flies in the face of everything Southern. For those of you entirely unaware of what was on the tablet that Moses lost coming down the mountain, it said, "Thou shalt add neither flour nor sugar to cornbread." Well, this one has both . . . and some. Flour makes the bread a little less course and sugar masks the bitterness cornmeal can have, or maybe it is acid reacting with the cast iron. Whatever the case, a little sugar helps.

Please don't fart around with anything else but cast iron to cook your cornbread. This is not cute Southern cliché. The simple fact is that batter poured into a hot skillet produces a crispy crust you will not get in a lighter weight pan. Serve this with Spicy Summer Pea Soup (page 47) or simply drizzle with a little molasses.

"I Love You" —Asie Payton

Preheat the oven to 350°F and heat a 12-inch cast-iron skillet for 20 minutes. Remove the skillet from the oven and coat the inside liberally with bacon fat. Return the pan to the oven until ready to bake.

In a large mixing bowl, combine the cornmeal, flour, sugar, baking powder, baking soda, and salt and blend well. In a separate bowl, whisk together the eggs, buttermilk, sour cream, and melted butter until fully combined. Stir the wet mixture into the dry mixture and combine well. Blend in the Crusted Chicken Cracklin's and black pepper. Pour the mixture into the hot skillet and bake for 30 minutes or until fully set and golden brown.

Note:

For Chicken Cracklin's, save the skin from 12 to 14 chicken breasts and thighs (freeze them until you have enough). Layer the thawed skin flat on parchment paper in single layers on a baking pan. Stack as many as 4 or 5 sheets on each baking pan. Sprinkle each layer lightly with salt, black pepper, and cayenne. Cover the top layer of skins with parchment and place a second baking sheet on top; add weight with a sauté pan. Place the pan in a 350°F oven for 12 to 15 minutes, or until the skins turn golden brown. Remove, drain, and crumble. Try not to eat one. It can't be done.

ingredients

1½ tablespoons bacon fat
3 cups yellow cornmeal
1 cup all-purpose flour
4 tablespoons sugar
2 teaspoons baking powder
2 teaspoons baking soda
1½ teaspoons salt
5 whole eggs, whisked lightly
4 cups buttermilk
1 cup sour cream
½ cup melted butter
1½ cups Crushed Chicken Cracklin's *(see Note)*
1½ tablespoons freshly ground black pepper

MAKES ENOUGH FOR 8 TO 10 PEOPLE

CHOCOLATE CHESS PIE WITH WOODFORD RESERVE ICE CREAM

There is a diner in Farmville, Virginia, called Walker's. It has a counter and eight stools and served one of the best "meat and three" lunch plates I have ever had. When I was at Hampden-Sydney College in the early 1980s, Mr. and Mrs. Walker would allow the H-SC boys to keep a running tab, which they would bill home to our parents monthly. And at about $3 a plate, it could not be beat for quality or value, especially for our folks. I would go almost every day with my two roommates for fried chicken, a griddled burger with a fried egg, or a bowl full of canned green beans cooked to death with ham hock and bacon. The prize though every trip was the chocolate chess pie. We lived by and swore by that pie. We accosted Mrs. Walker for a year, trying to get the recipe, before she finally told us that they were made by a local church group and she wasn't privy to the recipe. So we set our sites on the local Baptist church ladies and went to work on them. They were surprisingly forthcoming with their secret, which was immediately scrawled on the wall in our kitchen with a permanent marker. We kept a stash of frozen pie shells in our freezer and all the ingredients to make said pie, so a regular late-night activity was making and destroying a chocolate chess pie. I am not sure if we ever actually let one cool all the way down before devouring it, but I do remember loving every bite of this delightfully simple decadence.

ingredients

"Landslide" —The Smashing Pumpkins

PIECRUST

1½ cups all-purpose flour, plus more for dusting the work surface

3 tablespoons sugar

¼ teaspoon salt

¼ cup plus 2 teaspoons unsalted butter

¼ cup plus 2 teaspoons lard *(see page 136)*

2 large egg yolks

2 to 4 tablespoons ice water

PIE FILLING

5 large eggs

½ cup whole milk

4 tablespoons unsalted butter, melted

1 teaspoon vanilla extract

1¾ cups sugar

½ cup Dutch-process cocoa powder

2 tablespoons all-purpose flour

1 tablespoon yellow cornmeal

¼ teaspoon salt

MAKES ONE 9-INCH PIE
AND 2 QUARTS ICE CREAM

To make the piecrust: Preheat the oven to 400°F. In a stainless-steel bowl, combine the flour, sugar, and salt. Place the dry mixture in the refrigerator. Cut the butter into small pieces and place in the freezer along with the lard for 15 minutes. When the butter and lard are cold, cut them into the flour mixture using a pastry blender or fork until it reaches the consistency of coarse meal. Then mix in the egg yolks and 2 tablespoons ice water and blend until a ball forms. Add more water, 1 tablespoon at a time, if needed to help the dough come together.

Turn the dough out onto a lightly floured surface and gently knead (just 3 or 4 folds) until it comes together smoothly. If you tear the dough, you should be able to see relatively visible layers. Gather the dough into a disk, wrap well in plastic wrap, and chill for 30 minutes. This gives the dough the chance to rest so it will be less likely to shrink when baked.

Remove the dough from the refrigerator and place on a lightly floured surface. Roll out to a ¼-inch thickness and arrange it in a 9-inch pie pan. Crimp the edges decoratively as you like.

Dock the crust with a fork (prick holes all around the bottom of it without completely piercing the crust). Line the crust with parchment paper, fill with dried beans or pie weights, and bake for 15 minutes. Remove the pie weights and parchment and let the crust cool.

To make the pie filling: Preheat the oven to 325°F. In a stainless-steel bowl, whisk together the eggs, milk, butter, and vanilla until smooth.

In a separate bowl, blend together the sugar, cocoa powder, flour, cornmeal, and salt. Whisk the wet mixture into the dry mixture until fully combined. Pour the filling into the pie shell and bake for 35 minutes, until the center is set (shake the pie lightly to see if the center is fully cooked). Remove from the oven, let cool, and serve with a scoop of the bourbon ice cream.

WOODFORD RESERVE ICE CREAM

4 cups half-and-half
3 cups heavy cream
2 whole vanilla beans, split
14 egg yolks
2½ cups sugar
1 tablespoon vanilla extract
Pinch of salt
½ cup Woodford Reserve bourbon
(any bourbon will do, but Woodford adds bourbon flavor without some of the sweetness you might get otherwise)

In a medium saucepan, warm the half-and-half and cream with the vanilla beans over medium heat until bubbles begin to form around the edges of the pot. Remove from the heat.

Lay the vanilla beans on a cutting board. Pull the cut sides apart, exposing the soft inside of the vanilla beans, scrape the seeds out with the back side of a small sharp knife, and stir them into the warm cream mixture. You can discard the vanilla bean pods or drop them into a bottle of cheap bourbon. A couple of dozen pods allowed to sit for about 3 weeks will make you enough vanilla extract for the next 5 years.

In a stainless-steel bowl, whisk together the egg yolks and sugar until pale and well combined. Slowly whisk the hot cream mixture into the egg yolks and stir in the vanilla. Place the bowl on top of a simmering double boiler over low heat and continue to whisk until the custard begins to thicken and coats the back of a spoon. Stir in the salt and bourbon and refrigerate the custard until chilled.

Freeze in an ice-cream maker according to the manufacturer's directions. Transfer to a covered container and freeze for at least 2 hours and up to 6 weeks. Make sure you place a layer of plastic wrap directly on the surface of the ice cream, pressing out all of the air bubbles. This will keep the finished product from getting freezer burn.

BREAD PUDDING

10 large eggs
2 cups heavy whipping cream
1¼ cups whole milk
1 tablespoon plus 1 teaspoon vanilla extract
1¼ cups unsalted butter, melted
2¼ cups granulated sugar
¼ teaspoon salt
2 tablespoons plus 2 teaspoons ground cinnamon
2 teaspoons freshly grated nutmeg
¼ cup banana liqueur
10 cups torn stale bread
(any variety of white bread will do)
3 large bananas, thinly sliced

Preheat the oven to 350°F. In a large bowl, whisk together the eggs until well blended. Whisk in the cream, milk, vanilla, and melted butter and combine well.

In another large bowl, blend together 2 cups of the sugar, the salt, 2 tablespoons of the cinnamon, and the nutmeg. Stir in the egg mixture and blend well. Stir in the banana liqueur. Add the bread, combine well, and let rest for 10 minutes. Mash the bread pudding mixture with your hands to make sure all the bread is soaked through. Stir in the bananas.

Butter a deep 10-inch square baking pan. In a small bowl, blend the remaining ¼ cup sugar and 2 teaspoons cinnamon. Pour the bread pudding mixture into the prepared pan and sprinkle the top with the cinnamon sugar. Cover with aluminum foil and bake for 45 minutes. Remove the foil and bake for an additional 10 minutes. Grab the edge of the pan with a dry towel and give it a shake. Look to the center of the pan; if it doesn't jiggle and looks firm, it is cooked through.

BANANAS FOSTER BREAD PUDDING WITH BROWN SUGAR–RUM SAUCE AND CANDIED PECAN "SOIL"

Sunday brunch after church when I was a youngster was a *huge* deal. Mom and Dad cooked all the time, and eating out was definitely not routine for us. Brunch, after the fanfare that church was, always seemed like a circus to me. There were dining rooms full of guéridon at Commander's Palace, Brennan's, and Antoine's preparing café brûlot, cherries jubilee, baked Alaska, crepes suzette, and our favorite, bananas Foster. This was a deft creation of flambéed bananas with loads of rum, brown sugar, butter, and a dollop of vanilla ice cream. It was magic.

Turning this into a bread pudding, when we first opened the Grocery, took about as much creativity as, I'm sure, coming up with the McRib did, but it is still a serious crowd-pleaser 20 years later. Top with a dollop of sweetened whipped cream and drizzle with the Brown Sugar–Rum caramel to finish.

"Still New" —Smith Westerns

ingredients

To make the pecan "soil": Preheat the oven to 375°F. In a stainless-steel bowl, mix the pecans with the butter and then spread them into a single layer on a baking sheet. Bake, stirring every 4 minutes, for about 12 minutes, or until you can begin to smell them cooking. They will give off a distinct "toasted-nut" smell. Remove from the oven and let cool.

In another bowl, blend both sugars, the salt, cayenne, paprika, cinnamon, and cloves.

Beat the egg white with 1 tablespoon water until frothy in a large bowl. Stir in the pecans to coat evenly. Transfer the pecans to another bowl and toss with the sugar mixture until evenly coated. Spread the sugared pecans into a single layer on a baking sheet coated with nonstick spray. Bake for 30 minutes, stirring occasionally. Remove from the oven and let cool, separating the nuts as they cool. When completely cool, place the nuts in a food processor and pulse until broken into a "soil" consistency. Set aside until ready to serve.

While the bread pudding is baking, make the sauce: In a small saucepan over medium heat, warm the melted butter to a simmer. Stir in the brown sugar and vanilla, combine well, and simmer for 10 minutes.

Stir in the rum and simmer for an additional 3 minutes. Swirl in the cream and the split vanilla bean and simmer for 5 minutes. Remove the vanilla bean and, with a small sharp knife, scrape the seeds from inside the pod and blend them into the sauce. Discard the empty pod or rinse and add it to a bottle of bourbon to make your own extract (see page 227). Simmer for 5 to 6 minutes more, stirring constantly, or until the sauce thickens.

To serve, scoop a large, warm spoonful of bread pudding into a bowl, drizzle with the sauce, and sprinkle with the pecan "soil."

CANDIED PECAN "SOIL"

4 cups pecan halves
½ cup unsalted butter, melted
¼ cup granulated sugar
3 tablespoons dark brown sugar
½ teaspoon salt
2 pinches of cayenne
⅛ teaspoon smoked paprika
⅛ teaspoon ground cinnamon
Pinch of ground cloves
1 large egg white, at room temperature

BROWN SUGAR–RUM SAUCE

½ cup unsalted butter, melted
1½ cups dark brown sugar
1 tablespoon vanilla extract
1 cup dark rum
½ cup heavy cream
1 whole vanilla bean, split

SERVES 8

PEACH RICE PUDDING BRÛLÉE WITH BRANDY CHANTILLY CREAM

About 10 years ago, on a trip to Washington, D.C., a friend directed me to a Thai restaurant near DuPont Circle. He instructed me to "get through" dinner because the mango rice pudding they had was absolutely spectacular. So I did just that, and the rice pudding was very nice, if slightly short of transcendent. My issue was simply in the lack of textural variation, and I immediately started thinking about what might result if I crossed it with a crème brûlée and used local peaches. The result was excellent, and the crunchy layer of caramelized sugar works perfectly with the tender grains of starchy rice. It's a great vehicle for fresh, sweet summer peaches.

ingredients

½ cup raisins

1 cup bourbon

5 cups whole milk

1 cup heavy cream

1¼ cups dark brown sugar

Pinch of ground cinnamon

Pinch of ground cloves

2 whole vanilla beans, split

1 tablespoon vanilla extract

4 tablespoons unsalted butter

3 cups Arborio rice

¾ cup dry white wine

3 cups peeled, small-dice peaches

Granulated sugar, for topping

Brandy Chantilly Cream *(recipe follows)*, for serving

SERVES 6 TO 8

"Venus" —Shocking Blue

Combine the raisins and ½ cup of the bourbon in a small saucepan and bring to a simmer over medium heat. As soon as the bourbon simmers, remove from the heat and set aside.

In a medium saucepan, combine the milk, cream, brown sugar, cinnamon, cloves, and vanilla beans. Bring to a simmer over medium heat. As soon as the mixture begins to bubble around the edges, remove the vanilla beans, scrape the seeds from the pods with a small sharp knife, and return the seeds to the milk mixture. Discard the empty pods or rinse and add to a bottle of bourbon to make your own extract (see page 227). Whisk in the vanilla.

In another medium saucepan over medium heat, melt the butter, toss in the rice, and stir until it is warmed and coated with butter. Stir in the white wine and the remaining ½ cup bourbon and stir until the liquid is absorbed. Begin stirring in the milk mixture, ½ cup at a time, stirring and cooking until each addition is completely absorbed. Continue until the rice is just barely fully cooked, then stir in the raisins and peaches and distribute into six to eight 4-ounce ovenproof ramekins or brûlée dishes and let cool to room temperature.

Preheat the broiler. When ready to serve, coat the top of the rice pudding with a thin layer of granulated sugar. Place the dishes on the top rack of the oven and, watching carefully, brown the sugar lightly. Serve immediately with a spoonful of the Chantilly cream.

BRANDY CHANTILLY CREAM

1 cup heavy cream

3 tablespoons confectioners' sugar

2 teaspoons vanilla extract

Pinch of salt

2 tablespoons Cognac

Place the cream, sugar, vanilla, and salt in the bowl of a stand mixer fitted with the whisk attachment. Whisk on high speed until soft peaks form. Blend in the Cognac and whisk again on high speed until stiff peaks form.

LOUISIANA STRAWBERRY AND MEYER LEMON CREPES

Making crepes is all about patience and trust. Patience is a necessity because you will certainly screw a few of these up on your way to getting them right. However, once you hit the correct heat and your pan is nicely seasoned, you'll want to keep going all night because they are just that simple. Crepe dough can be a little tricky because it only works at the right temperature and when given the proper amount of time to rest. It requires trust, because you will look at the batter and wonder how anything that looks that much like skim milk could ever become a crepe. It will, I promise. You'll also be surprised at how little batter it takes to make a crepe. So, believe and you will thrive, at least as far as crepes are concerned. I do hope that success bleeds over into other areas of your life as well, of course.

"Rock You Like a Hurricane" —Scorpions

To make the crepes: In a stainless-steel bowl, whisk the eggs until smooth and creamy. Blend in the milk, ½ cup water, the butter, vanilla, and Cognac.

In another bowl, blend together the flour, sugar, and salt. Whisk the wet mixture into the flour mixture and combine well. Cover with plastic wrap and place the crepe batter in the refrigerator for 1 hour. This allows the bubbles to subside and the batter to relax so that the crepes will be less likely to tear during cooking. This batter will keep for up to 48 hours.

Heat an 8- to 9-inch nonstick pan. Add the clarified butter and swirl to coat the pan. Pour 1 ounce of batter into the center of the pan and swirl to spread evenly. Cook for 30 seconds and flip. Cook for another 10 seconds and transfer to a cutting board. Lay them out flat so they can cool. Continue until all the batter is gone. After they have cooled, you can stack them, separated with wax paper, and store in ziplock plastic bags in the refrigerator for several days or in the freezer for up to 2 months.

To make the mascarpone filling: Gently toss the strawberries in a small bowl with the sugar. Place in the refrigerator and let sit for 1 hour. At the end of the hour, pour off the syrup that has accumulated in the bowl and reserve. Place the strawberries in a food processor and puree. Add the mascarpone and salt and process again until smooth. Place, covered, in the refrigerator. Let chill for 20 minutes, or as long as overnight.

Pour the reserved strawberry syrup into a small saucepan and bring to a simmer over medium heat. Decrease the heat to low and simmer until the strawberry syrup thickens.

To make the lemon filling: In a medium sauté pan over medium heat, melt the butter. Add the strawberries, sugar, and lemon zest and juice. Swirl until the sugar is dissolved. Swirl in the vodka and salt and reduce for 1 minute.

To assemble the crepes: Lay the crepes out on a cutting board and spoon 3 tablespoons of the mascarpone filling down the center of each. Repeat with the lemon filling, spreading about 1 tablespoon per crepe. Roll the crepes into cylinders, or fold the four sides in toward the center and invert. Place two stuffed crepes on each plate and distribute the sliced strawberries over the top of each. Drizzle with the strawberry syrup, spoon a dollop of whipped cream over each crepe, and dust with confectioners' sugar.

ingredients

CREPES

2 large eggs

¾ cup whole milk

3 tablespoons unsalted butter, melted

1 teaspoon vanilla extract

2 tablespoons Cognac

1 cup all-purpose flour

5 teaspoons granulated sugar

Pinch of salt

Clarified unsalted butter *(see page xxiii)*, for coating the pan

STRAWBERRY-MASCARPONE FILLING

1 cup fresh strawberries, stems removed and sliced

¼ cup granulated sugar

1 pound mascarpone cheese *(or substitute cream cheese)*

Pinch of salt

STRAWBERRY-MEYER LEMON FILLING

3 tablespoons unsalted butter

2 cups fresh strawberries, stems removed and sliced

¼ cup granulated sugar

Finely grated zest and juice of 1 Meyer lemon

2 tablespoons vodka

Pinch of salt

ASSEMBLY

1 cup fresh strawberries, stems removed and sliced

Sweetened whipped cream

Confectioners' sugar

SERVES 6

BANANA-WALNUT LAYER CAKE WITH VANILLA CREAM CHEESE ICING

New Orleans used to have an excellent chain of bakeries around the city called McKenzie's. In their heyday, there were some 50 locations, and they served everything from thin sandwich white bread to petit fours, from chocolate/pecan turtles to buttermilk "drop" doughnuts. It is the only quality bakery chain I can recall, and their demise is a mystery, as their products were exceptional. One of the few surviving facades is located just half a block from the house where I grew up. The milk bottle green glass that covers the front of the building is unmistakable. Its dated look stands testament to the love for tradition that outweighs changing times, styles, and attitudes. It is an ice-cream shop now that offers a product of equal quality to its predecessor. I like to imagine that it is a bit of a tribute to McKenzie's memory.

When I was little, about once a month my mom would give my brother Richard and I a few dollars for breakfast, and we would tear down the block for doughnuts and whatnot. One of my favorite things they used to have was an iced banana and pecan coffee cake. They came wrapped in plastic in a disposable cake pan and could not have been any more delicious. This recipe was one I developed to mimic those flavors and textures, and for the first few years we were open it was the only dessert John Grisham would order when he and his family came in to eat. We always kidded that dessert time was *A Time to Eat . . . Cake*.

ingredients

"Bodies" —Sex Pistols

5 large overripe bananas
¾ cup buttermilk
2½ teaspoons vanilla extract
1¼ cups unsalted butter, softened
2¼ cups sugar
3 large eggs
3 cups all-purpose flour
1½ teaspoons baking soda
1½ teaspoons baking powder
¾ teaspoon salt
1¼ cup walnuts, toasted and chopped

SERVES 12 TO 14

Preheat the oven to 350°F. Butter two 9-inch round, straight-sided cake pans with butter and lightly dust with flour.

Place the bananas, buttermilk, and vanilla in a food processor and blend until smooth. Set the banana mixture aside.

In the bowl of a stand mixer fitted with the paddle attachment, cream the butter, blend in the sugar, and combine until light and fluffy, 3 to 4 minutes. On low speed, add the eggs, one at a time, allowing each to fully incorporate before adding the next.

In a stainless-steel bowl, combine the flour, baking soda, baking powder, and salt and blend together well. With the machine on medium-low speed, alternate blending the flour mixture and the reserved banana mixture into the butter mixture, 1 cup at a time. Be sure to fully incorporate after each addition. When finished, fold in the walnuts by hand.

Pour the cake batter into the prepared pans and bake on the center rack of the oven for 25 to 30 minutes, until a cake tester comes out clean. Remove from the oven and let cool for 10 minutes in the pans. Turn the cakes out onto a cooling rack and cool completely. Slice each of the layers in half crossways using a serrated knife, so that you end up with four layers.

Spread the icing on one layer and place a second on top; repeat until all four layers are stacked, and then spread the icing over the entire cake.

VANILLA CREAM CHEESE ICING

2 pounds cream cheese, softened
2 cups unsalted butter, softened
6½ cups confectioners' sugar
Pinch of salt
1 tablespoon plus 1 teaspoon vanilla extract

In a stand mixer fitted with the paddle attachment, beat the cream cheese on medium-high speed until smooth and fluffy. Beat in the butter on medium-high speed and combine well. Decrease the speed to low and slowly add the confectioners' sugar, ½ cup at a time, and combine fully. Add the salt and vanilla, return the speed to medium-high, and blend together well until smooth.

BOURBON-PECAN PIE WITH TONKA BEAN ICE CREAM

There really isn't much more that can be said on the subject of pecan pie. It is at the heart of the Southern dessert canon, and everyone has a slightly different version. There's your grandmother's version, there's their mother's version, there's somebody else's great-grandmother's recipe, and each is better than the other. It is a lot like gumbo in that way.

For our version, I wanted to use molasses to knock down some of the cloying sweetness that some pecan pies typically have, frequently masking the flavor of the pecans entirely.

Tonka beans, seeds from a flowering hardwood indigenous to northern South America, have a brilliant aroma of vanilla and almond. When used with restraint, they deliver an intense flavor and aroma of clove that lends a perfumy quality to its profile. They are technically illegal in the United States but are widely available on the Internet and at specialty stores. Apparently, consumed in large doses, it can cause liver damage in rodents, but then again, so can aspirin, bourbon, and Coca-Cola. This recipe is wonderful without the tonkas, but I discovered these little gems in France about 15 years ago and wanted to share.

"Saturday Night" —Schoolly D

ingredients

3 large eggs

2 large egg yolks

1¼ cups sugar

4 tablespoons unsalted butter

½ cup unsulfured molasses

2 cups pecan pieces, toasted

2 teaspoons vanilla extract

¼ cup Buffalo Trace bourbon
(any bourbon will do, but Buffalo Trace brings a little sweetness and a lot of bourbon flavor)

½ teaspoon salt

1 (9-inch) blind-baked piecrust *(page 226)*

Tonka Bean Ice Cream *(recipe follows)*

MAKES ONE 9-INCH PIE

Preheat the oven to 350°F. Whisk the eggs, egg yolks, and sugar together in a large stainless-steel or glass bowl until smooth and creamy. Blend in the butter, molasses, pecans, vanilla, bourbon, and salt until smooth. Pour into the pie shell. Bake for 35 minutes, or until the center is set. Serve warm with a scoop of the ice cream.

TONKA BEAN ICE CREAM

4 cups heavy cream

3⅓ cups half-and-half

2 whole vanilla beans, split

14 large egg yolks

2½ cups sugar

5 tablespoons honey

2 teaspoons vanilla extract

1 teaspoon tonka beans, finely grated on a Microplane *(optional)*

Pinch of salt

MAKES ABOUT 2 QUARTS

Combine the cream and half-and-half in a large saucepan with the vanilla beans and bring to a simmer. As soon as the cream begins to bubble around the edges, remove from the heat. Carefully remove the vanilla beans and scrape the seeds back into the cream, stirring well to combine. Discard the empty pods or rinse and add to a bottle of bourbon to make your own extract (see page 227).

In a large stainless-steel bowl, whisk the egg yolks and sugar together until pale and well combined. Slowly whisk in the hot cream. Stir in the honey, vanilla, and tonka beans. Place the bowl over a simmering double boiler set over low heat. Whisk constantly until the custard coats the back of a spoon. Stir in the salt and refrigerate until cold.

Freeze in an ice-cream maker according to the manufacturer's directions. Transfer the ice cream to a covered container and freeze for at least 1 hour before serving. The ice cream will keep in the freezer for up to 4 months. Make sure you place a layer of plastic wrap directly on the surface of the ice cream, pressing out all of the air bubbles. This will keep the finished product from getting freezer burn.

PHYLLO-WRAPPED
BOURBON-CLOVE POACHED PEARS À LA MODE

The first summer we were open at City Grocery, I was really digging as deep as I could, with my limited dessert knowledge, to create something interesting for our menu. My neighbor's pear tree hung over into my yard and, as I understand it, according to the law, falling pears become the property of the person who lives where they fall. I had pears coming out of my ears. I've never been terribly fond of the texture of pears (they feel a little like a cat's tongue to me), but I love the flavor. This was what came out of trying to manipulate the texture and enhance the flavor.

"(White Man) in Hammersmith Palais" —The Clash

ingredients

Preheat the oven to 350°F. Butter a baking dish large enough to hold the phyllo-wrapped pears in a single layer.

Combine 1 cup water, the bourbon, ½ cup of the sugar, the cloves, cinnamon, and peppercorns in a medium saucepan and bring to a simmer over medium heat. Gently lower the pear halves into the poaching liquid and poach for 4 to 5 minutes, until easily pierced with a knife. Transfer the pears to a cooling rack and let drain.

Strain the poaching liquid, discarding the solids, into a small saucepan and bring to a boil. Lower the heat and simmer until the syrup thickens. Set aside until ready to serve.

Working quickly, brush a piece of phyllo dough with the melted butter and sprinkle lightly with some of the remaining ½ cup sugar and pecans. Lay another sheet on top, and repeat the process until you have 3 sheets. Place a pear half, cut side up, in the center. Wrap the dough around the sides, up the edges of the pear but leaving the cut side of the pear completely exposed. Repeat with the remaining 3 pear halves. Brush the phyllo again with melted butter. Place the phyllo packages in the baking dish with the buttered phyllo on the bottom and the exposed pear side facing up. Bake for 12 to 15 minutes, until the phyllo begins to brown.

Serve immediately with a scoop of vanilla ice cream and drizzle with the reduced syrup.

Note:
For vanilla ice cream, use the recipe for Woodford Reserve Ice Cream (page 227). Omit the bourbon and add ½ cup sugar. Alternatively, substitute store bought.

3 cups bourbon
1 cup sugar
6 whole cloves
1 stick cinnamon
2 teaspoons black peppercorns
2 pears, peeled, halved, and cored
12 (14 by 18-inch) sheets phyllo dough
¾ cup unsalted butter, melted
½ cup pecans, toasted and finely crushed
Vanilla ice cream, for serving *(see Note)*

SERVES 4

KITCHEN SINK COOKIE ICE-CREAM SANDWICHES

At the risk of getting in the doghouse with my sweet bride, I am going to say it loud and proud. I love you, Christina Tosi! If you don't love her right along with me, well then, that's only because you haven't 1) met her or 2) tasted her food. She is both an inspiration in her ability in the kitchen *and* in that she is the sane anchor at the center of the swirling insanity that is the David Chang circus of success. Bless you, my dear, and thank you for what you give to the world.

When I got Tosi's book, I read it cover to cover twice before I made anything. It is packed with great secrets, like how glucose makes a cookie chewy forever. The recipe for these cookies is the result of experimenting with her totally addictive Cereal Milk creations. My problem is that I cannot stand to throw anything away, so we started trying to recycle the old cornflakes after soaking them to make Cereal Milk. These cookies started to be a joke because we were putting everything we could think of into them . . . until someone suggested soy sauce. The experiment stopped there, and what we had was everything but the kitchen sink. They are amazing sandwiched around our vanilla ice cream.

"Then I Met You" —The Proclaimers

ingredients

To make the cookies: Preheat the oven to 350°F. Line 2 baking sheets with parchment paper. In a stand mixer fitted with the paddle attachment, cream the butter and lard with the brown and granulated sugars on high speed until creamy. Add the glucose syrup and the vanilla and almond extracts, and combine well. Beat in the eggs, one at a time, until completely blended.

Stir together the flour, oats, baking soda, and salt in a medium bowl. Reduce the mixer speed to low and add the flour mixture, ½ cup at a time, to the butter mixture until fully combined and smooth. Blend in the cornflakes, marshmallows, potato chips, peanuts, sesame seeds, coffee granules, and chocolate chips and combine fully again.

Drop 2 tablespoons at a time onto the baking sheets, about 1½ inches apart. Bake for 7 to 10 minutes, until the edges begin to darken. Remove from the oven and let cool for 5 to 7 minutes on the pans. Transfer to a rack to finish cooling.

To assemble: Cut the ice cream into chunks, put in a bowl, and mash with the back of a spoon until softened. Line a small baking pan with plastic wrap, spread the ice cream evenly onto the pan, cover with plastic wrap, and refreeze.

Once refrozen, remove the ice cream from the pan. Cut out circles using a cookie cutter that's about the same size as the cookies. Sandwich the ice cream disks between two cookies. These can be individually wrapped in plastic wrap and frozen for up to 2 weeks.

Note:
For vanilla ice cream, use the recipe for Woodford Reserve Ice Cream (page 227). Omit the bourbon and add ½ cup sugar. Alternatively, substitute store bought.

¾ cup unsalted butter

4 tablespoons lard *(see page 136)*

¾ cup dark brown sugar

¾ cup granulated sugar

½ cup glucose syrup
(available at specialty baking stores and on the Internet; if you must, substitute light cane syrup or light corn syrup)

2 teaspoons vanilla extract

½ teaspoon almond extract

2 large eggs

1½ cups all-purpose flour

½ cup instant oats

1 tablespoon baking soda

½ teaspoon salt

1½ cups crushed cornflakes

1½ cups mini marshmallows

1 cup crushed thin-cut, salted potato chips

¼ cup crushed roasted peanuts

3 tablespoons sesame seeds, toasted

1 tablespoon instant coffee granules

1 cup semisweet chocolate chips

6 cups vanilla ice cream *(see Note)*

MAKES 4 SANDWICHES
(WITH A HANDFUL OF COOKIES LEFT TO SNACK ON)

CHOCOLATE–PEANUT BUTTER CAKE

Chocolate and peanut butter almost killed me. Or, at least, that's what I tell people. I was living on a steady diet of coffee, Jif extra-crunchy peanut butter, and Baskin-Robbins chocolate and peanut butter ice cream through half of 2008 and most of 2009, as we were opening Snackbar and trying to shape Big Bad Breakfast. Precisely one month after winning the James Beard Award and an alcoholic goodwill tour to celebrate, I collapsed and spent a month in the hospital.

My pancreas had gone off like a bomb, as my doctor explained it, due partly to the poor dietary choices, but largely a result of a really shitty conspiracy of bad genetic material. I blame my parents (rightly, unless I don't actually belong to them) and am still looking for legal counsel to help me settle my "reparations."

This cake was not developed to mark the occasion of my deficient DNA, but rather exists as recognition of my enduring love of the combination of these flavors together, in spite of their crushing effect on my pancreas a few years back. If this doesn't translate to you, may God have mercy on your soul.

ingredients

"Surrender (Live)" —Cheap Trick

¾ pound semisweet chocolate, chopped
1 cup unsalted butter
3 large eggs
1 cup granulated sugar
2 teaspoons vanilla extract
¾ cup all-purpose flour
1 teaspoon baking powder
2 pinches of salt

SERVES 10

Preheat the oven to 325°F. Butter and lightly flour two 9-inch round cake pans and set aside.

Place a stainless-steel or glass bowl over a pan of gently simmering water. Melt the chocolate and butter together in the bowl.

On medium speed, beat the eggs in a stand mixer fitted with the paddle attachment until smooth. Add the sugar and vanilla and beat on medium speed for 5 minutes. Scrape down the sides of the bowl and beat for an additional 5 minutes. Beat in the chocolate mixture on medium speed until well blended.

Stir together the flour, baking powder, and salt in a bowl. With the mixer running on low speed, add the flour mixture 2 tablespoons at a time, making sure to fully incorporate each addition before adding the next.

Divide the batter between the prepared pans and bake for 20 to 25 minutes, until set. Fully cool the layers in the pans. When cool, invert onto cardboard cake circles or baking sheets and place uncovered in the freezer to chill while making the mousse and ganache. A cold cake will make the mousse easier to spread.

Put one of the cake layers, bottom side up, on a cake circle or serving plate. Spread the peanut butter mousse evenly over the top. Place the second layer on top of the first, bottom side down, and return the cake to the freezer while preparing the ganache.

Remove the cake from the freezer and smooth the thickened ganache over the top and down the sides of the cake. Chill until the ganache hardens.

PEANUT BUTTER MOUSSE

½ cup heavy cream
¼ cup confectioners' sugar
¾ teaspoon vanilla extract
1 cup creamy peanut butter

Whisk the heavy cream, confectioners' sugar, and vanilla on high speed in a stand mixer fitted with the whisk attachment until stiff peaks form. Transfer to a medium bowl and set aside.

In the same bowl on the stand mixer, beat the peanut butter until smooth. Gently fold in the whipped cream, one-third at a time, until fully combined.

GANACHE

1½ cups heavy cream
3 tablespoons granulated sugar
¾ pound dark chocolate, chopped

Warm the cream, sugar, and chocolate in a saucepan over low heat until the sugar begins to dissolve. Stir well with a heatproof spatula until the chocolate is fully melted and then remove from the heat. Allow the ganache to rest and cool for 15 minutes.

CAYENNE-PRALINE ICE CREAM

I made these pralines as a takeaway for the Southern Foodways Alliance fall symposium about 10 years ago. Shortly afterward, I was flooded with requests for the recipe. The cayenne adds just enough heat to catch up at the end, but not enough to really burn. The pralines keep for a long time and make good presents. The process sounds a little tedious, but it is actually very simple and quick. At this very moment, you are one candy thermometer away from some of the easiest homemade holiday gifts you can imagine.

For this recipe, we crumble the pralines and stir them into homemade bourbon ice cream. Just try it.

ingredients

"Just Like Heaven" —Dinosaur Jr.

3 cups granulated sugar

3 cups dark brown sugar

2¼ cups heavy cream

3 tablespoons unsalted butter

2 tablespoons vanilla extract

1 teaspoon cayenne

Pinch of salt

4 cups whole pecans, toasted and roughly chopped

Woodford Reserve Ice Cream
(page 227; bourbon optional)

MAKES ABOUT 2 QUARTS

Combine the granulated and brown sugars and cream in a medium saucepan and bring to a simmer over medium heat. Place a candy thermometer in the sugar mixture and cook, swirling constantly, until the thermometer registers 247°F. Whisk in the butter, vanilla, cayenne, and salt and whisk by hand until creamy.

Stir in the toasted pecans with a wooden spoon, scoop out onto a nonstick baking sheet, and let cool. The mixture will harden immediately into pralines. With your hands, roughly crush enough pralines to make 2½ cups. Reserve the rest for another use.

If you made the ice cream ahead of time, let it soften a bit at room temperature. Transfer the soft-frozen ice cream to a covered container if necessary, stir in the crushed pralines, and freeze for at least 1 hour before serving. This will keep for up to 4 months, if stored properly (see page 227).

COMPRESSED SUMMER MELON WITH COUNTRY HAM POWDER

Ever since the Cryovac machine became a fixture in restaurants, chefs have been compressing melon. The act takes a delicious summer melon cube and transforms it into something with the original texture of the fruit, but a flavor more like that of a Jolly Rancher. This is a sweet but salty interpretation.

"What a Wonderful World" —Joey Ramone

ingredients

To make the crema: Whip the cream in a medium bowl until soft peaks form. Stir in the sugar and salt and whip until stiff peaks form. Slowly blend in the buttermilk. Place in the refrigerator.

To make the ham powder: Place the ham in a dehydrator and dry for 12 hours. Alternatively, place on a cooling rack on a baking sheet in your oven on its lowest setting with the door propped open with something nonflammable. When dry, remove the ham and grind in a spice grinder to a fine powder. Set aside.

To make the melon: Place the watermelon and honeydew in separate FoodSaver bags, spread them out in a single layer, and vacuum-seal as tightly as possible. Place these bags in the refrigerator and let chill for several hours.

When ready to serve, divide the melon evenly among serving bowls, sprinkle with a little ham powder, and top with a spoonful of the buttermilk crema.

BUTTERMILK CREMA

½ cup heavy cream

2 tablespoons confectioners' sugar

2 pinches of salt

3 tablespoons buttermilk

HAM POWDER

20 paper-thin slices country ham, trimmed of fat

COMPRESSED MELON

16 (1-inch square) watermelon cubes

16 (1-inch square) honeydew melon cubes

SERVES 4

VANILLA BEAN–BUTTERMILK PANNA COTTA WITH BOURBON-MARINATED SUMMER CHERRIES

For the longest time I pushed back against gelatin. It was one of those ingredients I just buried because of my preconceived opinions about its texture. About 20 years ago, on a trip through northern Italy, I finished dinner with a chestnut panna cotta that just blew my mind. Gelatin was officially back in the game.

My friend Joe York turned me onto the Cruz Family Dairy buttermilk. The Cruzes, who operate just outside of Knoxville, do for buttermilk what Allan Benton does for ham and Julian Van Winkle does for bourbon. It is absolutely one of the finest things that will ever cross your lips. This marriage is perfect because it elevates the texture of the Cruz buttermilk to an otherworldly creaminess and carries the flavor perfectly.

"Shipbuilding" —Elvis Costello

Put the gelatin in a small bowl with 2 tablespoons water and set aside to soften.

In a small saucepan, heat the cream with the sugar, lemon zest and juice, and vanilla bean over medium heat. As soon as bubbles begin to form around the edges of the pot, carefully remove the vanilla bean, scrape the seeds from the pod with a sharp knife, and stir the seeds into the cream mixture. Discard the pod, or rinse and use to make your own extract (see page 227). Stir in the gelatin and whisk until completely dissolved and incorporated. Let cool until warm (not hot) and then whisk in the buttermilk.

Spray four 8-ounce ramekins or dessert cups with nonstick cooking spray and divide the panna cotta mixture among them. Refrigerate for several hours, until set. Turn out onto plates and serve with the bourbon cherries and a drizzle of the cherry-bourbon syrup.

Note:
Once you have tasted Earl Cruz's buttermilk, absolutely nothing else will do as a substitute. Unfortunately, you have to be somewhere in the area surrounding Knoxville, Tennessee, to get it, so reality dictates substituting a store-bought brand. Given the opportunity, get your hands on some Cruz Family Dairy buttermilk. The good thing is that it has a shelf life of months in the refrigerator . . . and it gets better the longer it sits.

ingredients

PANNA COTTA
1½ teaspoons unflavored powdered gelatin
1 cup heavy cream
½ cup plus 2 tablespoons sugar
Finely grated zest and juice of 1 lemon
1 whole vanilla bean, split
2 cups Cruz Family Dairy buttermilk *(see Note)*

SERVES 4

BOURBON-MARINATED CHERRIES

¼ pound fresh summer cherries
1½ cups bourbon
1 tablespoon freshly squeezed lemon juice
2 tablespoons sugar
½ teaspoon vanilla extract

Stem the cherries and cut a small slit in the top of each. Alternatively, you can remove the pits, if you like. In a small saucepan, combine the bourbon, lemon juice, sugar, and vanilla and bring to a simmer. The minute bubbles begin to form around the edge, remove from the heat and add the cherries. Refrigerate, covered, overnight.

PORK FAT BEIGNETS WITH BOURBON CARAMEL

Though dessert beignets could absolutely not be any more New Orleans, you rarely catch them on anyone's menu in the city. Considering the line that builds up almost every night at Café Du Monde (it's the *only* item on their menu), you'd think they'd be on every menu around. This is a simple twist on that classic. The pork fat adds a little depth of flavor, and the cayenne helps cut through a little of the richness.

"The Sharpest Thorn" —Allen Toussaint and Elvis Costello

To make the caramel: In a medium heavy-bottomed saucepan, combine the sugar and 3 tablespoons water over medium heat. Swirl the sugar as it begins to boil *(do not stir it)*. Continue swirling the sugar until it begins to change color. As it approaches a medium amber color, remove from the heat and whisk in the cream. Be careful: This mixture will bubble up furiously at first, but it will settle. Whisk in the butter, salt, and bourbon. Set aside.

To make the beignets: Mix the water, sugar, and yeast in a large bowl and let sit for 10 minutes, or until it foams.

In another bowl, beat the eggs, salt, cream, and milk together. Mix the egg mixture into the yeast mixture.

Add 3 cups of the flour and the cayenne to the yeast mixture and stir to combine. Add the lard and butter and continue to stir while adding the remaining 4 cups flour. Remove the dough from the bowl, place onto a lightly floured surface, and knead until smooth. Lightly rub a large bowl with vegetable oil. Put the dough into the oiled bowl and cover with plastic wrap or a kitchen towel. Let rise in a warm place for at least 2 hours.

Preheat 2½ inches of peanut oil in a deep fryer to 350°F. Roll the dough out to about a ¼-inch thickness and cut into 1-inch squares. Carefully place a few pieces of the dough in the deep fryer at a time, flipping constantly and frying until they turn golden. Transfer with a slotted spoon to a plate lined with paper towels to drain. Serve immediately, dusted heavily with confectioners' sugar and drizzled with the caramel.

ingredients

BOURBON CARAMEL

1 cup granulated sugar
¾ cup heavy cream
4 tablespoons unsalted butter
½ teaspoon salt
2 tablespoons bourbon

BEIGNETS

1½ cups lukewarm water *(100° to 105°F)*
½ cup granulated sugar
1 (¼-ounce) envelope active dry yeast
2 large eggs, lightly beaten
1¼ teaspoons salt
½ cup heavy cream
½ cup whole milk
7 cups all-purpose flour
1 teaspoon cayenne
4 tablespoons lard *(see page 136)*
2 tablespoons unsalted butter, softened
Peanut oil, for deep-frying
3 cups confectioners' sugar

SERVES 6 TO 8

LEMON-ROSEMARY SORBET WITH BENNE SEED SHORTBREAD

The summer of 1992, when we opened, was oppressively hot, as was our kitchen. This sorbet was one of our first dessert menu items. The greatest challenge we faced was getting it to the table before it melted.

Rosemary and lemon play so nicely together that this was just a must-do combination. The sorbet is tangy and the shortbread is a little earthy. Together they make an ideal end to a summer meal.

ingredients

"Sick Bed of Cuchulainn" —The Pogues

ROSEMARY SIMPLE SYRUP
(MAKES ABOUT 6 CUPS)

4 cups sugar

6 large fresh rosemary sprigs

SORBET

4 cups Rosemary Simple Syrup

2½ cups freshly squeezed lemon juice

½ cup vodka

2 large egg whites

MAKES 2 QUARTS SORBET

To make the simple syrup: Simmer 4 cups water with the sugar and rosemary in a large saucepan over low heat for 10 minutes. Let cool, then strain the syrup and discard the solids.

To make the sorbet: Whisk the simple syrup, lemon juice, 2 cups water, and the vodka together in a stainless-steel bowl and chill for several hours.

Spin the lemon mixture in an ice-cream maker according to the manufacturer's directions for 15 minutes. Add the egg whites and spin until the sorbet is soft-frozen. Transfer to a shallow plastic container (this will help the sorbet finish freezing more quickly) and freeze until firm. Serve with a shortbread cookie on the side.

BENNE SEED SHORTBREAD

2 cups all-purpose flour

¼ cup sesame seeds, toasted

2 teaspoons toasted sesame oil

1 cup sugar, plus more for sprinkling

¾ teaspoon smoked paprika

½ teaspoon salt

1 cup unsalted butter, cubed and frozen

½ teaspoon vanilla extract

Preheat the oven to 375°F. Combine the flour, 2 tablespoons of the sesame seeds, the sesame oil, sugar, paprika, and salt in a food processor and pulse to combine. Add the butter and pulse until it resembles a coarse meal. Blend in the vanilla.

Pour the dough out onto a work surface and gather it into a ball. Knead with the palm of your hands until smooth. Roll the dough out to a ½-inch thickness and sprinkle with the remaining 2 tablespoons sesame seeds. Roll the rolling pin lightly over the dough to gently push the seeds into the top of the dough. Sprinkle the dough lightly with some sugar. Cut the shortbread into whatever shapes you like. Place the shapes on a baking sheet, about 1 inch apart, and bake for 25 minutes or until golden brown. Remove from the oven and let cool on a rack.

METRIC CONVERSIONS & EQUIVALENTS

Metric Conversion Formulas

TO CONVERT	MULTIPLY
Ounces to grams	Ounces by 28.35
Pounds to kilograms	Pounds by 0.454
Teaspoons to milliliters	Teaspoons by 4.93
Tablespoons to milliliters	Tablespoons by 14.79
Fluid ounces to milliliters	Fluid ounces by 29.57
Cups to milliliters	Cups by 236.59
Cups to liters	Cups by 0.236
Pints to liters	Pints by 0.473
Quarts to liters	Quarts by 0.946
Gallons to liters	Gallons by 3.785
Inches to centimeters	Inches by 2.54

Approximate Metric Equivalents

VOLUME

¼ teaspoon	1 milliliter
½ teaspoon	2.5 milliliters
¾ teaspoon	4 milliliters
1 teaspoon	5 milliliters
1¼ teaspoons	6 milliliters
1½ teaspoons	7.5 milliliters
1¾ teaspoons	8.5 milliliters
2 teaspoons	10 milliliters
1 tablespoon (½ fluid ounce)	15 milliliters
2 tablespoons (1 fluid ounce)	30 milliliters
¼ cup	60 milliliters
⅓ cup	80 milliliters
½ cup (4 fluid ounces)	120 milliliters
⅔ cup	160 milliliters
¾ cup	180 milliliters
1 cup (8 fluid ounces)	240 milliliters
1¼ cups	300 milliliters
1½ cups (12 fluid ounces)	360 milliliters
1⅔ cups	400 milliliters
2 cups (1 pint)	460 milliliters
3 cups	700 milliliters
4 cups (1 quart)	0.95 liter
1 quart plus ¼ cup	1 liter
4 quarts (1 gallon)	3.8 liters

WEIGHT

¼ ounce	7 grams
½ ounce	14 grams
¾ ounce	21 grams
1 ounce	28 grams
1¼ ounces	35 grams
1½ ounces	42.5 grams
1⅔ ounces	45 grams
2 ounces	57 grams
3 ounces	85 grams
4 ounces (¼ pound)	113 grams
5 ounces	142 grams
6 ounces	170 grams
7 ounces	198 grams
8 ounces (½ pound)	227 grams
16 ounces (1 pound)	454 grams
35.25 ounces (2.2 pounds)	1 kilogram

LENGTH

⅛ inch	3 millimeters
¼ inch	6 millimeters
½ inch	1.25 centimeters
1 inch	2.5 centimeters
2 inches	5 centimeters
2½ inches	6 centimeters
4 inches	10 centimeters
5 inches	13 centimeters
6 inches	15.25 centimeters
12 inches (1 foot)	30 centimeters

Common Ingredients and Their Approximate Equivalents

1 cup uncooked rice = 225 grams
1 cup all-purpose flour = 140 grams
1 stick butter (4 ounces • ½ cup • 8 tablespoons) = 110 grams
1 cup butter (8 ounces • 2 sticks • 16 tablespoons) = 220 grams
1 cup brown sugar, firmly packed = 225 grams
1 cup granulated sugar = 200 grams

Oven Temperatures

To convert Fahrenheit to Celsius, subtract 32 from Fahrenheit, multiply the result by 5, then divide by 9.

DESCRIPTION	FAHRENHEIT	CELSIUS	BRITISH GAS MARK
Very cool	200°	95°	0
Very cool	225°	110°	¼
Very cool	250°	120°	½
Cool	275°	135°	1
Cool	300°	150°	2
Warm	325°	165°	3
Moderate	350°	175°	4
Moderately hot	375°	190°	5
Fairly hot	400°	200°	6
Hot	425°	220°	7
Very hot	450°	230°	8
Very hot	475°	245°	9

Information compiled from a variety of sources, including *Recipes into Type* by Joan Whitman and Dolores Simon (Newton, MA: Biscuit Books, 2000); *The New Food Lover's Companion* by Sharon Tyler Herbst (Hauppauge, NY: Barron's, 1995); and *Rosemary Brown's Big Kitchen Instruction Book* (Kansas City, MO: Andrews McMeel, 1998).

INDEX

A

Absinthe Frappé, 14
acorn squash, 39
Airline Motors, 17
alcoholic beverages
    Absinthe Frappé, 14
    Bourbon Milk Punch, 15
    City Grocery Bloody Mary, 4, 5
    Deadliest Sin Champagne Punch, 22
    Last-Word Fizz, 10, 11
    Mint Julep Redux, 24
    New Old-Fashioned, 16, 17
    "Smoked" Sazerac, 12, 13
    Spiced Cider, 18, 19
    University Grays Punch, 20, 21
    The Volunteer, 25
Anson Mills, 186
Apple, Johnny, 157
apples
    Apple Cider Reduction, 159
    Lemon-Pickled Honeycrisp Apples, 82
    Maryland-Style Crab Cakes with
        Green Apple–Celery Salad,
        164, 165
    Mustard-Crusted Pork Tenderloin with
        Apple Cider Reduction, 159
    Pork Belly Rillons with Spiced Apple
        Butter, 114
    Smoked Center-Cut Pork Chops with
        Roasted Clove Applesauce,
        206, 207
    Spiced Cider, 18
Ashley Farms, 183
Aurora, Chapel Hill, 160

B

bacon
    Bacon and Tomato Jam, 166
    Brown Sugar–Black Pepper Bacon,
        116, 117
    fat, xxii
Bailey, Coyt, 68
Baking & Spinning
    Bananas Foster Bread Pudding with
        Brown Sugar–Rum Sauce and
        Candied Pecan "Soil," 228, 229
    Banana-Walnut Layer Cake with
        Vanilla Cream Cheese Icing,
        232, 233
    Bourbon-Pecan Pie with Tonka Bean
        Ice Cream, 234
    Bread Pudding, 228, 229

Cayenne-Praline Ice Cream, 240
Chicken Skin Cornbread, 225
Chocolate Chess Pie with Woodford
    Reserve Ice Cream, 226, 227
Chocolate-Espresso "Jolt" Cake,
    242, 243
Chocolate–Peanut Butter Cake,
    238, 239
Compressed Summer Melon and
    Country Ham Powder, 240
Grillades and Grits Casserole,
    222, 223
Kitchen Sink Cookie Ice-Cream
    Sandwiches, 236, 237
Lemon-Rosemary Sorbet with Benne
    Seed Shortbread, 248, 249
Louisiana Strawberry and Meyer
    Lemon Crepes, 231
Peach Rice Pudding Brûlée with
    Brandy Chantilly Cream, 230
Phyllo-Wrapped Bourbon-Clove
    Poached Pears à la Mode, 235
Pork Fat Beignets with Bourbon
    Caramel, 246, 247
Sweet Corn Pudding, 224
Szechuan Pepper–Blueberry Cobbler
    with Five-Spice Buttermilk Crema,
    244, 245
Vanilla Bean–Buttermilk Panna Cotta
    with Bourbon-Marinated Summer
    Cherries, 241
*Ball's Complete Book of Home
    Preserving*, 82
bananas
    Bananas Foster Bread Pudding with
        Brown Sugar–Rum Sauce and
        Candied Pecan "Soil," 228, 229
    Banana-Walnut Layer Cake with
        Vanilla Cream Cheese Icing,
        232, 233
Barker, Ben, 97
basic recipes, xxvi–xxvii
Bayona, xiii
beans
    Bourbon-Pecan Pie with Tonka Bean
        Ice Cream, 234
    green beans, 207
    Red Beans and Rice "Gumbo," 42
    vanilla, 241
    white, 163
Beard, James, xxi
Beard House, xiv, xv
"Beat on The Brat," xx

the Beatles, xix
Bee Gees, xx
Beef
    Beef and Vegetable "Punish"
        Stew, 38
    Grillades and Grits Casserole,
        222, 223
    Smoked Whole Beef Tenderloin,
        208, 209
Beefheart, xx
beets, 211
Beignets, 246, 247
Benne Seed Shortbread, 248, 249
"Bennie and the Jets," xx
Benton, Allan, 173, 241
beverages. *See* shrubs; Stirring, Shaking
    & Muddling; *specific beverage*
Bhatt, Vishwesh, 96, 157
Big Bad Breakfast, xvi, 42, 105, 116,
    166, 238
Big Bad Smokehouse, 119
biscuits, 127, 244, 245
Bistro, Maison de Ville, xiii
Black, Jeff, 121
black pepper, xxi
    Black Pepper Buttermilk Ranch, 139
    Black Pepper Pappardelle, 160, 161
    Black Pepper Steen's Cane
        Syrup, 135
    Brown Sugar–Black Pepper Bacon,
        116, 117
black vinegar, 147
Bloody Mary, 4, 5
Bloody Pig, 4
Bloomfield, April, 203
Blue Plate mayonnaise, 93
Bluegrass Soy Sauce, 146
Bob's Red Mill, 102
Boiling & Simmering. *See* soups
    and stews
Boos, John, xxiv
Boos Blocks, xxiv
boudin, 122, 123
Boulud, Daniel, xiii, 211
bourbon
    Bourbon Caramel, 246, 247
    Bourbon Milk Punch, 15
    Bourbon-Braised Pork Cheeks, 186
    Bourbon-Marinated Cherries, 241
    Bourbon-Pecan Pie with Tonka Bean
        Ice Cream, 234
    Phyllo-Wrapped Bourbon-Clove
        Poached Pears à la Mode, 235

Pork Fat Beignets with Bourbon Caramel, 246, 247
Bourbon Barrel Foods, 63, 146
braising. *See* Roasting & Braising
Brandy Chantilly Cream, 230
bread
    bread pudding, 190, 228, 229
    cornbread, 225
    homemade, xxi
Bread-and-Butter Pickles, 79
Brightsen, Frank, xiii
Brightsen's, xiii
Brining & Smoking
    Hickory-Smoked Salmon Cakes with Marinated Lentils and Dill Aioli, 205
    No-Fail Thanksgiving Turkey, 200
    Pecan-Smoked Duck with Molasses Lacquer, 210
    Smoked Beets with Charred Pecans and Buttermilk–Goat Cheese Crema, 211
    Smoked Center-Cut Pork Chops with Roasted Clove Applesauce, 206, 207
    Smoked Chicken Salad, 204
    Smoked Endive, 214, 215
    Smoked Glazed Baby Carrots, xvii, 212, 213
    Smoked Mushroom Tamales, 216, 217
    Smoked Scallop "Crudo," 202, 203
    Smoked Whole Beef Tenderloin, 208, 209
Brock, Sean, 63, 150
Brown Sugar–Black Pepper Bacon, 116, 117
Brown Sugar–Rum Sauce, 229
Buddy Ward and Sons 13 Mile Seafood, 50
buttermilk
    Black Pepper Buttermilk Ranch, 139
    Buttermilk Crema, 240, 244, 245
    Buttermilk–Goat Cheese Crema, 211
    Herbed Buttermilk Biscuits, 127
    Smoked Beets with Charred Pecans and Buttermilk–Goat Cheese Crema, 211
    Szechuan Pepper–Blueberry Cobbler with Five-Spice Buttermilk Crema, 244, 245
    Vanilla Bean–Buttermilk Panna Cotta with Bourbon-Marinated Summer Cherries, 241

C

Café Du Monde, 247
Cajun roux, 43
cake
    Banana-Walnut Layer Cake with Vanilla Cream Cheese Icing, 232, 233
    Chocolate-Espresso "Jolt" Cake, 242, 243
    Chocolate–Peanut Butter Cake, 238, 239
Camerons smoker, 203
Canale, Dee, 125
Candied Pecan "Soil," 229
cane syrup. *See* Steen's Pure Cane Syrup
canning. *See* Pickling & Canning
cantaloupe, 25
caramel, 246, 247
Carpenters, xix
carrots
    Chilled Grilled Carrot Soup, 36
    Lemon-Dill Baby Carrots, 44
    Smoked Carrots, xvii
    Smoked Glazed Baby Carrots, xvii, 212, 213
cast iron pans, 43
Cat Stevens, xix
catfish, 144, 174, 175
cayenne
    Cayenne pepper, 102
    Cayenne-Praline Ice Cream, 240
    Cayenne–Sweet Corn Puree, 168, 169
celery, 46, 164, 165
Cereal Milk, 237
champagne, 22
Chang, David, 58, 63, 237
charcuterie program, 113
charentais, 25
Chase, Leah, 41
cheese. *See also* cream cheese; goat cheese; ricotta
    Creamy Garlic-Parmesan Grits, 186
    Pimento Cheese Fritters, 151
    Spinach-Ricotta Gnudi, 44
    Strawberry-Mascarpone Filling, 231
cherries
    Bourbon-Marinated Cherries, 241
    Roasted Cherry Tomato Marinara, 84, 85
    Rosemary-Cherry Lemonade, 6, 7
    Warm Cherry-Juniper Vinaigrette, 162
chestnuts, 124, 125
chicken
    Chicken Cracklin's, 225
    Chicken Skin Cornbread, 225
    Chicken-Fried Duck with Caramelized Onion Gravy, 140

Coca-Cola Brined Fried Chicken Thighs, 137
    Confit of Chicken Gizzards with Herbed Buttermilk Biscuits and Grainy Mustard, 127
    Dark Chicken Stock, 31, 32
    Fried Chicken Liver Pâté Salad, 138
    Herb and Garlic Roasted Poulet Rouge, 183
    Smoked Chicken Salad, 204
    Top-Shelf Chicken and Dumplings, 45
chiffonade, 85
Chilled Grilled Carrot Soup, 36
Chimichurri (rustic), 98, 99
Chimichurri (smooth), 98, 99
chive oil, 48
chocolate. *See also* white chocolate
    Chocolate Chess Pie with Woodford Reserve Ice Cream, 226, 227
    Chocolate-Espresso "Jolt" Cake, 242, 243
    Chocolate–Peanut Butter Cake, 238, 239
    Ganache, 239
cholesterol, 136, 144
Chowchow, 100, 101
Christensen, Ashley, ix, 151
cider, 18, 19, 159
Citrus-Strawberry Shrub, 22, 23
City Grocery, xiv, xvii, 9, 25, 28, 55, 151, 166, 183, 191, 235
City Grocery Bloody Mary, 4, 5
clarified butter, xxiii
Cleopatra, 58
clove, 182, 206, 207, 235
Coal-Roasted Sweet Potatoes, 210
cobbler, 244, 245
Coca-Cola Brined Fried Chicken Thighs, 137
Cochon, 42, 122
cold smoking, 113
collards, 63, 120, 121
Comeback Sauce, 150
Commander's Palace, xiii, 50
Compressed Summer Melon and Country Ham Powder, 240
condiments. *See also* mayonnaise; sauces; vinaigrettes
    Black Pepper Buttermilk Ranch, 139
    Blue Plate mayonnaise, 93
    Chimichurri (rustic), 98, 99
    Chimichurri (smooth), 98, 99
    Comeback Sauce, 150
    Corn and Red Pepper Chowchow, 100, 101
    Fresh Herb Tartar Sauce, 107
    Garam Masala, 157
    Ginger Tartar Sauce, 174, 175
    Grainy Mustard, 94, 95, 127

condiments *(continued)*
    Homemade "Duke's" Mayonnaise, 91, 92, 93
    Jalapeño Hot Sauce, 102
    New Orleans–Style Rémoulade, 106
    Peach Relish, 118
    Roasted Jalapeño Tartar Sauce, 144
    Roasted Red Pepper Harissa, 96
    Roasted Tomato Ketchup, 148, 149
    Salt-Roasted Turnip Puree, 159
    Spiced Apple Butter, 114
    Super-Bonus Gravy, 201
    Tabasco, 102
    Tomato Jam, 105, 166
    Vinegar Reduction, 107
    Whole-Grain Guinness Mustard, 94
    Worcestershire Sauce, 97
    Yellow Mustard, 93
Confit of Chicken Gizzards with Herbed Buttermilk Biscuits and Grainy Mustard, 127
cooking
    exercise of, xix
    techniques, xxv
cookware, xxiii
Cooter Brown's, 128
corn
    Corn and Red Pepper Chowchow, 100, 101
    Pickled Sweet Corn, 80, 81
    Porcini-Dusted Seared Gulf Grouper with Cayenne–Sweet Corn Puree, 168, 169
    Sweet Corn Pudding, 224
corn dogs, 148, 149
cornbread, 225
cornmeal, 139
Cornmeal-Fried Oysters with Black Pepper Buttermilk Ranch, 139
countertop, xxiv
Country Ham Powder, 240
Country-Style Pork Pâté with Chestnuts, 124, 125
crab, 191
    cakes, 164, 165
    meat, xxii
cream cheese
    Creole Cream Cheese Grits, 170, 171
    Vanilla Cream Cheese Icing, 232, 233
Cream of Roasted Salsify Soup, 48, 49
Creamy Garlic-Parmesan Grits, 186
Creole Cream Cheese Grits, 170, 171
Creole roux, 43
Creole Seasoning, xxvi
crepes, 231
Crisco, 136
Crispy Pig's Ears "Frites" with Comeback Sauce, 150

Crook's Corner, Chapel Hill, North Carolina, xiii, 28, 39, 101, 244
Cruz, Earl, 241
Cruz Family Dairy, 241
Curing, Preserving & Stuffing. *See* preservation techniques, for proteins
Currence, Becky, 28
Currence, Bess, 2, 28
Currence, John, xi, 104
    family photos, xii–xiii, xvi, 38
Currence, Mamie, ix
Currence, Richard, 194
Currence, Richard Jr., 75, 145, 232
cutting boards, xxiv
Cyprus Black Lava salt, xxi

D
"Dancing Queen," xx
Dark Chicken Stock, 31, 32
dashi, 146
Deadliest Sin Champagne Punch, 22
Deep South "Ramen" with Fried Poached Eggs, 146, 147
Des Jardins, Traci, 203
desserts. *See* Baking & Spinning
Deviled Pickled Eggs, 70
Deviled Pickled Eggs with Sunburst Trout Roe, 71
Dill Aioli, 205
Dill Slices, 78
Dooky Chase, 41
Dory, John, 203
drink, for mood enhancement, xix
drinks. *See* Stirring, Shaking & Muddling
duck
    Chicken-Fried Duck with Caramelized Onion Gravy, 140
    Duck Confit with Peach Relish, 118
    Duck Prosciutto, 113
    Garlic-Duck Sausage with Collard "Choucroute Garni," 120, 121
    Pan-Fried Duck Rillettes, 141
    Pan-Roasted Duck Breast "Frisée" Aux Lardons, xvii, 184, 185
    Pecan-Smoked Duck with Molasses Lacquer, 210
    Pickled Duck Legs (Escabeche), 66
    Tea-Smoked Duck Stir-Fry, 158
Duke's mayonnaise, xxi. *See also* Homemade "Duke's" Mayonnaise
dumplings, 45

E
Edge, John T., xi, 151
Egerton, John, 8
eggs
    Deep South "Ramen" with Fried Poached Eggs, 146, 147

Deviled Pickled Eggs, 70
Deviled Pickled Eggs with Sunburst Trout Roe, 71
Egg Wash, xxvii
Poached Eggs, 185
Elie, Lolis, 42
Emilia, Reggio, 193
endive, 214, 215
enjoyment, xix
equipment, xxiii–xxiv
Escabeche, 66
Eugene Walter's Iced Tea, 8

F
Faulkner, William, xi
fennel pollen, 203
fermenting. *See* Pickling & Canning
Fernando (chef), 193
FIG restaurant, 138
filé powder, 41
finishing salt, xxi
fish. *See* seafood
Five-Spice Buttermilk Crema, 244, 245
flavored oils, 172
Fleer, John, 151
Flounder Pontchartrain, 172
flour, xxii, xxvi
Food, Inc., xxi
FoodSaver, xxiv
"Freaky Tales" (Too \$hort), xx
French Vidalia Onion Soup, 52, 53
French's yellow mustard, xxi
Fresh Herb Tartar Sauce, 107
Fresh Herb Vinaigrette, xxvii
Fried Chicken Liver Pâté Salad, 138
Fried Poached Eggs, 146, 147
fritters, 151
frog's legs, 145
frying
    Chicken-Fried Duck with Caramelized Onion Gravy, 140
    Coca-Cola Brined Fried Chicken Thighs, 137
    Crispy Pig's Ears "Frites" with Comeback Sauce, 150
    Deep South "Ramen" with Fried Poached Eggs, 146, 147
    Fried Chicken Liver Pâté Salad, 138
    Cornmeal-Fried Oysters with Black Pepper Buttermilk Ranch, 139
    Garlic-Fried Frog's Legs Sauce Piquant, 145
    Okra and Green Onion Hush Puppies, 142, 143
    Pan-Fried Catfish with Roasted Jalapeño Tartar Sauce, 144
    Pan-Fried Duck Rillettes, 141
    Pimento Cheese Fritters, 151
    Quail and Waffles, 134–35

Shrimp and Lobster Corn Dogs, 148, 149
tips, 134

G

Ganache, 239
Garam Masala, 157
garlic, xxvi, 186
    Creamy Garlic-Parmesan Grits, 186
    Garlic Olive Oil, xxvi
    Garlic-Duck Sausage with Collard "Choucroute Garni," 120, 121
    Garlic-Fried Frog's Legs Sauce Piquant, 145
    Herb and Garlic Roasted Poulet Rouge, 183
Gautreau's, xiii, xiv, xx, 212
Ginger Tartar Sauce, 174, 175
gnudi, 44
goat cheese, 221
Grainy Mustard, 94, 95, 127
grapes, 72, 73, 204
gravy, 140, 201
Green Apple–Celery Salad, 164, 165
green beans, 207
green onions, 142, 143
Grillades and Grits Casserole, 222, 223
grits
    Creamy Garlic-Parmesan Grits, 186
    Creole Cream Cheese Grits, 170, 171
    Grillades and Grits Casserole, 222, 223
grouper, 168, 169, 187
grown-up drinks, 9
Guarnaschelli, Alex, 191
gumbo
    Gumbo Z'Herbes, 40, 41
    Red Beans and Rice "Gumbo," 42

H

Hagar, Sammy, 220
ham. *See also* prosciutto
    Compressed Summer Melon and Country Ham Powder, 240
    Ham Powder, 240
    Ham Stock, 33
    Tasso Ham, 119
Hamilton, Gabrielle, 203
Hannah, Chris, 11
harissa, 96
Hastings, Chris, 45
Hawaiian Big Flake salt, xxi
Henckels knives, xxiii
Herb and Garlic Roasted Poulet Rouge, 183
herb vinaigrette, xxvii
Herbed Biscuits, 127
Herbed Buttermilk Biscuits, 127
Herbs de Provence, 48

Hickory-Smoked Salmon Cakes with Marinated Lentils and Dill Aioli, 205
Higgins, Gwen, 160
Hill Country Cioppino, 167
Himalayan Pink salt, xxi
Homemade "Duke's" Mayonnaise, 91, 92, 93
honeycrisp apples, 82
hot sauce, 102
hothouse tomatoes, xxii
Hurricane Katrina, xi, 25, 42, 128
hush puppies, 142, 143

I

ice cream. *See also* sorbet
    Cayenne-Praline Ice Cream, 240
    Chocolate Chess Pie with Woodford Reserve Ice Cream, 226, 227
    Kitchen Sink Cookie Ice-Cream Sandwiches, 236, 237
    Phyllo-Wrapped Bourbon-Clove Poached Pears à la Mode, 235
    Tonka Bean Ice Cream, 234
iced tea, 8
icing, 232
Indian spice trade, 157
Individual Quick Freezing (IQF), 144
Ingraham, Dwayne, 220
ingredients, buying good, xx–xxi
IQF. *See* Individual Quick Freezing
Italian Sausage and Black Pepper Pappardelle, 160, 161
Iuzzini, Johnny, 244

J

jalapeños
    Jalapeño Hot Sauce, 102
    Pan-Fried Catfish with Roasted Jalapeño Tartar Sauce, 144
jam, 105, 166
Jambalaya "Boudin," 122, 123
Jamie, Matt, 63, 105
Jasmine Rice, 158
Jean Georges, 244
jelly, 86
Joe Petrossi's, 50
John, Elton, xx
Jolt Cola, 242, 243
Joy of Cooking, xix

K

Kentucky Soy-Collard Kimchi, 63
ketchup, 148, 149
Kewpie mayonnaise, xxi
kimchi, 63
Kitchen Confidential, xiv
Kitchen Sink Cookie Ice-Cream Sandwiches, 236, 237
KitchenAid mixer, xxiv

knives, xxiii
kosher salt, xxi

L

Lagasse, Emeril, xiii
Lake Pontchartrain, 172
Lamb
    Seared Boneless Loin of Lamb with Wilted Rosemary Spinach and White Bean Puree, 163
    Satsuma and Clove-Braised Lamb Shanks, 182
    hearts, 69
lard, xxii, 136, 184
lardons, xvii, 184, 185
Lardo-Sautéed Green Beans, 207
Lasseter, Mary Beth, 151
Last-Word Fizz, 10, 11
Lata, Mike, 63, 138
le Cep, Beaune, France, xv
Lee, Ed, 63
lemonade, 6, 7
lemons
    Lemon-Dill Baby Carrots, 44
    Lemon-Pickled Honeycrisp Apples, 82
    Lemon-Rosemary Sorbet with Benne Seed Shortbread, 248, 249
    Lemon-Sherry Vinaigrette, xxvii
    Lemon-Thyme Shrub, 21
    Louisiana Strawberry and Meyer Lemon Crepes, 231
lentils, 205
"light," xxi
Light in August (Faulkner), xi
lime, pickling, 79
Link, Donald, 42, 115, 122
Live from San Quentin, xx
lobster, 148, 149
Louisiana Strawberry and Meyer Lemon Crepes, 231
Lovejoy, Kirk, 113
"low-fat," xxi
Lucy (grandmother), 204

M

Magnolia Grill, 97
The Maille Boutique, 94
Maldon salt, xxi
mandoline, xxiv, 165
Maras, Gerard, 170, 200
marinara sauce, 84, 85
Marinated Lentils, 205
Maryland-Style Crab Cakes with Green Apple–Celery Salad, 164, 165
mascarpone, 231
Mayan Sun salt, xxi
mayonnaise, xxi, 91, 92, 93, 128–29
McConnell, Jayce, 21
McIlhenny, Paul, 102, 105

McIlhenny Company, 102
McKenzie's, 232
McPhail, Tory, 50
Meat Loaf, xx
meat pies, 128–29
Meat Puppets, xx
melon, 25, 87, 240
Meuller, Fred, 39, 220
Meyer lemons, 231
microplane, xxiv
Milliken, Mary Sue, xxi, 203
Ministry, xx
Minor Threat, xx
Mint Julep Redux, 24
Molasses Lacquer, 210
Momofuku Noodle Bar, 58
Montegoterro, Jean-Marc, 211
mood, xix
Moody Blues, xix
Mozart, xx
Mr. B's Bistro, 170, 200
Muscadine grapes, 204
mushrooms
    Porcini-Dusted Seared Gulf Grouper
        with Cayenne–Sweet Corn Puree,
        168, 169
    shiitake, 64, 65
    Smoked Mushroom Tamales,
        216, 217
music, xix–xx
mustard
    Confit of Chicken Gizzards with
        Herbed Buttermilk Biscuits and
        Grainy Mustard, 127
    Grainy Mustard, 94, 95, 127
    Mustard-Crusted Pork Tenderloin with
        Apple Cider Reduction, 159
    Whole-Grain Guinness Mustard, 94
    Yellow Mustard, xxi, 93

N
Neal, Bill, xiii, xiv, 55, 67, 101, 136, 143,
    157, 220, 244
New Old-Fashioned, 16, 17
New Orleans–Style Rémoulade, 106
New York Times, 157
No-Fail Thanksgiving Turkey, 200
NOLA Oyster Stew, 51
NOLA-Style Barbecued Shrimp with
    Creole Cream Cheese Grits, 170, 171
The Nutcracker, xxii

O
oils
    chive oil, 48
    Crisco, 136
    flavored, 172
    Garlic Olive Oil, xxvi
    olive oil, xxiii

okra
    Okra and Green Onion Hush Puppies,
        142, 143
    Spicy Pickled Okra, 60, 61
    Stewed Okra and Tomatoes,
        54, 55
onions
    Chicken-Fried Duck with Caramelized
        Onion Gravy, 140
    French Vidalia Onion Soup,
        52, 53
    Okra and Green Onion Hush Puppies,
        142, 143
open fire cooking, xxv
Orange Bitters, 17
Osso Buco with Rosemary and English
    Pea Risotto, 188, 189
Osteen, Louis, xxii
oysters, 50
    Nola Oyster Stew, 51
    Cornmeal-Fried Oysters with Black
        Pepper Buttermilk Ranch, 139
    oyster root, 48

P
Palm Court, Palm Beach, Florida, xiii
Pan-Fried Catfish with Roasted Jalapeño
    Tartar Sauce, 144
Pan-Fried Duck Rillettes, 141
Panna Cotta, 241
Pan-Roasted Duck Breast "Frisée" Aux
    Lardons, xvii, 184, 185
Pan-Roasted Soft Shells with Roasted
    Tomato-Vermouth Pan Butter, 191
pappardelle, 160, 161
Pascal's Manale, 170
pâté, 124, 125, 138
peaches
    Peach Rice Pudding Brûlée with
        Brandy Chantilly Cream, 230
    Pickled Peach Relish, 118
    Pickled Peaches, 76, 77
peanut butter
    Chocolate–Peanut Butter Cake, 238
    Peanut Butter Mouse, 239
pears, 235
peas, 47, 188, 189
pecans
    Bananas Foster Bread Pudding with
        Brown Sugar–Rum Sauce and
        Candied Pecan "Soil," 228, 229
    Bourbon-Pecan Pie with Tonka Bean
        Ice Cream, 234
    Pecan-Smoked Duck with Molasses
        Lacquer, 210
    Smoked Beets with Charred Pecans
        and Buttermilk–Goat Cheese
        Crema, 211
pepper grinders, xxi

peppers, 102. See also black pepper
    jelly, 86
    red, 96, 100, 101
    Szechuan, 174, 175, 244, 245
Petrossi's, 50
Peugeot pepper grinders, xxi
Phyllo-Wrapped Bourbon-Clove Poached
    Pears à la Mode, 235
Pickling & Canning
    Bread-and-Butter Pickles, 79
    canning process, 82
    Deviled Pickled Eggs, 70
    Deviled Pickled Eggs with Sunburst
        Trout Roe, 71
    Dill Slices, 78
    Kentucky Soy-Collard Kimchi, 63
    Lemon-Pickled Honeycrisp Apples, 82
    Pickled Duck Legs (Escabeche), 66
    Pickled Grapes, 72, 73
    Pickled Peach Relish, 118
    Pickled Peaches, 76, 77
    Pickled Pig's Ears, 68
    Pickled Shrimp, 67
    Pickled Sweet Corn, 80, 81
    Pickled Sweet Potatoes, 62
    Pickled Watermelon Rind, 87
    Roasted Cherry Tomato Marinara,
        84, 85
    Rosemary-Pickled Lamb Hearts, 69
    Soy-Pickled Shiitakes, 64, 65
    Spicy Pepper Jelly, 86
    Spicy Pickled Okra, 60, 61
pies. See also cobbler
    Bourbon-Pecan Pie with Tonka Bean
        Ice Cream, 234
    Chocolate Chess Pie with Woodford
        Reserve Ice Cream, 226, 227
    Spicy Hill Country Meat Pies with
        Sriracha Mayonnaise, 128–29
pig's ears, 68, 150
Pimento Cheese Fritters, 151
Poached Eggs, 146, 147, 185
Polish Smoked Sausage, 115
Pollan, Michael, xxi
pontchartrain, 172
Porcini-Dusted Seared Gulf Grouper
    with Cayenne–Sweet Corn Puree,
    168, 169
pork. See also bacon; pig's ears
    Bourbon-Braised Pork Cheeks, 186
    Country-Style Pork Pâté with
        Chestnuts, 124, 125
    Grillades and Grits Casserole,
        222, 223
    Mustard-Crusted Pork Tenderloin with
        Apple Cider Reduction, 159
    Pork Belly Rillons with Spiced Apple
        Butter, 114

Pork Fat Beignets with Bourbon
    Caramel, 246, 247
Pork Rillettes, 126
Smoked Center-Cut Pork Chops
    with Roasted Clove Applesauce,
    206, 207
Steen's Syrup-Braised Pork Belly,
    180, 181
Portale, Alfred, xiii
poulet rouge, 183
poultry. *See* chicken; duck; rabbit; turkey
Poultry Brine, 200
pralines, 240
preservation techniques, for proteins
    Brown Sugar–Black Pepper Bacon,
    116, 117
    Confit of Chicken Gizzards with
      Herbed Buttermilk Biscuits and
      Grainy Mustard, 127
    Country-Style Pork Pâté with
      Chestnuts, 124, 125
    Duck Confit with Peach Relish, 118
    Duck Prosciutto, 113
    Garlic-Duck Sausage with Collard
      "Choucroute Garni," 120, 121
    Jambalaya "Boudin," 122, 123
    Polish Smoked Sausage, 115
    Pork Belly Rillons with Spiced Apple
      Butter, 114
    Pork Rillettes, 126
    Spicy Hill Country Meat Pies with
      Sriracha Mayonnaise, 128–29
    Tasso Ham, 119
preserving. *See* Pickling & Canning
pressure cooker, xxiv
prosciutto, 113, 173
proteins, xxi. *See also* preservation
    techniques, for proteins
Prudhomme, Paul, xiii
pudding
    Bananas Foster Bread Pudding with
      Brown Sugar–Rum Sauce and
      Candied Pecan "Soil," 228, 229
    Peach Rice Pudding Brûlée with
      Brandy Chantilly Cream, 230
    Sweet Corn Pudding, 224
punch
    Bourbon Milk Punch, 15
    Deadliest Sin Champagne Punch, 22
    University Grays Punch, 20, 21
"Punish" Stew, 28, 37, 38
"Purple Haze," xx

Q
Quail and Waffles, 134–35
quatre épices (spice blend), 121

R
Rabbit Cacciatore, 192, 193
ramen noodles, 146, 147
recipe, reading, xx
Red Beans and Rice "Gumbo," 42
red peppers, 96, 100, 101
relish, xxi, 118
rémoulade, 106
rice, 42, 158. *See also* risotto
    Rice Pilaf, 43
    rice pudding, 230
ricotta, 44
rillettes, 126, 141
rillons, 114
risotto, 188, 189
Roasting & Braising
    Bourbon-Braised Pork Cheeks, 186
    Herb and Garlic Roasted Poulet
      Rouge, 183
    Osso Buco with Rosemary and
      English Pea Risotto, 188, 189
    Pan-Roasted Duck Breast "Frisée"
      Aux Lardons, xvii, 184, 185
    Pan-Roasted Soft Shells with Roasted
      Tomato-Vermouth Pan Butter, 191
    Rabbit Cacciatore, 192, 193
    Roasted Acorn Squash Bisque, 39
    Roasted and Stuffed Speckled Trout,
      194, 195
    Roasted Cherry Tomato Marinara, 84, 85
    Roasted Clove Applesauce, 207
    Roasted Jalapeño Tartar Sauce, 144
    Roasted Quail Stuffed with Truffle
      Bread Pudding, 190
    Roasted Red Pepper Harissa, 96
    Roasted Tomato Ketchup, 148, 149
    Roasted Tomato-Vermouth Pan
      Butter, 191
    Satsuma and Clove-Braised Lamb
      Shanks, 182
    Steen's Syrup-Braised Pork Belly,
      180, 181
    Tomato-Braised Grouper, 187
Roberts, Glenn, 186
Rogers, Craig, 69
rosemary
    Lemon-Rosemary Sorbet with Benne
      Seed Shortbread, 248, 249
    Osso Buco with Rosemary and
      English Pea Risotto, 188, 189
    Rosemary Simple Syrup, 248
    Rosemary-Cherry Lemonade, 6, 7
    Rosemary-Pickled Lamb Hearts, 69
    Seared Boneless Loin of Lamb with
      Wilted Rosemary Spinach and
      White Bean Puree, 163
Roth, David Lee, 183, 220
roux, 43

S
salad, 184
    Fried Chicken Liver Pâté Salad, 138
    Green Apple–Celery Salad, 164, 165
    Smoked Chicken Salad, 204
salmon, 205
salsify, 48, 49
salt, xxi
Salt-Roasted Turnip Puree, 159
Satsuma and Clove-Braised Lamb
    Shanks, 182
sauces
    Bluegrass Soy Sauce, 146
    Brown Sugar–Rum Sauce, 228, 229
    Comeback Sauce, 150
    Dill Aioli, 205
    Fresh Herb Tartar Sauce, 107
    Garlic-Fried Frog's Legs Sauce
      Piquant, 145
    Ginger Tartar Sauce, 174, 175
    Homemade "Duke's" Mayonnaise, 91,
      92, 93
    Jalapeño Hot Sauce, 102
    marinara sauce, 84, 85
    Roasted Jalapeño Tartar Sauce, 144
    Super-Bonus Gravy, 201
    Worcestershire Sauce, 97
Sauer Company, 93
sausage, 42
    casings, 115
    Garlic-Duck Sausage with Collard
      "Choucroute Garni," 120, 121
    Italian Sausage and Black Pepper
      Pappardelle, 160, 161
    Polish Smoked Sausage, 115
Sautéing & Searing
    Flounder Pontchartrain, 172
    Hill Country Cioppino, 167
    Italian Sausage and Black Pepper
      Pappardelle, 160, 161
    Maryland-Style Crab Cakes with
      Green Apple–Celery Salad,
      164, 165
    Mustard-Crusted Pork Tenderloin with
      Apple Cider Reduction, 159
    NOLA-Style Barbecued Shrimp with
      Creole Cream Cheese Grits,
      170, 171
    Porcini-Dusted Seared Gulf Grouper
      with Cayenne–Sweet Corn Puree,
      168, 169
    Seared Benton's American Prosciutto-
      Wrapped Gulf Yellowfin Tuna, 173
    Seared Boneless Loin of Lamb with
      Wilted Rosemary Spinach and
      White Bean Puree, 163
    Seared Gulf Swordfish with Bacon
      and Tomato Jam, 166

Sautéing & Searing (continued)
    Szechuan Pepper–Crusted Farm-
        Raised Catfish with Ginger Tartar
        Sauce, 174, 175
    Tea-Smoked Duck Stir-Fry, 158
    Tournedos of Venison with Warm
        Cherry-Juniper Vinaigrette, 162
    Veal Country Captain, 156, 157
scallops, 202, 203
Scarlet Frills, 185
Scotch bonnets, 102
seafood. See also specific seafood
    Flounder Pontchartrain, 172
    Hickory-Smoked Salmon Cakes with
        Marinated Lentils and Dill Aioli, 205
    Hill Country Cioppino, 167
    NOLA Oyster Stew, 51
    NOLA-Style Barbecued Shrimp
        with Creole Cream Cheese Grits,
        170, 171
    Pan-Roasted Soft Shells with Roasted
        Tomato-Vermouth Pan Butter, 191
    Porcini-Dusted Seared Gulf Grouper
        with Cayenne–Sweet Corn Puree,
        168, 169
    Roasted and Stuffed Speckled Trout,
        194, 195
    Seared Benton's American Prosciutto-
        Wrapped Gulf Yellowfin Tuna, 173
    Seared Gulf Swordfish with Bacon
        and Tomato Jam, 166
    Smoked Scallop "Crudo," 202, 203
    Szechuan Pepper–Crusted Farm-
        Raised Catfish with Ginger Tartar
        Sauce, 174, 175
    Tomato-Braised Grouper, 187
searing. See also Sautéing & Searing
    Seared Benton's American Prosciutto-
        Wrapped Gulf Yellowfin Tuna, 173
    Seared Boneless Loin of Lamb with
        Wilted Rosemary Spinach and
        White Bean Puree, 163
    Seared Gulf Swordfish with Bacon
        and Tomato Jam, 166
Seasoned Flour, xxvi
seasoning, xxv, xxvi
Seider, Greg, 12
Selman, Larkin, xiii, 118, 212
Serrano peppers, 102
shiitake mushrooms, 64, 65
shortbread, 248, 249
Shoup, John, 191
shrimp
    NOLA-Style Barbecued Shrimp
        with Creole Cream Cheese Grits,
        170, 171
    Pickled Shrimp, 67
    Shrimp and Lobster Corn Dogs, 148, 149
    Shrimp Stock, 34

shrubs, 21, 22, 23
Shun knives, xxiii
simmering. See soups and stews
Simon and Garfunkel, xix
Slathering, Squirting & Smearing. See
    condiments; sauces
Smoked Beets with Charred Pecans
    and Buttermilk–Goat Cheese
    Crema, 211
Smoked Center-Cut Pork Chops
    with Roasted Clove Applesauce,
    206, 207
Smoked Chicken Salad, 204
Smoked Endive, 214, 215
Smoked Glazed Baby Carrots, xvii,
    212, 213
Smoked Mushroom Tamales, 216, 217
smoked sausage, 115
"Smoked" Sazerac, 12, 13
Smoked Scallop "Crudo," 202, 203
Smoked Whole Beef Tenderloin,
    208, 209
smoking. See Brining & Smoking;
    preservation techniques, for
    proteins
Snack, Johnny, xii, 12, 132
Snackbar, 157, 238
soft shell crabs, 191
sorbet, 248, 249
soups and stews
    Celery Heart Velouté, 46
    Chilled Grilled Carrot Soup, 36
    Cream of Roasted Salsify Soup, 48, 49
    Dark Chicken Stock, 31, 32
    French Vidalia Onion Soup, 52, 53
    Gumbo Z'Herbes, 40, 41
    Ham Stock, 33
    NOLA Oyster Stew, 51
    "Punish" Stew, 28, 37, 38
    Red Beans and Rice "Gumbo," 42
    Roasted Acorn Squash Bisque, 39
    Shrimp Stock, 34
    Spicy Summer Pea Soup, 47
    Stewed Okra and Tomatoes, 54, 55
    Top-Shelf Chicken and Dumplings, 45
    Veal Stock, 30
    Vegetable Stock, 35
Southern Foodways Alliance, 128, 150,
    151, 240
soy, 63
    sauce, 146
    Soy-Pickled Shiitakes, 64, 65
Spahr's Seafood, 145
Spiced Apple Butter, 114
Spiced Cider, 18, 19
Spicer, Susan, xiii
spices. See also salt; seasoning; specific
    spice
    Creole Seasoning, xxvi

    Garam Masala, 157
    quatre épices (spice blend), 121
Spicy Hill Country Meat Pies with
    Sriracha Mayonnaise, 128–29
Spicy Pepper Jelly, 86
Spicy Pickled Okra, 60, 61
Spicy Summer Pea Soup, 47
spinach
    Seared Boneless Loin of Lamb with
        Wilted Rosemary Spinach and
        White Bean Puree, 163
    Spinach-Ricotta Gnudi, 44
spinning. See Baking & Spinning
Spiral Staircase, 206
spotify.com, xx
Spotted Pig, 203
squash, 39
sriracha, 128
Sriracha Mayonnaise, 128
Ssäm Bar, 63
Stan's Meat Market, xvi
Steen's Pure Cane Syrup, xxii, 135
    Steen's Syrup-Braised Pork Belly,
        180, 181
Steen's Syrup Mill, 180
Stewed Okra and Tomatoes, 54, 55
stews. See soups and stews
stir-fry, 158
Stirring, Shaking & Muddling
    Absinthe Frappé, 14
    Bourbon Milk Punch, 15
    Citrus-Strawberry Shrub, 22, 23
    Deadliest Sin Champagne Punch, 22
    Eugene Walter's Iced Tea, 8
    Last-Word Fizz, 10, 11
    Lemon-Thyme Shrub, 21
    Mint Julep Redux, 24
    New Old-Fashioned, 16, 17
    "Smoked" Sazerac, 12, 13
    Spiced Cider, 18, 19
    University Grays Punch, 20, 21
    The Volunteer, 25
Stitt, Frank, xiii, 126
stocks
    Dark Chicken Stock, 31, 32
    Ham Stock, 33
    making good, 31
    Shrimp Stock, 34
    Veal Stock, 30
    Vegetable Stock, 35
strawberries
    Citrus-Strawberry Shrub, 22, 23
    Louisiana Strawberry and Meyer
        Lemon Crepes, 231
    Strawberry-Mascarpone Filling, 231
    Strawberry-Meyer Lemon Filling, 231
Stryjewski, Stephen, 115
stuffing. See preservation techniques,
    for proteins

Sunburst Trout Farm, 70
Super-Bonus Gravy, 201
Sweet Corn Pudding, 224
sweet potatoes
    Coal-Roasted Sweet Potatoes, 210
    Pickled Sweet Potatoes, 62
swordfish, 166
syrups
    Citrus-Strawberry Shrub, 22, 23
    Lemon-Thyme Shrub, 21
    Rosemary Simple Syrup, 248
Szechuan Pepper–Blueberry Cobbler
        with Five-Spice Buttermilk Crema,
        244, 245
Szechuan Pepper–Crusted Farm-Raised
        Catfish with Ginger Tartar Sauce,
        174, 175

T
Tabasco, 102
tamales, 216, 217
tartar sauce
    Fresh Herb Tartar Sauce, 107
    Ginger Tartar Sauce, 174, 175
    Pan-Fried Catfish with Roasted
        Jalapeño Tartar Sauce, 144
Tasso Ham, 119
Tea-Smoked Duck Stir-Fry, 158
Thompson, Wright, 66, 209
tomatoes, xxii
    Pan-Roasted Soft Shells with Roasted
        Tomato-Vermouth Pan Butter, 191
    Roasted Cherry Tomato Marinara,
        84, 85
    Roasted Tomato Ketchup, 148, 149
    Roasted Tomato-Vermouth Pan
        Butter, 191
    Stewed Okra and Tomatoes, 54, 55
    Tomato Aspic, 66
    Tomato Jam, 105, 166
    Tomato-Braised Grouper, 187
Tonka Bean Ice Cream, 234
Too $hort, xx

Top-Shelf Chicken and Dumplings, 45
Tosi, Christina, 237
Tournedos of Venison with Warm Cherry-
        Juniper Vinaigrette, 162
transglutimanase, 173
trout
    Deviled Pickled Eggs with Sunburst
        Trout Roe, 71
    Roasted and Stuffed Speckled Trout,
        194, 195
Truffle Bread Pudding, 190
tuna, 173
turkey, 200, 201
turnips, 159

U
Universal Life Church, 186
University Grays Punch, 20, 21

V
vacuum sealer, xxiv
Van Halen, 220
Van Winkle, Julian, 241
Vanilla Bean–Buttermilk Panna Cotta
        with Bourbon-Marinated Summer
        Cherries, 241
Vanilla Cream Cheese Icing, 232, 233
veal, 156, 157
Veal Stock, 30
vegetables. See also specific types
    "Punish" Stew, 28, 37, 38
    Vegetable Stock, 35
venison, 162
Vic Firth pepper grinder, xxi
vinaigrettes, 184
    Fresh Herb Vinaigrette, xxvii
    Lemon-Sherry Vinaigrette, xxvii
    Warm Cherry-Juniper Vinaigrette, 162
vinegar, 107, 147
Vitamix blender, xxiv
Vlasic relish, xxi
The Volunteer, 25

W
waffles, 134–35
Walker's, 226
walnuts, 232, 233
Walter, Eugene, 8
Warm Cherry-Juniper Vinaigrette, 162
watermelon rind, 87
Waxman, Jonathan, xiii
Weems, Jim, 143
wet/dry ingredient mixing, xxv
White, Barry, 178
White Bean Puree, 163
white beans, 163
white chocolate, xxii
White House, xvi
Whole-Grain Guinness Mustard, 94
Willie Mae's Scotch House, xi, 25, 128
Wilted Rosemary Spinach, 163
wood chips, soaking, 206
Woodford Reserve Ice Cream, 226, 227
Worcestershire Sauce, 97
Wüstof knives, xxiii

X
xantham gum, 102

Y
Yates, Randy, 4, 183
Yellow Mustard, xxi, 93
yellowfin tuna, 173
York, Joe, 241

Z
Zuperpollo, 66